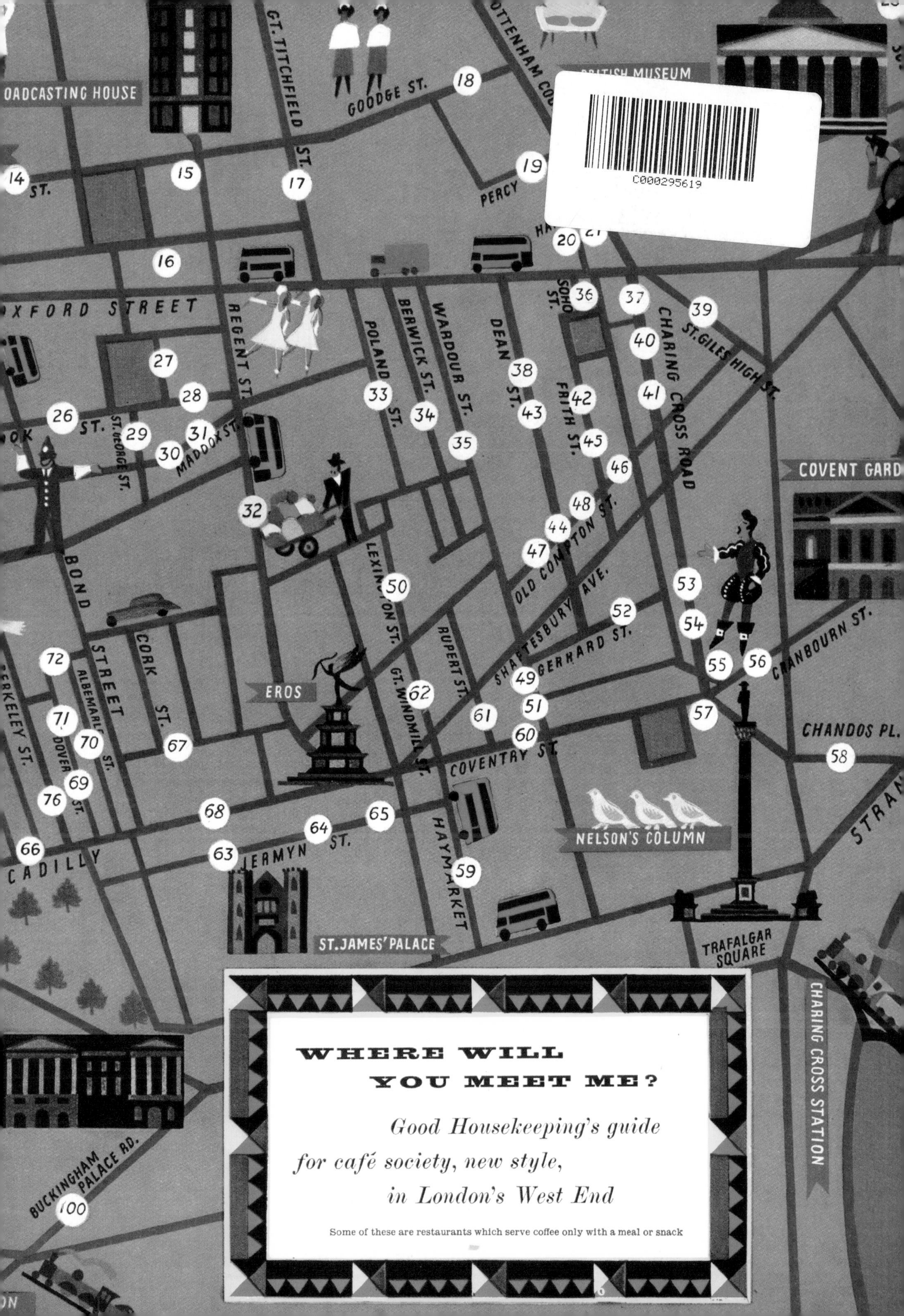
WHERE WILL YOU MEET ME?
Good Housekeeping's guide
for café society, new style,
in London's West End
Some of these are restaurants which serve coffee only with a meal or snack
BRITISH MUSEUM
C000295619
OADCASTING HOUSE
GT. TITCHFIELD ST.
GOODGE ST.
PERCY
OXFORD STREET
REGENT ST.
POLAND ST.
BERWICK ST.
WARDOUR ST.
DEAN ST.
SOHO ST.
FRITH ST.
CHARING CROSS ROAD
ST. GILES HIGH ST.
COVENT GARD
MADDOX ST.
ST. GEORGE ST.
BOND STREET
CORK ST.
ALBEMARLE ST.
DOVER ST.
BERKELEY ST.
LEXINGTON ST.
OLD COMPTON ST.
SHAFTESBURY AVE.
GERRARD ST.
RUPERT ST.
GT. WINDMILL ST.
CRANBOURN ST.
CHANDOS PL.
COVENTRY ST.
EROS
JERMYN ST.
CADILLY
HAYMARKET
NELSON'S COLUMN
ST. JAMES' PALACE
TRAFALGAR SQUARE
CHARING CROSS STATION
STRAN
BUCKINGHAM PALACE RD.

The Best of the 1950s

First published in the United Kingdom
in 2008 by
Collins & Brown
10 Southcombe Street
London W14 0RA

An imprint of Anova Books Company Ltd

The Good Housekeeping website address is
www.allaboutyou.com/goodhousekeeping

ISBN 978-1-84340-488-0

A CIP catalogue for this book is available from the British Library.

10 9 8 7 6 5 4 3 2 1

Archival Scans by Hollingworth & Moss Ltd UK

Reproduction by Rival Colour Ltd UK
Printed and bound in Thailand by Imago

Keep updated.
Email sales@anovabooks.com for FREE email alerts on forthcoming titles.

This book can be ordered direct from the publisher. Contact the marketing department, but try your bookshop first.

www.anovabooks.com

Good Housekeeping

The Best of the 1950s

COLLINS & BROWN

I have to be

particular . . .

I help to make CHIVERS JAM and everything has to be just right. It's prepared in silver-lined pans like these.

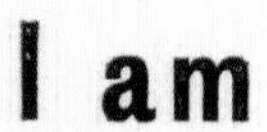

I am

particular . . .

With Jam, mother taught me to look for the fruit first and then ask the price— now I just say "CHIVERS".

CHIVERS JAMS

are particularly good

they are made by particular *people for* particular *people.*

CHIVERS & SONS LTD., The Orchard Factory, HISTON, CAMBRIDGE and at Montrose, Huntingdon and York

Introduction

After the deprivation and austerity of the war years, 1950s Britain was the era of booming optimism, invention and technology. Women's concerns moved from scrimping and rationing to creating domestic bliss in the home as people began to earn more and enjoy a considerably better quality of life. Although women had been encouraged to return to the home after the war, many still continued to work and contribute to the family income.

With little domestic help, the middle-class woman was now striving to be the perfect wife, mother, hostess and cook, and new labour-saving devices flooded the market offering to improve her life, from easy-to-wipe Formica, spin driers and steam irons to fridges, freezers and heated hostess trolleys. One of the most popular additions to the home was the fitted, colour-coordinated kitchen, which gave the 1950s kitchen its distinctive look. Household chores, such as the laundry, became easier as front-loading washing machines became affordable and clothes were made of easy-to-wash synthetic fabrics.

The standard of living rose and people were warmer, better fed and better dressed than ever before. The growth of television and TV and magazine advertising broadened horizons and raised expectations so that few disagreed with the Prime Minister Harold Macmillan when he announced in 1957 that Britons had 'never had it so good'.

The Best of the 1950s is a fascinating collection of pages from *Good Housekeeping's* archive. This nostalgic reproduction of the food, fashion, fiction and fitness features and numerous advertisements from the period, provides an insightful chapter in the history of the British home.

Louise

LOUISE CHUNN

WHITE TO WEAR

White is the thing to wear, in considered moderation, for early Spring sunshine. Here are nine ideas; run them up in a few hours, to lighten dark clothes

To be ready for the earliest spring sunshine, make yourself little odds and ends of white, and use them to light up a dark outfit. A white piqué waistcoat under a dark jacket is a crisp change from the usual blouse. A knitted, tightly-ribbed white tube makes a strapless top for a dark evening skirt now, goes sun-bathing later. A stiff white cummerbund—the only light accent on a sombre dress. A starched white piqué rose for

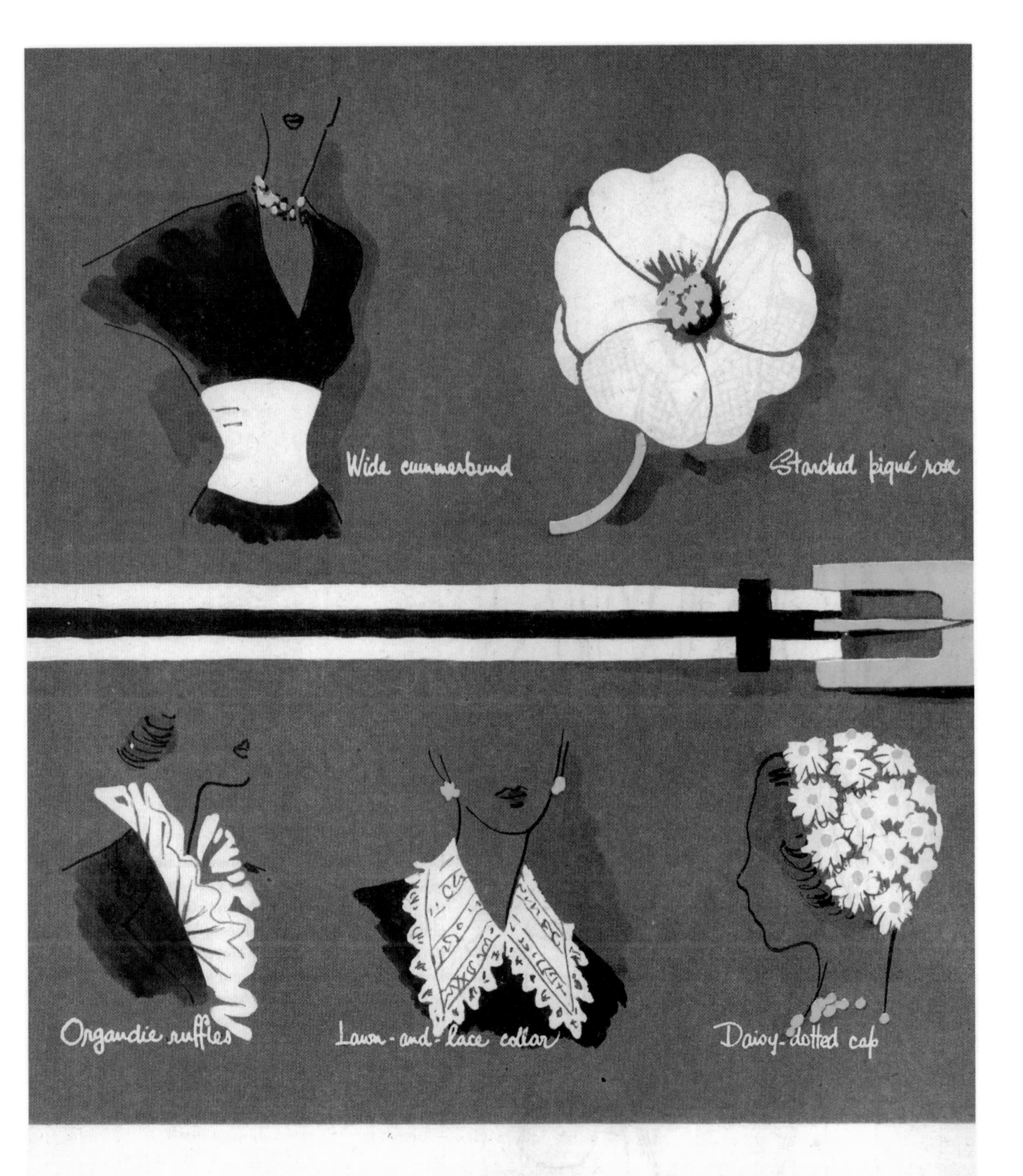

your lapel (we give you the shape of the petal here, and don't forget the starch !). Hand-rolled double ruffles of white organdie to stand stiffly up around your spring-time face, or a flat collar of batiste, with white insertion whipped in at intervals, edged with narrow lace. If you are very young, make a skull-cap of stiff muslin, cover it entirely with big white daisies. Take two lengths of white grosgrain ribbon, sandwich a dark ribbon between them for a white-buckled belt. And don't let your umbrella stay out of key—make a tight cover for it of snowy piqué, frilled stiffly below the handle. Having assembled your chosen fripperies, wear them with discretion, and singly. The considered touch of white on a dark suit is like the flicker of garlic in a good salad —correctly used, both are spicily delicious, but over-insistence on either is a disaster. Keep white for a single accent, use it with delicacy and finesse.

the things you FALL for

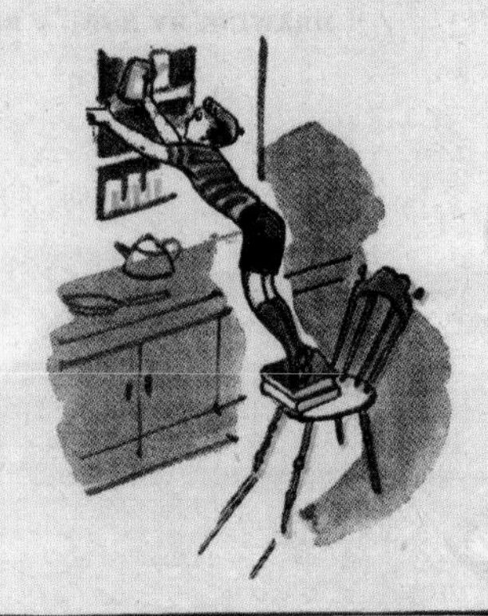

Every year thousands of people in this country are injured in home accidents—many hundreds permanently or fatally. Falls head the list—falls caused by familiar hazards such as we show here. Jam-stealing Tommy defies gravity from a rickety perch. But he's taking a risk and you will, too, unless you take precautions. Before you start climbing, get a ladder. It's a nuisance, but so is a broken leg.

Don't use small loose rugs where they can trip the unwary, particularly not at the head and foot of stairs. Stitch strips of sheet rubber or linoleum on the back of the rug at either end, to render them "non-skid." Waxed floors may be slippery when the wax is not properly applied. Spread it thinly, and unless it's the "no-rub" kind buff it long and well. Hard paste polish can be diluted with turpentine for easy spreading.

"Better light—better sight," says the slogan. And better safety, if passages, stairs and halls are kept illuminated with even a low wattage lamp. It is then easy to find the light switches of rooms you are entering without stumbling over obstacles. Bedrooms need bedside switches or lamps. Long extension cords trailing about are another dangerous hazard. Avoid this by having wall outlets installed, if possible.

Some say they would sooner keep a rattlesnake than a stairway in poor repair and there's some sense in it. Lack of a hand rail on stairs, front porch or back-door steps invites accidents, too. Be doubly careful on stairs when you are carrying heavy or bulky loads that need two hands or that hide your feet. A firm hand on the banister rail aids balance at any time and can prevent a bad fall.

THE ART OF MAKING Idle CONVERSATION

Wise words for the socially shy on how to say much without meaning anything

BY A. A. MILNE

Conversation, as you may have noticed, requires two people, one at each end. Many years ago, before most of you were born (and how the world go on without you has always been a puzzle to me), it would sometimes happen to a young man like myself that he would be invited to a dinner-party. Now a dinner-party in those far-off days was a solemn business. Dismiss at once from your mind the picture of yourself, cigarette between fingers, drinking gin and orange in the bed-sitting room with your host, while your hostess bustles in and out of the kitchenette telling you that the soup is just coming in, and have you ever tried snoek pie because it's rather fun—" Oh, and Peter, could you do something constructive about the pineapple chunks, because the thing you're supposed to open it with doesn't seem to work?" It was nothing like that.

There would be nineteen people in the drawing-room when the Shy Young Man was announced by the butler in a loud authoritative voice as " Mr. Million." The Hostess, possibly remembering where she had seen him before, possibly not, would advance beneath a forest of chandelier and over an acre of parquet flooring, to give him a languid hand and say: " So glad you could come, let me see, I think you're taking Miss Postlethwaite in, ah there she is, Muriel dear, this is Mr. Melon "—and there, poor devil, he was.

There were no cocktails in those days: nothing to loosen the tongue, nothing to occupy the hands. Had Mr. Melon lit a cigarette, the ladies would have swooned and the men muttered that it wasn't cricket; " Parkinson," the Host would have said, " remove Mr. Mullins." Smoking was for the dining-room only, (*Continued on page* 93)

DRAWING BY Dekk

The Beauty Clinic

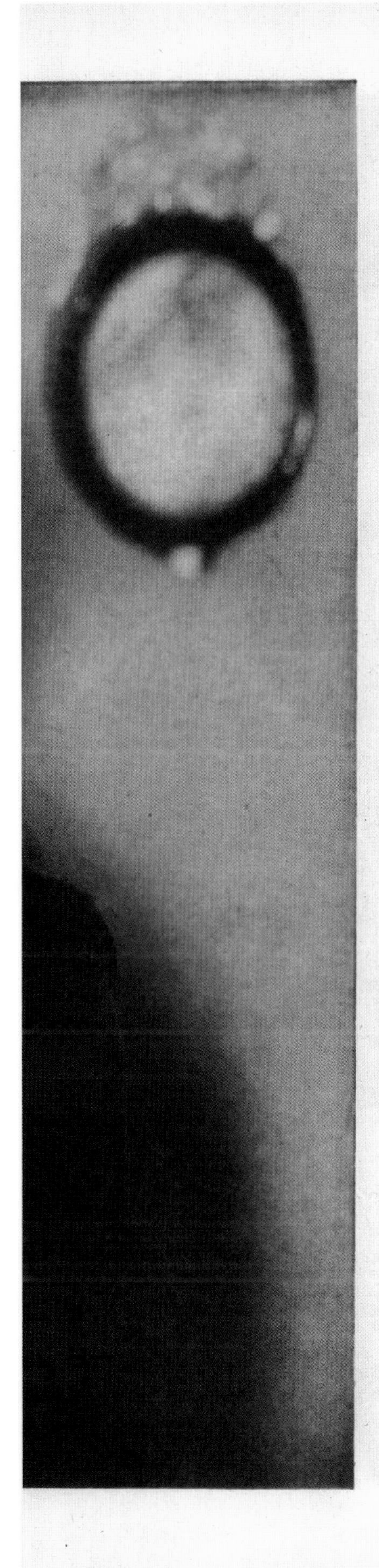

FINDING YOURSELF

Ethne Davies discusses a woman we all know well—the one everyone likes, the one we all want to be, the one you could be

There are few things in life more pleasing or more satisfying than the company of an attractive, serene and self-possessed woman. Such a woman is in constant demand. She draws men and women alike towards her, anxious to please her wherever she goes. Her friends may be young or old and range from the high-powered business executive to the grocer in the shop on the corner. She is the woman we should all like to be. When we look for her secrets, we find that they are not really secrets at all, but equally they are not gifts. For each darling of the gods, born with enviable qualities, there are hundreds who must discover what potentialities they have and study how to develop them.

1 Our ideal woman is seldom a great beauty, but she is certain to have made the utmost of her assets. Keenly interested in the present day, she does not aspire to lead a fashion, but follows quietly, considering, discarding and adapting. Her make-up, hairstyles, dresses, all are reflections of her personal taste. The myriad points of grooming have become habits practised daily so that now their upkeep is a matter of moments for her and she has an easy conscience. She will never offend with a strident voice or an ungraceful gesture, and she is always fresh as a snowdrop from her skin to her topcoat and her hat.

2 Poise is high on her list of requirements, but she is careful never to lapse into the brusque or blasé, nor seem too sure of herself. As we have said, that is the ideal, but if, with you, shyness and lack of confidence have not been left behind where they belong—in early 'teens—the time has come for some simple self-analysis. Why are you worrying? If your manners are good and your choice of clothes correct for the occasion, there is no cause for concern and your timidity can be overcome by a little firm self-discipline. Try to forget your fears and start a conversation next time you feel overcome by shyness. Encourage others to talk about themselves and you will rapidly earn the reputation of being a friendly woman and a charming conversationalist!

3 Fortunately, age has little to do with popularity. One of the most delightful women we know recalls many agonizing early mistakes. Her children were growing up, she tells us, before she found the way to make and keep good friends. Certainly she does not lack them now, and so we have studied her with closer care. Pettiness and affectation, we find, have no part in her; she can be depended upon for her tact and kindness in any situation, for her sympathy and her generous sense of humour; and, as they always will, these endearing qualities have helped to trace the lines of real beauty in her face.

The Institute • Principal, Phyllis L. Garbutt, A.R.I.C.

Curries

The Indian cuisine is renowned throughout the world for its savour and piquancy. A great variety of spices are used in the preparation of dishes, the selection of which depends entirely upon the experience and skill of the cook. The sauce, highly seasoned but not necessarily very hot, in which the fresh foods are cooked is called in one Indian language *kari*—corrupted into our *curry*.

Whatever the dish that is to be prepared, the following ingredients are always included—chilli powder, which gives the curry its hotness, bayleaf, cinnamon, onion or garlic and cloves, and then a selection of other spices such as ground coriander seed (*dhaniya*), cardamom, turmeric powder (*haldi*), cummin powder (*jeera*) and ginger (*udruk*). These ingredients are often mixed to a paste with a little tamarind pulp or water. Then they are thoroughly fried in fat.

At one time the spices were pounded or ground just as needed, but now they are frequently bought ready for use. Few grocers stock them all, but we know of an Indian emporium where they may be bought. A good curry is a careful blend of the most universally popular spices, but the discriminating prefer to blend their own so that particular flavours can predominate when required.

In different parts of India and according to the social position and religion of the people, the curries are served differently, and, as one would expect in such a vast country, the dishes are called by different names. Our picture shows a meal that might be served to a member of a well-to-do family in Bengal.

Each person has, on a silver *thali* or tray, a number of little bowls which a servant fills and replenishes with the selected dishes. When the meal is eaten, rice is first taken from the bowl and put on the *thali*, and some of the contents of the other bowls put on top. It is then eaten with the fingers and the help of a broken *puri* (or a *chuppatie*).

Here are the recipes for the variety of dishes shown in the picture, except the chutney and rice, and they might all be served at the same time, or any of the curried dishes, served with rice, would make an appetizing course.

Dry Beef Curry (Ghosht Bhuma)

1 lb. beef steak
1 tablespoonful ground coriander
1 teaspoonful ground turmeric
1 bayleaf and 2 cloves
½ teaspoonful cummin seed
¼ teaspoonful ground chillies
Pinch ground cinnamon
Tamarind water or vinegar
2 oz. dripping
1 onion and 1 clove garlic
½ pint stock or water
Salt to taste

Cut the beef into neat pieces. Mix together the spices with a little weak vinegar or tamarind water to form a paste. Melt the fat and fry the chopped onion and finely sliced garlic. Then fry the curry paste very thoroughly, stirring well. Add the meat and allow to cook slowly, continuing to stir and extracting some of the juices from the meat. Then add the liquid and cover the pan, allowing the meat to cook gently for another hour. Add a little salt and further seasoning if needed. By the time the curry is cooked, it will have absorbed all the liquid.

Curried Lentils (Dhall)

½ lb. lentils
1 small onion finely chopped
2 red chillies and 1 bayleaf
1-in. stick cinnamon and 3 cloves
2 whole cardamoms
1 oz. fat
1 clove garlic
½ teaspoonful ground turmeric
½ teaspoonful ground cummin seed
Pinch of ground chillies
Pinch of ground ginger
Tamarind water or vinegar
¼ pt. tomato juice
1 dessertspoonful ground coriander

Put the lentils to cook with the onion, chillies, bayleaf, cinnamon, cloves and cardamoms in salt water. Cook until the lentils are soft but not mushy. Melt the fat in a pan and fry the very finely chopped garlic, and meanwhile mix the other dry ingredients to a smooth paste with a little tamarind water or vinegar. Fry for 5 minutes in the fat, then add the tomato juice and lentil mixture and continue cooking for 15–20 minutes. The *Dhall* will be thick or thin according to how much liquid is added. If it is too liquid, it can be boiled rapidly to reduce it.

H—3

Vegetable Curry (Chitchlee)

½ lb. prepared mixed vegetables
1 oz. fat
1 onion and 1 clove garlic
½ tablespoonful ground coriander
½ teaspoonful ground turmeric
½ a bayleaf
Pinch chilli powder
2 to 3 cloves
Pinch ground cummin seed
½ teaspoonful ground ginger
Little mustard seed
Tamarind water

Dice the vegetables. Melt the fat and fry the thinly sliced onion and garlic. Make a paste of the other ingredients and fry it for 5 minutes. Then add vegetables and liquid and simmer until cooked. Season well and serve.

Spinach (Bhaji)

1 lb. spinach
2 oz. margarine
Lemon juice and seasoning
Red pepper and nutmeg

Thoroughly wash and prepare the spinach. Melt half the margarine in the pan and put in the wet spinach. Toss now and again and cook for 10 minutes until the spinach is thoroughly cooked. Drain off the liquid, chop in remaining margarine, sprinkle with lemon juice and season well. Serve with some red pepper and grated nutmeg shaken over.

Puri

4 oz. wholemeal flour
4 oz. plain flour
1 teaspoonful salt
Water to mix
Fat for frying

Mix together the dry ingredients and mix to a stiffish dough with the water. Knead well and shape into flat round biscuits ⅛ inch thick and about 3–4 inches in diameter. Heat some fat or oil in a small pan (about 3 inches of fat) and when smoking hot put in a cake, baste well and allow the *puri* to puff. Turn and fry the other side until crisp and brown. Drain well and serve immediately.

BY BETTY COY
(*Combined Domestic Subjects Diploma, London*)

trading on TRUST

Have you ever stopped to think how much trust you place in your tradespeople? The butcher delivers the weekly joint, the coal merchant dumps your order of anthracite in the shed, the draper runs his yardstick along your length of dress goods, the "manufacturer" sends you his "spun silk slip" as per his newspaper small ad, the barrow boy weighs out "three pounds for two bob," at the grocer's you ask for a large packet of soap powder substitute . . . and you pay what is asked of you.

What have you got for your money? Have you even paused to check and see? If you're the average shopper, you haven't.

But, for the moment, let us assume you are one of those rare shoppers who does inquire into her purchases. The answers come back: "four and sixpenny'orth lamb shoulder," "ten hundredweights of anthracite," "three yards of taffeta," "a silk slip," "three pounds of oranges," "a packet of substitute soap powder" . . . Yet, are you any the wiser for having asked?

Perhaps you did get what you paid for. On the other hand the butcher may have overcharged you *2d.* a pound on the lamb shoulder. The coal merchant may have shorted you one bag of anthracite. The draper's three yards may in reality have been only eight-and-a-half feet. The "spun silk" may be artificial silk. The barrow boy's three pounds of oranges may have included a half pound of thumb. And that largest packet of synthetic soap powder may actually contain less powder than most of the smaller packets around it.

A pretty state of affairs, you will say indignantly. So let me hasten to point out that here in one paragraph I have lumped together sharp trading practices which it might take thousands of individual purchases to produce in the normal course of daily shopping. In an article gathering together information on any special set of circumstances—in this instance trade dishonesty—it is very easy to slip into the illusion that these circumstances are representative of conditions generally.

In the main, tradespeople and merchants are honest citizens. But every pack of cards has its knaves, and it's against these knaves that to be forewarned is to be forearmed.

One of the most flagrant swindles practised by dishonest traders is the giving of short weight and measure. There are laws designed to punish such offenders. The enforcement of these laws is entrusted to the Weights and Measures Offices of the various local authorities. I picked the largest of these, the London County Council Weights and Measures Office, as a first-hand source of information. My first impression was that the Inspectors there were rather surprised—pleasantly so—that I called in to see them.

"The average person," they told me, "isn't even aware that we exist. Yet day and night, seven days a week—including Sundays and Bank Holidays—we are on the alert to protect shoppers against short weight and measure."

Their principal function is to check the accuracy of and stamp every single weight and measure and weighing and measuring machine used in trade in London County. At the same time they keep an eye on the weighing and measuring practices of tradesmen and haul into court any they find indulging in skullduggery. They know every trick and ruse of merchant cheats. Last year the

19 inspectors visited 38,000 shops one or more times and inspected about one-half million appliances. In only 249 instances was it necessary to institute legal proceedings.

I visited the Weights and Measures Office with the naïve impression that, as a person with a scientific eye, I was too canny to be swindled by a dishonest man at a weighing machine. I was very quickly disillusioned.

Before my piercing (as I fondly imagined) gaze, one of the Inspectors weighed out three pounds of apples for me on a typical barrow scale. I could see nothing wrong with the operation and had it been done at a barrow I would have happily paid for my purchase and trotted blithely along.

Imagine my chagrin, then, when taking the bag of apples back and re-weighing it on an official checking scale, the Inspector showed me I had been short-weighted by almost a pound. A number of short-weighing tricks had been perpetrated on me and I had been none the wiser.

"In the first place," the Inspector explained, "I (*Continued on page* **50**)

Do you know that . . .

Shady traders have seven stock ways of giving short weight ?

Weights sold with cheap kitchen scales are seldom correct ?

A big packet sometimes has less inside it than a smaller one ?

Weights and measures laws don't cover post office scales ?

BY GEORGE GLENWOOD

The London Collections

THE 1950 LOOK

The London Export Collections this season set the stage for the 1950 look. There is no great or drastic change—nothing sensational or dramatic—but the difference between 1949 and 1950 is very real. One has more the feeling that lines are *beginning* to change than that they have already done so. These subtle differences are apparent in detail rather than in mass, in tendencies rather than in arbitrary changes of direction. It is from gentle hints and details that the 1950 look emerges. Casual coats are still loose and easy—but they are narrower. There is that about their cut which makes one remember the tube-like, wrapped-around coats of Lorelei in *Gentlemen Prefer Blondes*. The big loose coat for travelling is still much loved, but the vast amplitude of the past few seasons is being pared down. The fitted, big (*Continued on page* **133**)

● **VICTOR STIEBEL**

The romantic look for evening in a dress with the du Maurier air. Black faille is moulded into a bodice which fits like a second skin, into a pulled-back apron drapery, into a great spreading underskirt. Frosty white eyelet embroidery edges the slashed neckline and ripples round the skirt. A pink rose nestles at the bosom

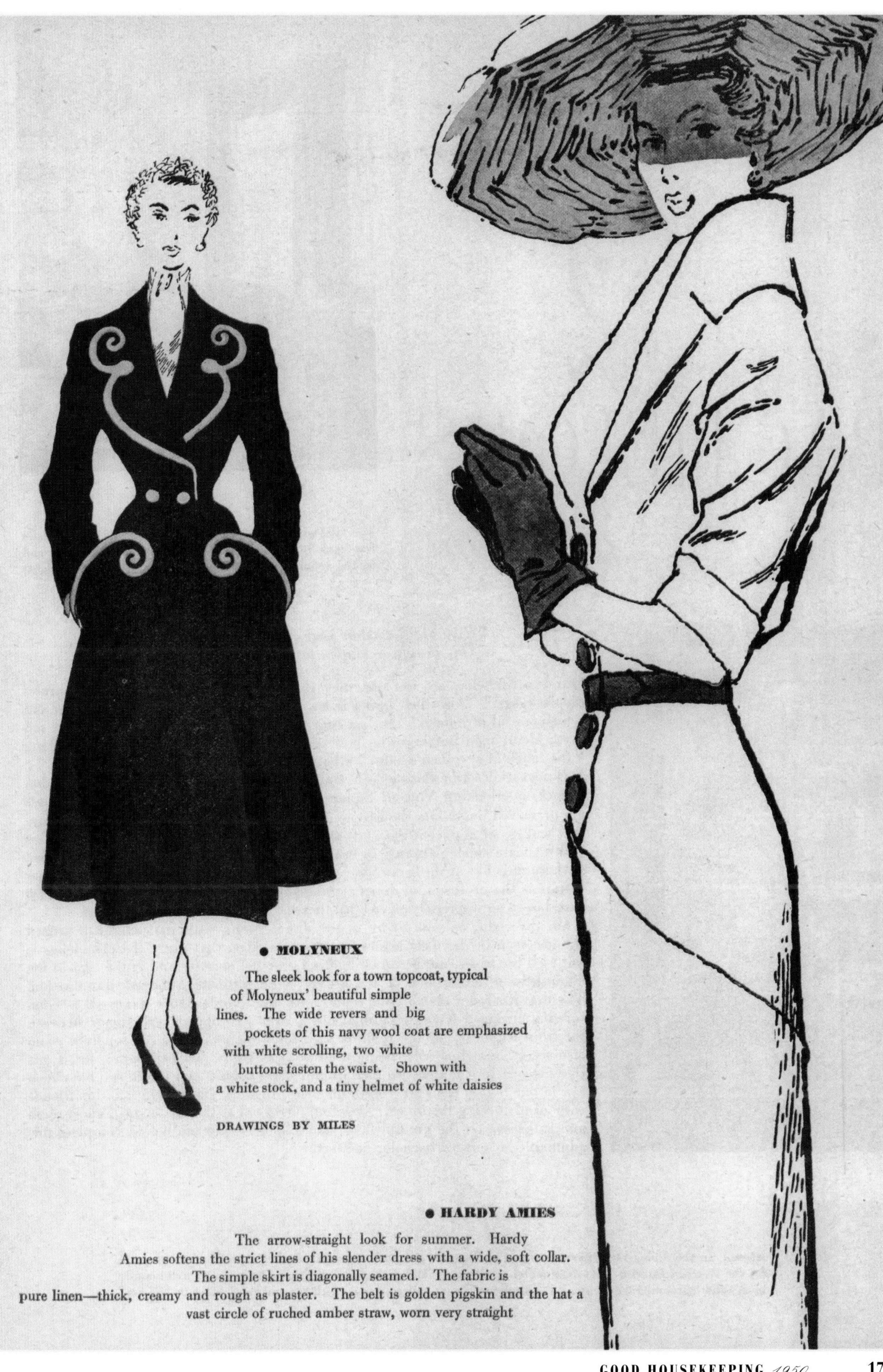

• MOLYNEUX

The sleek look for a town topcoat, typical of Molyneux' beautiful simple lines. The wide revers and big pockets of this navy wool coat are emphasized with white scrolling, two white buttons fasten the waist. Shown with a white stock, and a tiny helmet of white daisies

DRAWINGS BY MILES

• HARDY AMIES

The arrow-straight look for summer. Hardy Amies softens the strict lines of his slender dress with a wide, soft collar. The simple skirt is diagonally seamed. The fabric is pure linen—thick, creamy and rough as plaster. The belt is golden pigskin and the hat a vast circle of ruched amber straw, worn very straight

Your second skin

1. SPECTATOR. COTTON SUNSUIT IN VIVID GREEN, BLACK-PRINTED.
ABOUT £7 13*s.* 6*d.* AT HARRODS

2. MARTIN WHITE. ELASTICATED COTTON—WIDE SHOULDER STRAPS.
ABOUT £1 16*s.* AT JAY'S

3. JANTZEN. BRIGHT WOOL ONE-PIECE, HALF-SKIRTED, CLOSE-FITTING.
ABOUT £2 11*s.* 10*d.* AT PETER ROBINSON

4. JANTZEN. AN ADJUSTABLE TOP, A HALF-SKIRT, A FAINT SHEEN.
ABOUT £2 9*s.* 11*d.* AT PETER ROBINSON

We admit that you don't wear a great deal for facing up to sun and sea-water. But what you *do* wear fits you like the paper on the wall. Your sun-and-swim suit is designed to give you the freedom and the neatness of a fish—but very few fishes will look as pretty as you do, this summer. Left to right, 1. Spectator's peacock-green cotton sunsuit has a wide, black-lined sash. Wear it with a huge raffia sombrero (Eaton Bag Co., Manette St., W.1) and Bollé sun-glasses from Fenwick's. 2. An elasticated cotton swimsuit, scarlet on white, from Martin White. 3. Pale parrot-green with a herringbone pattern for those who like a wool swimsuit—by Jantzen. 4. The big fashion flash of the season—a starkly plain, exquisitely cut black maillot by Jantzen. N.B.—Two-piece swimsuits are still with us, and still very good, but the simple one-piece suit is the best suit, this year

John French

*
Big news
this year—
the plain black swimsuit

★

An American story: we believe a great story. We publish it with enthusiasm

★

Hazen said, " I didn't say you're unreasonable. I said it's unreasonable of me to expect you to understand."

His wife, leaning across the breakfast table with the percolator, gave him an amused glance.

" Darling," Nancy said pleasantly. " It's just too early in the morning for us to split hairs."

Hazen wished, as he nodded his thanks for the coffee, that Nancy had not decided to be amused by the situation. It gave him no excuse to grow angry. And Hazen felt that, after what he had gone through during the past twelve days, the chance to ease the tension by growing angry would do him good.

" I'm not splitting hairs," he said. " I'm merely stating facts. This dinner for tonight was arranged by G. G. himself. G. G. said no wives. G. G. said the guests would be absolutely limited to eighteen. G. G. said that number included himself and Lord Edgeworth. G. G. said the figure could not be changed, because that's as many people as the private dining-room at The Swindon Club can possibly hold. G. G. said—I beg your pardon ? "

" Nothing," Nancy said. " I was just wondering whether anyone noticed a white light, coming from a mysterious source, playing about G. G.'s brow while he was saying all that."

In spite of his desire to grow angry, Hazen found himself forcing back a rueful smile. Grover Grange, who was always identified by his staff as G. G., was the publishing genius who had founded, and ruled with an iron hand, the empire of fabulously successful magazines known to the world at large as *Universe, Inc.* There were times when Hazen, like his wife, felt uneasily that G. G. had taken on a disturbing number of characteristics that people usually attribute to divinity.

" I wouldn't know about mysterious white lights," Hazen said, as he reached for the cream. " All I know is that G. G. put the whole thing in a memorandum, on his own private stationery, twelve days ago, that the memorandum was sent up to me, and that it's a matter of simple arithmetic. Lord Edgeworth, the guest of honour, and G. G. himself, add up to two. If you deduct them from the number eighteen, you're left with sixteen. Our last Executive Census indicated that *Universe, Inc.* now has two hundred and eighty-six staff members who fall in Upper Echelon, Category A. Every one of those two hundred and eighty-six people feels that he or she has had something to do with making (*Continued on page* 88)

BY JEROME WEIDMAN

ILLUSTRATED BY JOAN MARTIN MAY

to go alone to
the tiny flat and
say his say.
What he saw whe
he got there
surprised him as
much as it
may surprise you
way to perform it

The WOMAN'S

★ Representative housewives give us their opinions on monarchy, the Church, football pools, the divorce laws, conscription, sex education

92% APPROVE OF MONARCHY

In January last year we published the results of a survey which Mass-Observation had made especially for GOOD HOUSEKEEPING magazine. Its object was to discover and define the difficulties with which middle-class housewives had to contend when carrying out their important duties as homemakers. We dealt then with highly practical matters such as the effect of rationing on the average family, the cost of living and the shortage of domestic help.

This year we asked Mass-Observation to make a second survey, but directed this time at discovering what middle-class housewives are thinking on various topics of current and fairly controversial interest—such as sex education, the value of the monarchy, the influence of the Church, the pros. and cons. of the welfare state and so on. This month we present the first part of this latest report, dealing with housewives' opinions on a number of general topics. Next month the second part will be devoted to one particular subject —their views on the welfare state.

One of the stock jokes of the public-opinion polls humorist concerns the number of people, especially the number of housewives, who " don't know." It is true that the number who " don't know " what the United Nations is, or the name of their M.P., or who Sherlock Holmes was, is larger than might be thought: and it is equally true that those who most often say they " don't know "

A MASS-OBSERVATION SURVEY FOR GOOD HOUSEKEEPING

tend to be housewives. But does it follow from this that housewives as a group are necessarily ignorant, particularly on matters on which they have some sort of personal experience?

Results of our current survey certainly highlight the "don't knows": 52 per cent, for instance, didn't know what the welfare state was, and 40 per cent didn't know how they felt about football pools. But such groups are not constant. There is no common core of ignorance, and, though few people in the sample said "I don't know" to *most* questions, most said "I don't know" to *some*.

But the "don't know" of these housewives was not necessarily a profession of ignorance. Frequently the implication was that the subject of enquiry was too complex to be embraced in the answer to a single question.

As far as the general topics dealt with in this first section were concerned, it soon became clear that on most there was little unanimity of opinion among housewives. Although 92 per cent of those interviewed approved of the monarchy, and a fairly large majority (74 per cent) agreed that sex instruction should be given to children, on other subjects opinion was much divided. For instance, 55 per cent stated that they approved of conscription, and 46 per cent of football pools; 32 per cent thought the churches were doing a good job. A question on the divorce laws drew out a variety of opinions but was not couched in a form that invited "yes" or "no" for an answer.

Sex Instruction

Taking each of these subjects in detail, this is the picture revealed by our survey of how people feel about the idea of sex instruction. It was found that 74 per cent of those questioned approved the idea; 12 per cent had mixed feelings; 10 per cent disapproved; and 4 per cent had no opinion on the matter.

32% THINK CHURCHES ARE DOING A GOOD JOB

Older people were much more inclined to disapprove than the younger ones. Among those under twenty-five, 79 per cent approved, but among those over sixty only 55 per cent were in favour.

Approval is not always whole-hearted. As many as one in four add the proviso that sex instruction should be given by parents, and three in twenty emphasize that children should reach a certain age before they are given such instruction. Ideas about the "right" age vary from person to person, but only a few feel that the child should be told as soon as he asks. People generally seem aware that it is a ticklish subject to handle. "*If it is taught in a special set class,*" said an insurance official's wife, "*I think you get the children into a silly state before they get there.*"

It is interesting here to mention that, in another Mass-Observation survey, in which a national sample of more than 2,000 people were questioned, by far the greatest measure of approval for sex instruction came from those who had themselves received it; and though parents' approval of sex instruction was often accompanied by embarrassment at the thought of actually having to give it themselves, teachers for the most part not merely approved of the idea, but felt that there was no real difficulty in execution.

Some people feel that instruction *en masse* must be somewhat arbitrary and therefore dangerous. The manageress of a draper's shop said with some feeling, "*My sister's children come out with things and they don't know what they're saying.*" Even so, school instruction is usually regarded as the lesser of two evils, and few people now share the views of the wife of a shipping company official who said, "*I don't really agree with it. To a certain point, yes, but in the olden days they learnt all they needed without all this bother.*"

The Divorce Laws

Divorce is another topic that looms large in contemporary thought and a question in this survey that drew out some interesting facts was, "In what circumstances do you think that people in this country should be allowed to divorce one another?"

The basic answers were as follows (some people giving more than one reason): 20 per cent gave no answer; 23 per cent mentioned incompatibility, inability to get on, as grounds on which divorce should be granted; 20 per cent mentioned cruelty or desertion; 16 per cent mentioned adultery; 12 per cent mentioned mental unhappiness; 8 per cent mentioned insanity; 3 per cent mentioned drunkenness; 5 per cent said that the laws should be as they are now; 10 per cent said that divorce is always wrong; 4 per cent said that divorce is wrong if there are children.

Perhaps the most significant thing here is that "inability to get on" (which may or may not include sexual infidelity) is most often mentioned as legitimate reason for divorce, more often than either desertion or adultery. A timber merchant's wife, in fact, (*Continued on page* 88)

1

2

 Six good-looking, inexpensive dresses to prove that

Tea-set by Lawleys 3 Keith Ewart

THE PLEASANT HOURS

WHAT do you wear in your leisure hours at home? Do you cling for ever to a "comfortable" skirt and jumper, saving your "best" for rare occasions? Or have you found a little dress, not elaborate, not too plain, but "different" to give you a feeling of luxury and relaxation; perfect for the days when friends call unexpectedly. We rate the casual woollen dress an indispensable part of every woman's wardrobe, and we have chosen six for you to see. They are in the shops in jewel-bright or muted "background" colours, with all the latest fashion features, at prices well within your purse.

1. BEAUTIFUL GREY/BLUE DRESS BY DALTON FASHIONS. THE CURVED WRAP-OVER TUNIC IS BUTTONED FROM COLLAR TO KNEES, WHERE IT BURSTS INTO A SHORT FLARE. £6 4*s.* FROM JOHN BARKER, KENSINGTON HIGH STREET, LONDON, W.8.

2. A GINGER-BROWN WOOL AFGALAINE DRESS, PRETTILY FOLDED AT THE WAIST AND HELD BY A CHESTNUT PATENT BELT. BY MALCOLM BROWN, £5 AT DICKINS & JONES, REGENT STREET, W.1.

3. ROTERS' TURQUOISE WOOL-JERSEY DRESS HAS A NATURAL SHOULDER-LINE, FLY-FASTENING FROM COLLAR TO WAIST. THE SKIRT HAS A SINGLE PLEAT EACH SIDE. PRICE £5 9*s.* 5*d.* FROM SELFRIDGES, OXFORD STREET, W.1.

elegance is yours just for the looking

A 6-PAGE SECTION OF PRESENT-DAY FURNITURE

THE STUDIO

BY PETER LULING

PRESENT-DAY LIVING-ROOM

Since restrictions were lifted on the design of furniture for the home market, there has been a welcome improvement in choice and quality. In this section three rooms are illustrated, furnished with articles in current production : a living-room, a living-cum-dining-room, and a bed-sitting-room. Alternative pieces are shown separately. With few exceptions, items included are of British manufacture, featured in the Festival of Britain *Design Review,* and are tax-free. Each room was arranged and furnished by the author, with the co-operation of a leading store. If a piece is exclusive, this is mentioned. All shown on these two pages are from Liberty's of Regent Street. *Opposite :* Wing chair (foreground) with detachable head-rest, from £16 2*s.* 6*d.* Fireplace in oak with shelf and sliding glass doors, £17 10*s.* Wall desk in birch, £11. Windsor armchair with squab cushion, £3 4*s.* 8*d.* Buttoned-back wing chair in beech, £15 13*s.* 4*d.* Tray-top table, £12 17*s.* 6*d.* Mahogany floor standard with metal shade, £18 2*s.* 6*d.* Paper ceiling shade, 26*s.* 6*d.* Curtains, Liberty printed linen, 48 in. wide, 33*s.* 6*d.* per yard. (All prices correct at time of going to press.)

NEST OF TABLES DESIGNED BY KELVIN MACAVOY, FROM £11 6*s.* 8*d.* (LIBERTY'S EXCLUSIVE)

ARMCHAIR IN NATURAL BIRCH, COVERED IN VARIOUS TAPESTRIES. PRICE FROM £9 10*s.* 8*d.*

GLASS-TOPPED COFFEE TABLE IN SYCAMORE, CHESTNUT OR MAHOGANY, FROM £7 18*s.* 3*d.*

MAHOGANY TABLE LAMP, WITH SILK SHADE, 11 GNS. ; WITH A METAL SHADE, £9 15*s.* 9*d.*

COFFEE TABLE AND WORK-BOX, DESIGNED BY KELVIN MACAVOY, £12 0*s.* 6*d.* (LIBERTY'S EXCL.)

" BOOMERANG " TABLE, FROM 2 GNS. ; ALTERNATIVE SHAPE OPPOSITE. (LIBERTY'S EXCL.)

First-year wife

mainly for the First-year wife

A topic a month for the new housewife

Maurice Ambler

THIS MONTH: HOW TO BUY FOOD, AND WHAT TO KEEP IN THE STORE-CUPBOARD

To the new housewife, the problems of shopping and of stocking up a first store-cupboard seem to present major housekeeping headaches, but they needn't do so. "How much should I buy?" is usually the cry of the inexperienced housewife, so here is a rough guide to average quantities of some of the more basic foods needed per meal for two people.

MEATS

	Fresh	*Cooked*	*Sausages*
With bone:	about 8 oz.	4 oz.	8 oz.
Boneless:	4–6 oz.		

The above amounts of fresh meat cannot always be obtained under present rationing conditions and it must be eked out by serving with plenty of vegetables or with dumplings or Yorkshire pudding. Since fresh meat is rationed according to price, it is as well to get to know which are the inexpensive cuts, since you will get more meat by buying these. If you buy grilling or frying steak, for instance, you will get much less than of stewing steak. But don't forget the cheaper cuts need more care and attention in cooking if they are to be palatable, and they may consist of a relatively large amount of bone or fat.

FISH

With bone	*With little or no bone*	*For made-up dishes*
12–16 oz.	6–8 oz.	4–6 oz.

Haddock, cod, whiting, herring, mackerel and sometimes plaice are among the cheaper varieties. Turbot, sole, halibut and, of course, shellfish are more expensive.

VEGETABLES

Potatoes	*Root*	*Green*
12–16 oz.	12–16 oz.	12–16 oz. (this will allow for inevitable wastage).

FRUIT

Fresh	*Dried*
16 oz.	8 oz.

Greengroceries should be fresh and sound. Avoid any that are limp or, with fruits, any that are over- or under-ripe. Remember that foods are cheapest and best when in season. Out-of-season fruits and vegetables, for instance, are not only more expensive but often also lacking in flavour.

Knowing which foods are most useful and necessary to keep in the store-cupboard is another problem besetting the new housewife. A large, well-filled store cupboard was at one time the first essential to good housekeeping, but today circumstances have altered a great deal. Often storage space is limited, stores themselves are less plentiful and, even in remote country districts where there is no village shop, travelling motor stores generally make weekly visits. It is, therefore, no longer necessary for housewives to keep large stocks, and it is even unwise to do so since there is always risk of wastage through spoliation. Cereals, for instance, are liable to be attacked by mites and weevils if kept for any length of time; baking-powder may lose its strength if it becomes damp. Canned foods have a long shelf life, but there is no particular point in cumbering up your cupboards with unnecessarily large stocks of these.

Your store-cupboard should be in a cool, dry, airy position and kept scrupulously clean. Wash out store jars, bread bin, etc., at intervals and thoroughly dry before replacing stores. Always wipe up any spilt food at once and, of course, look over all stores at regular intervals for any signs of spoliation. If possible, avoid cupboards with too deep shelves; shallow ones are far easier to keep tidy and make it easier for you to find what you want. Some articles can be stored in the containers in which they are purchased—others require store jars. The least expensive are 1 or 2-lb. glass jam jars with plastic or metal covers. In these it is easy to identify the contents at a glance and to see when they require replenishment. It is important to keep such stores as salt, biscuits, coffee, baking-powder and spices in airtight containers. Bread should be kept in a bin with slight ventilation or merely wrapped in a clean tea towel.

Although the contents of the modern store-cupboard may be limited, they need to be carefully thought out so that you are not always having to run out for a missing ingredient. The following list is a general guide for those setting up a store-cupboard for the first time. Everyone will wish to make modifications to meet her own desires and requirements but most people find it useful to keep:

- Flour
- Rice
- Semolina
- Tapioca
- Macaroni
- Breakfast cereal
- Cornflour
- Custard powder
- Gelatine
- Tea
- Coffee
- Cocoa
- Sugar
- Preserves and syrup
- Dried fruits, including prunes
- Salt
- Baking-powder
- Pepper
- Mustard
- Vinegar
- Mixed herbs and spices
- Sauces
- Pickles
- Gravy browning
- Flavourings and colourings

A small reserve of tinned and prepared foods, e.g. tinned luncheon meat, sardines, soups, evaporated and condensed milks, fruit, vegetables, packet jellies, etc.

Phyllis L. Garbutt

What 1951 means to Me...

A fanfare for a Festival year by any young mother of today

My grandmother tells me that the Age of Gold is dead—my mother (she says) stopped concentrating and it slipped away, like a dream. For her, the Age of Gold meant sleek butlers, enormous Barons of Beef and shoulders of home-killed mutton; hunt balls in the 'Shires; Victoria on the throne. In 1851 money ruled the world.

1951 seems to me the most gloriously exciting year through which humanity has yet been privileged to live.

1951, for me, is the year when Miss Normanton, the first woman K.C. could smile blandly on a world where sex equality was an accomplished fact and promise she would "do her best to show justice to men": a year we nursed the children through measles, whooping cough, influenza without having to worry about the doctor's bill. And it was the year when I was one of the lucky people who got a ticket out of the Ballot from the Festival to hear Yehudi Menuhin play.

Of course life in 1951 is a conflict, and a frightening conflict too. But I wouldn't change any of it. When the world stands looking at ruin and disaster, it might even be some of *my* faith in the spiritual progress of the average, decent human being that may help us to make up our minds between Peace and War—Progress or Armageddon.

Perhaps the Age of Gold *is* dead. 1951 may mean the Age of Faith is just beginning....

KNOW YOUR OWN FIGURE

Exercise for figure faults, for vitality, for litheness of body, for a lilt in your walk ; to stay young, young, young

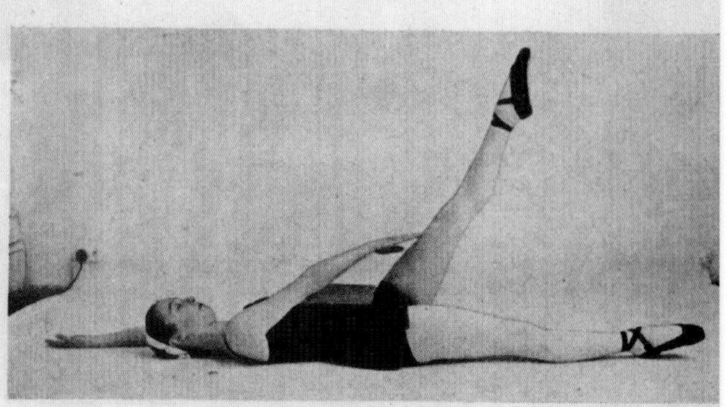

For a slender waist, stand with feet apart, left arm overhead, right arm down. Now bend to the right at waist only. Reverse arms and bend left. Repeat this and all other exercises on this page 20 times. To flatten your abdomen, lie on floor with legs straight, arms overhead, book on tummy. Now raise right arm and left leg until the hand touches the knee. Repeat with alternating legs and arms

To slim hips, sit on floor, arms out, legs straight, heels together. Now use hip muscles to lift and rock first on one hip as far as you can, then on the other. Be sure to keep heels together. For slim legs and firm thighs, lie on one side with arm up under head, right one bracing you in front. Now, keeping knees straight, swing legs rapidly backwards and forwards from hips, scissors-wise

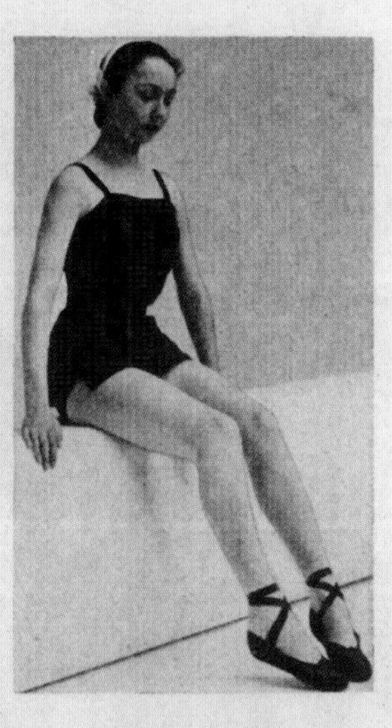

To keep ankles trim and strong, practise this often. Sit with feet in pigeon-toed position. Now raising the feet, tap your toes on the floor, then your heels. Remember to keep toes together, heels far apart. To lift the bosom, sit cross-legged in relaxed position. Place hands on lower ribs and without moving your hips lift up two inches

BE YOUR OWN MASSEUSE

Have you ever thought, if I could afford massage, I'd have a perfect figure? We're sorry, Madam, but you'd probably be doomed to failure. To melt away extra pounds and inches a diet is essential and an exercise routine a great help. Massage alone will not dissolve avoirdupois. It does have its place in reducing, however, for it helps to speed up the circulation and the removal of waste products. Moreover, if it can be arranged after exercise, it will lessen the possibility of a stiff, sore body.

In addition to reducing, massage relaxes tired muscles, soothes the nerves, tones the skin, rests and refreshes. If professional massage is within your pocket, very good; if not, let us show you how to work upon yourself. Top-to-toe massage is more effective than concentration on spots. It is not necessary to pummel yourself until you cry nor to work until you are exhausted. Enjoy it and you will derive far more benefit. Our pictures demonstrate hand movements and the Pifco massager.

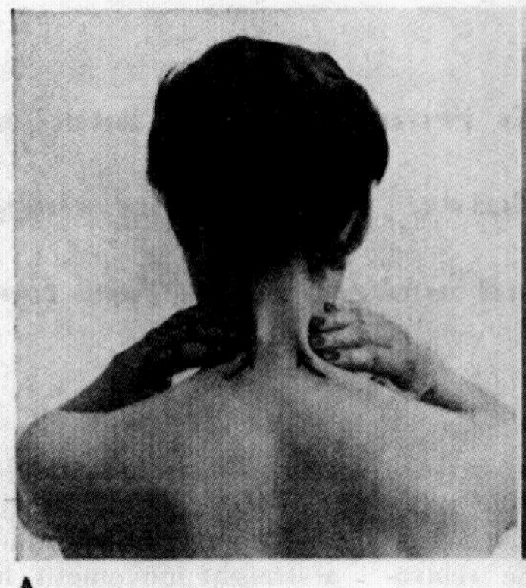

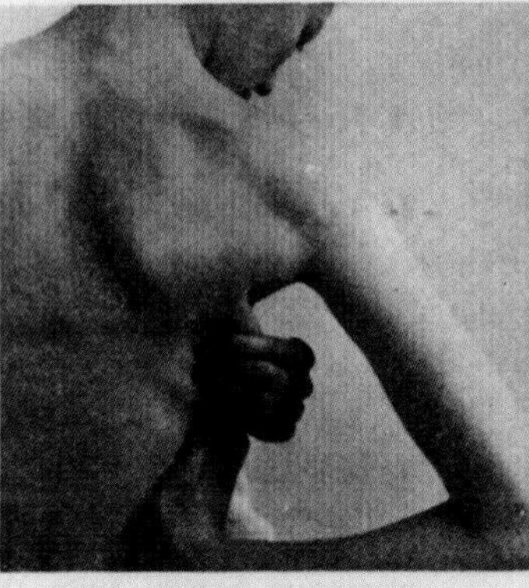

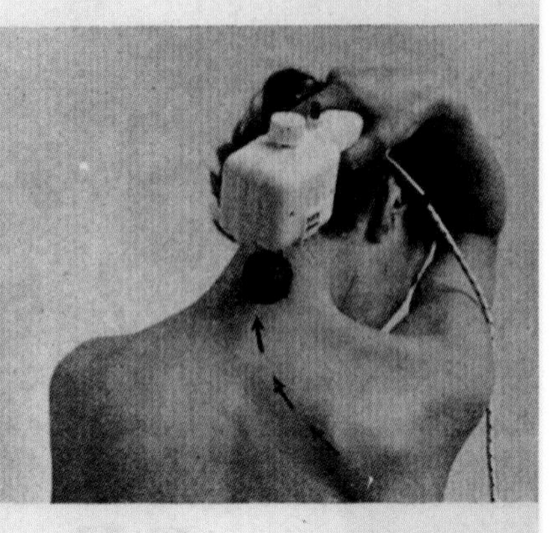

↑

To massage the neck and muscles behind the ears, place fingers at the collar-bone. Press deeply with a rotary motion into back of shoulders and up to hairline

Stroke or knead the abdomen lightly; deal more firmly with an over-the-waist roll. Then with pinching movements work from the waist-line up to each armpit

Now work over the top of your shoulder and massage the upper back as far as you can, transferring the machine from one hand to the other to extend your reach

Never massage the breasts. Move over upper chest and abdomen with light upward pressure. Stroke up from waist to armpits and finally hold vibrator on lower spine

To strengthen and soothe tired feet, massage the instep and the ball of the foot. Now work upward over the entire leg. Hips and buttocks take firm pressure

Use a hard, upward, wringing movement on the ankles and legs. End on the thighs, hips and buttocks, where a hard punching with doubled fists is most effective

↓

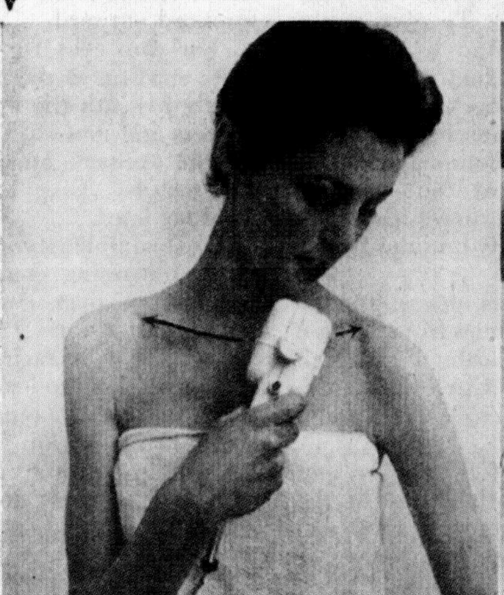

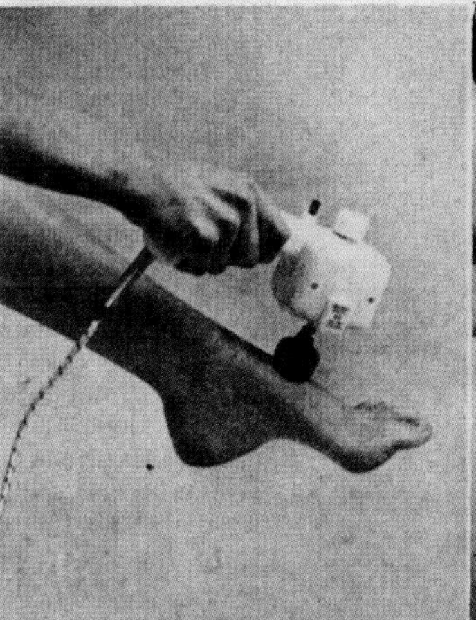

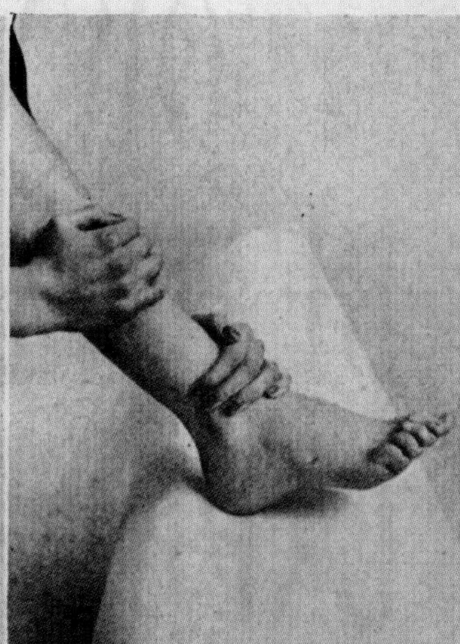

A GIRL *versus* LONDON

BY JANE DORLING

This is Sally. Have you met her—or her like—come to London from Newcastle, Dundee, Belfast or Penzance, perhaps? At 22 she is fighting for independence, security, contentment. She believes she can win in spite of the atom bomb

Those stockings must be cleared away and dried in her room because this bathroom is shared

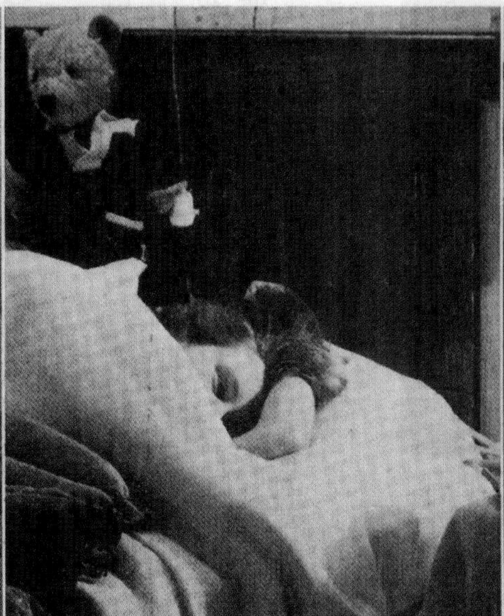

'Flu. No one to call the doctor. No friends. Will the landlady help? The teddy-bear is the only link with her home

Clothes are cheaper when you make them yourself. But *can* you? Sally hopes Joyce's experience may pull her through

Not much to live on, certainly, but she doesn't need money for courage, common sense, humour. She can't afford despair, illness, unhappiness, loneliness, idleness

Paris on the line! The boss has gone to lunch. It is the customer he was waiting for all morning. If she can cope with this, it may mean a rise. It's her chance

The sales. A £4 pair of shoes for 25*s*. Had she saved, she could also have a £20 suit for £8, overcoat £5. Could you save £14 5*s*. from £4 10*s*. a week? Sally did

Sunday. No cash. Bird-song. Sunshine. Dew on the grass. Trees budding. Spring in the air. No one to talk to. A strange dog the only other sign of life

This is the story of any girl in her first job in London—of her fight for existence, happiness and security.

There are hundreds of girls like Sally. She is 22. She has to keep herself alive, healthy, attractive on £4 10*s*. a week. Hers is the story of the extravagance of the gallery queue, the glamour of the 2*s*. 8*d*. dance-hall, the free and glistening pavements and the bright lights that twinkle in the Thames from the Embankment: of the destroying boredom of lonely week-ends after the nervous strain of a busy office . . . and how and where she makes both ends meet.

Sally is a child of the twentieth century who came to London, not because she thought the great city was paved with gold. "It isn't," says Sally. "But it has something." It has something that her own home town—in Scotland, Ireland or the provinces—hasn't got. For Sally, like any other pretty girl, is talented. She fancies herself as a dancer, singer, actress. Sometimes she fancies she is all of them at once. In her home town she was lucky if she saw a show "Prior to London production" once a year. In London she can see the best plays, learn from the best dancing teachers (if she can afford them at a guinea a lesson), can rub shoulders in the street with the great. She once saw Vivien Leigh going into *The Ivy* and lived on it for days. She wouldn't go home for anything, wouldn't even admit that the struggle is pretty grim. How would *you* budget for £4 10*s*. a week?

I must leave you to work it out for yourself. Sally says that it leaves her with precisely 30*s*. a week to dress herself, amuse herself and keep healthy. And she only manages this margin by sharing a furnished double divan room with Joyce, and running their housekeeping jointly.

As for clothes, stockings are one of the biggest worries. A pair of decent nylons costs 15*s*. and they are pretty hard to come by. Sally goes to the same shop for her underclothes, buys one pair of nylons every two months. The lady who keeps the

Smile at the soaring temperature—in dresses made for coolness, comfort and fresh good looks

1. Sambo's cotton dress in yellow and grey stripes etched with navy. With big straw hat and worn over a stiffened petticoat, it is a summer standby. Price £3 8*s.* approx. Peter Robinson, Oxford Circus, W.1.
2. Malcolm Brown makes this charmer, simply styled, lavishly cut. In pure silk, the colours are lime, sky, musquash, gold and betel, as shown. £9 2*s.* 6*d.* at Dickins & Jones, Regent St., W.1.
3. From Brenner Sports comes this navy-and-white cotton two-piece touched with white lace at the neck. Add a wide white hat and white gloves for freshness. Elegant together and equally useful as separates. £3 9*s.* 11*d.* at Paige, 21 New Bond St., W.1.

4. John, Harold and Blanes' gold spun-rayon dress has the season's ample skirt, a wide collar and life-size apples appliquéd on the pockets. A dress for popularity, parties, picnics and hot, hot sun. £3 12*s*. 6*d*. approx. at Swan & Edgar, Regent St., W.1.
5. The bold design of Lorocco's cotton dress adds its own bright comment to the day. Made with graceful flaring skirt and important stiff revers. In navy, grey, moss and cherry on white. From £3 11*s*. 6*d*. at Swan & Edgar, Regent St., London, W.1.
6. Bijou's dress is the coolest we've ever handled. Slender in cut, prettily striped, made of featherweight handkerchief linen, happy in the wash and a dream to iron. Approx. £4 6*s*., D.H.Evans, Oxford St., W.1.
7. Carnegie's maize linen dress will be a favourite for the woman who likes a tailored look. Straight, with well-cut pleats, bodice horizontally tucked, it is at its best with black accessories. Approx. £3 15*s*. at Barnet Hutton, 368 Oxford St., W.1.
8. Dainty feminine dress in red-and-white fine washable cotton by Susan Small. The stripes cleverly flatter the bust, shoulders are curved, hem swirling. £11 0*s*. 6*d*. at Derry & Toms, High St., Kensington, W.8.
9. Rosecroft's slim classic dress in sky rayon with shantung finish. Bodice and hips are picked out with white lattice appliqué. Neat from morning till evening. £3 15*s*. 2*d*. at Selfridges, Oxford St., W.1.
10. A distinctive cotton dress by Percy Trilnick, with scooped neck, small white vest, nipped waist and generous skirt. White polka-dots on navy or red. Price approximately £3 at McDonald's, Glasgow.

DRAWING BY RUTH FREEMAN

Cherry Baskets
Fill short crust cases with a little jam and a lot of double-thick custard . . . and here's the trick! The custard must be as creamy, as colourful, as flavourful *as only Bird's can make it*. Use angelica for handles and cherries for decoration.
REGD.
Be sure of delicious fun . . . make these with
BIRD'S CUSTARD
Party Oranges
Cut oranges in half, leaving zig-zag edges. Mix orange pulp with chopped orange jelly (Bird's, of course) and put in shells. Fill up with Bird's rich, creamy custard and top with cherries. Bird's *unvarying* quality makes these a dream to prepare and eat!

Festival Footnote
Fine shoes for a fine occasion—Physical Culture present three new styles in happily appropriate colours. Made the Selby way to give you the joy of perfect fitting and a festival of foot comfort.
Five fittings to each Brannock size and half-size. Special slim fitting service for ladies with slender feet
And now—
PHYSICAL CULTURE
Juniors
These new children's shoes have all the famous Physical Culture qualities of style and fit. For infants up to teenagers.
Physical Culture
A SELBY SHOE
If you care to write us we'll gladly tell you your nearest retailer.
PHYSICAL CULTURE SHOES LTD., 17-18 OLD BOND ST., LONDON, W.1. Wholesale only

BY HECTOR BOLITHO

Portrait of A QUEEN

British monarchy in its present constitutional form is largely the creation of women; of Queen Victoria, and the queen consorts who have followed her. With the fading of its political power, the crown has depended more and more on the domestic example set by the Royal Family; the example described by Prince Albert when he wrote to his brother, in 1840, " I wish you could be here and see in us a couple joined in love and unanimity. . . . Become as happy as we are, more I cannot wish for you." This uncynical and old-fashioned conception of marriage, which has endured for more than a century, inspired Mr. Winston Churchill to say, of King George VI and Queen Elizabeth, " They have the rare talent of being able to make a mass of people realize, in a flash, that they are good."

To comprehend the importance of Queen Elizabeth's part in sustaining the strength of the monarchy after the shock of the Abdication, we must glance back over her private story, before January 14th, 1923, when the following notice appeared in the Court Circular:

It is with the greatest pleasure that the King and Queen announce the betrothal of their loved son, the Duke of York, to the Lady Elizabeth Bowes-Lyon, daughter of the Earl and Countess of Strathmore, to which the King has gladly given his consent.

Queen Elizabeth spent much of her childhood at Glamis Castle in the Highlands. Her first experiences of human relationships were among her father's tenants, keepers and servants, and under the guidance of a nurse who said that she was " an exceptionally easy child " to bring up. She developed among people who valued learning for learning's sake, and not as an investment for profit. Her family—descended from warriors of the fourteenth century—were painters and writers, and she was educated in the habit of intelligent conversation and thoughtful living, rather than dalliance and fashion. When John Sargent painted her, as a girl in her late 'teens, he described (*Continued on page* **95**)

A characteristic study of Her Majesty by Dorothy Wilding

the studio

CONDUCTED BY HARRIET REEDER

■ In the average English house without servants, mother spends half her time in solitary confinement in the kitchen, which usually means away from the rest of the family. Above is an American livingroom-kitchen, where family and guests can be near while you work. The combination of rough brick, rustic woodwork and modern kitchen equipment is typical

Surprisingly, this is the other end of the room opposite. Two colours only, rich red and simple white, have been used with striking effect. Though wood is still scarce in this country, wallpaper which gives a perfect imitation is available. Note the cleverly-contrived three-tiered curtains

KITCHEN IN AMERICA

where they have revived the dual-purpose room, of which we show a handsome example

Slip a band round the case or trunk and the wheels make transport easy

A grain mill to save labour and food. The pig works it himself, and stops pushing it when he is not hungry

This device makes carrying two pailfuls of water much simpler

INVENTIONS

About Television's nation-wide shop window for people with novel ideas for saving time, money, work and worry

Benjamin Franklin once observed that necessity never made a good bargain. A bargain—like a Christmas cracker—has two ends, and the best goes to the arm with the stronger pull. The other collapses unless something turns up to stiffen resistance; some help or outside support. Too, too familiar is the tale of family treasures "sold for a song" because the owner was simple and easily discomforted by the buyer. But it is not only over the disposal of personal treasures than an owner may lose heart. There is another kind of owner; the man looking for a market for his ideas: the inventor, an isolated and unprotected unit in society.

These islands contain a store of inventive energy which in the past, for lack of encouragement and support, has often been diverted with advantage to other countries, or else allowed to run to waste; an inventor has before this been known to take his secret with him to the grave, and it has died with him from sheer neglect. For these tragedies manufacturers are unfortunately responsible; they have often lacked enterprise and foresight; sometimes they have been hostile to new ideas and even ignoble in their dealings, offering the inventor terms he felt unable to accept.

This is why the progress of TV's experiment, *Inventors' Club*, should be watched; over the past four years it has shown stimulating results. Regular viewers will have followed the gradual growth of this programme since its beginning; they may also like to know something about its origin and purpose.

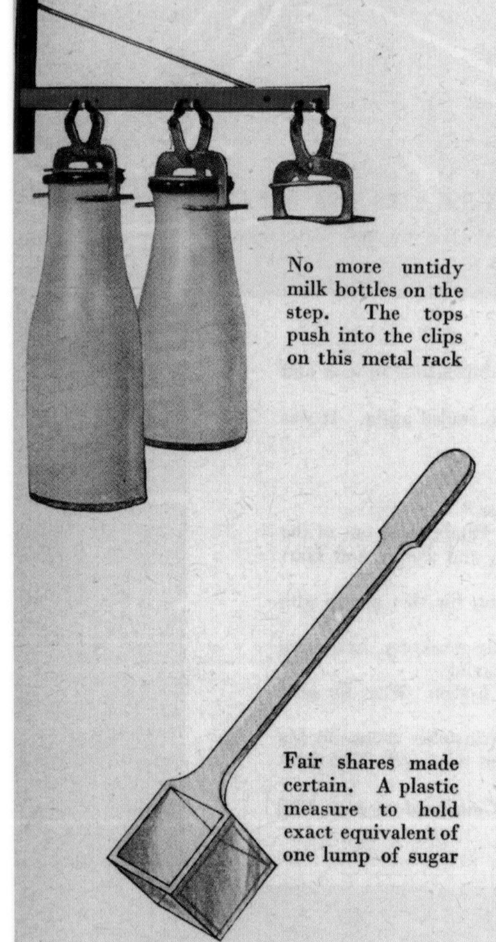

No more untidy milk bottles on the step. The tops push into the clips on this metal rack

Fair shares made certain. A plastic measure to hold exact equivalent of one lump of sugar

INVENTIONS NOT *ON VIEW*

Turn to page 114 for details of our August Housewives' Competition which invites you to give your personal instructions to an imaginary inventor. What would *you* ask him to invent to ease your daily round and lighten your duties as a housewife?

FIRST PRIZE: Singer electric iron with Pillar chrome-finished ironing board and Flexaway flex carrier; *or* Merry Go Home potato peeler and Princess Weylux scales; *or* £10.

SECOND PRIZE: Prestige kitchen tool set with Magirack magnetic holder; *or* Presto Meatmaster (pressure cooker with separators); *or* £5.

THIRD PRIZE: H.M.V. travelling iron; *or* Instant fruit press and refrigerator boxes and Puk Hexa cubes; *or* £3.

12 CONSOLATION PRIZES: Choice of a Dorridge plate drainer; *or* a Flexible Flo floor mop; *or* an Elizabeth Mckellar girdle with pastry cutters; *or* £1.

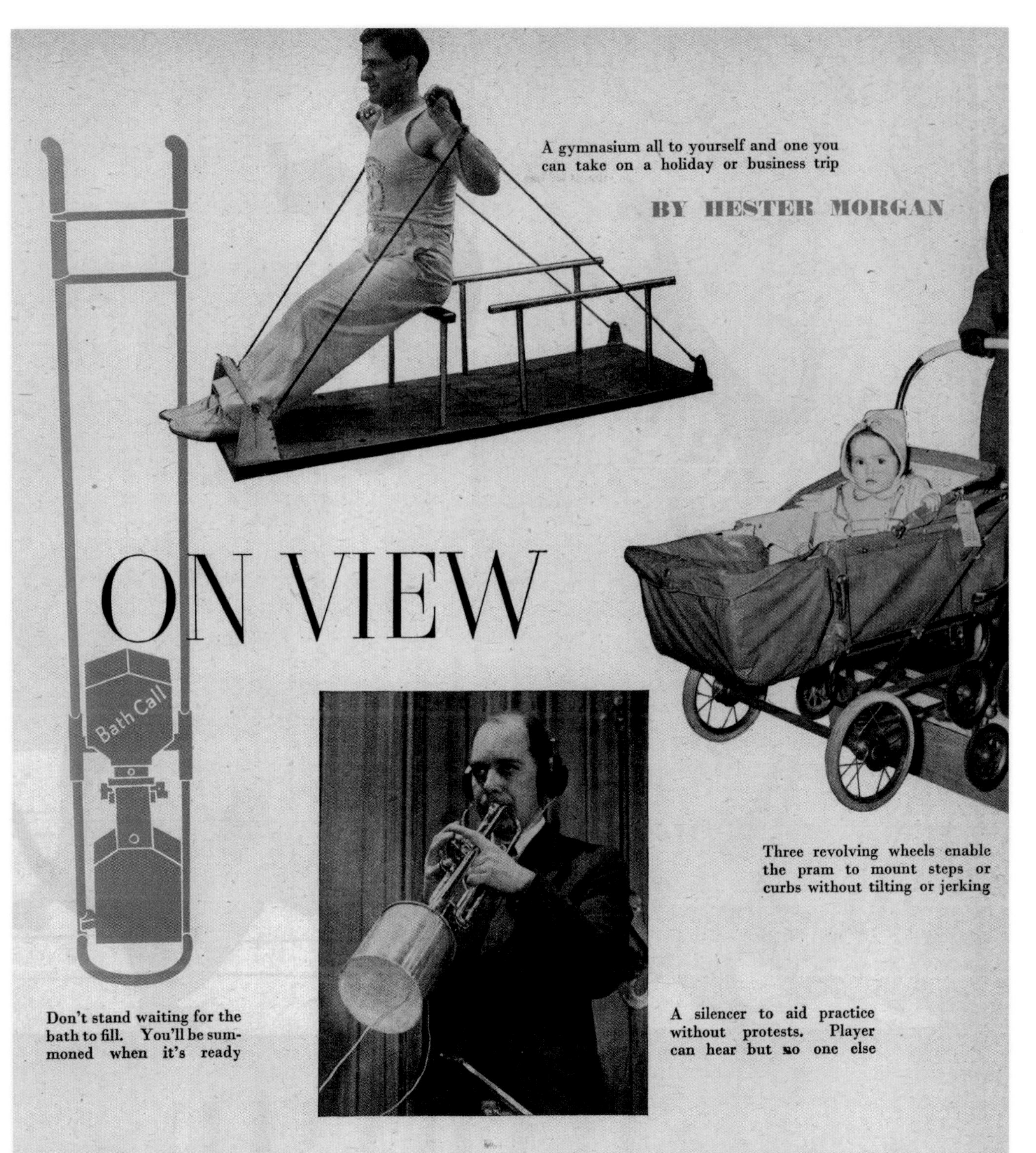

A gymnasium all to yourself and one you can take on a holiday or business trip

BY HESTER MORGAN

ON VIEW

Three revolving wheels enable the pram to mount steps or curbs without tilting or jerking

Don't stand waiting for the bath to fill. You'll be summoned when it's ready

A silencer to aid practice without protests. Player can hear but no one else

Inventors' Club developed out of a series of broadcast talks by Leslie Hardern on Design. These were continued as a series of television programmes, and perhaps naturally enough they tended to include Invention. The programme soon became a feature on rather unusual lines; ideas were its principal material, and before long Mr. Hardern was appealing for inventors to come forward and demonstrate their own, the aim being to televise the best, and bring them to the notice of manufacturers. Support was needed and obtained officially from the Board of Trade, from the Press and from bodies such as the Institute of Patentees. But response from the public was shy, at first.

The shyness was soon overcome, and the programme was successfully launched. There were no snags after this. Viewers' submissions now average one thousand a year. Descriptions are invited, accompanied by sketches or photographs and assessed by a panel consisting of the programme's experts: George Noordhof, producer; Leslie Hardern, founder and organizer; Geoffrey Boumphrey and John Gilbert are technical assessors responsible for design and engineering, electronics and motor-engines.

A drastic weeding-out by this panel of the original submissions leaves about ten per cent. for actual televising. Of this number, about one in four is eventually taken up by the trade, and in order that no risk is run by the inventor of piracy of his idea, Mr. Hardern insists on a provisional patent.

So much, then, for the organizing side, the brains behind TV's attempt to encourage national inventiveness by helping it strike roots in the somewhat (*Continued on page* **114**)

BY LINDSAY WILLIAMS

Last October none of the hospital staff or the patients of the busy Sea View Hospital on Staten Island, New York, thought that it would be anything other than a normal autumn month. The nurses busied themselves looking after their many patients and the doctors went on their rounds all little realizing that in a few months' time the eyes of an amazed and incredulous world would be turned upon them. Among the various topics of conversation of the Sea View doctors, the fact that an American firm had just passed on to the hospital a couple of drugs for testing, would be mentioned, discussed and then allowed to drop. After all, such matters were fairly routine happenings—all kinds of drugs had been tested before and reported on—there was nothing new in that.

This time the drugs, one known as " Rimifon " and the other a variation of it called " Marsilid," were to be tested to see what effect, if any, they would have in the treatment of tuberculosis in human patients. A good many so-called " wonder drugs" in this particular field have disappointed early expectations, and a good many researchers have had their hopes dashed, because the bacteria which cause T.B. are notoriously tough nuts to crack. So far only Streptomycin, its relative Dihydrostreptomycin and another drug called PAS have had any success, but at best these, it had been found, will only effect a cure of certain patients.

In the Sea View Hospital there were several T.B. patients on whom these three drugs had been tried but with no effect. They were desperate cases, thin, underweight, feverish and with their sputum full of the deadly T.B. microbes which were slowly and relentlessly sapping their vitality. In fact, as the doctors afterwards said, they were no longer candidates for any accepted form of therapy. Then Drs. Irving Selikoff and Edward Robitzek began dosing them with the two new drugs. There was no immediate effect. But after a couple of weeks the most amazing things began to happen. The patients developed voracious appetites, fever subsided and there were rapid gains in weight. In some, it was found, the dreadful lung cavities began to close up—and they all felt loads better.

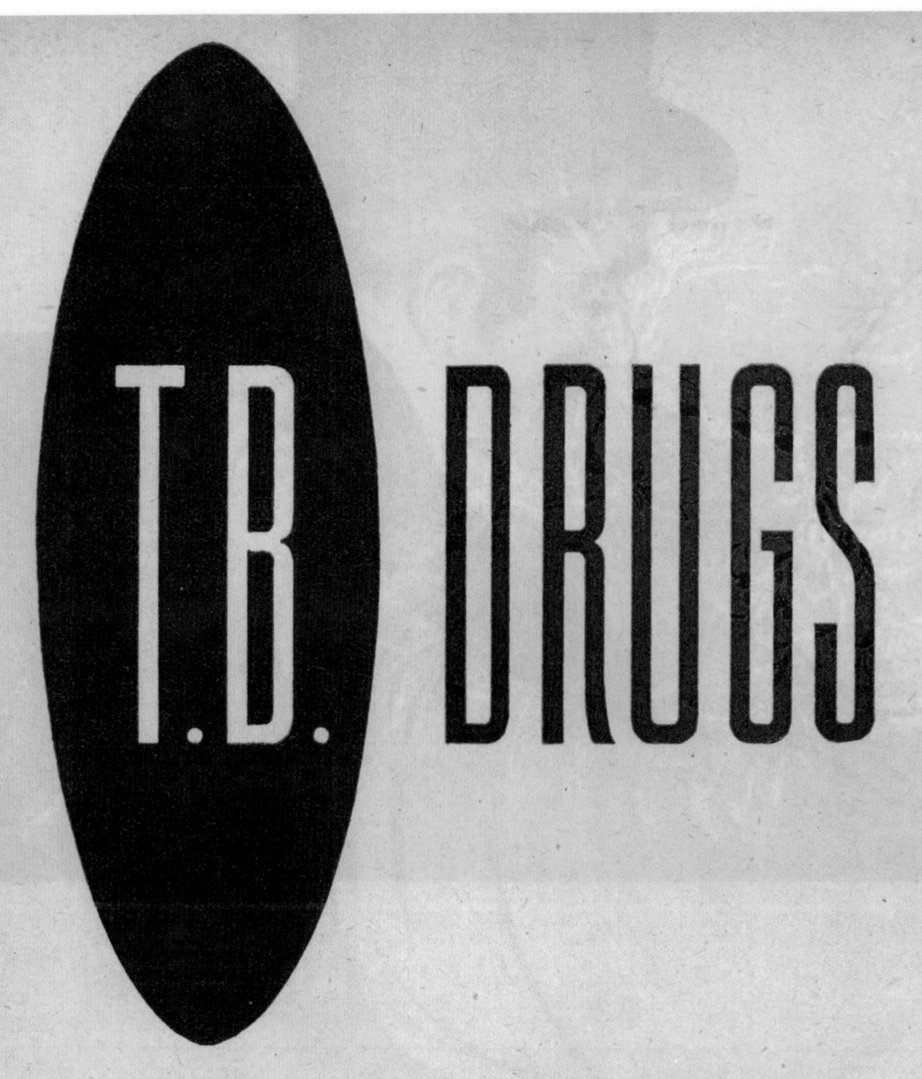

T.B. DRUGS

Their names are Nydrazid, Marsilid and Rimifon. Here we set out as fairly as we can what's known about them so far, and two big queries that still remain to be answered

A common feature was the striking reduction in the number of T.B. germs in the sputum. In some specimens doctors were unable to spot any of the rod-shaped bacteria at all under the microscope, and so were able to pronounce the verdict of "negative." Great news for the victims.

The first patient treated was a young negress, Hilda Carrion, both of whose lungs were badly affected. One soon significantly improved. Another patient promptly ate eleven eggs for breakfast, while another one, whose weight had dropped from thirteen stone to a mere seven, regained the six stones in nine weeks. Bedridden patients were able to get up and walk round the wards to visit one another. Some were even able to dance!

The New York Hospital was doing tests with another drug identical with Rimifon called Nydrazid which, strangely enough, had been produced at the same time, but quite independently, by another American pharmaceutical house, whose scientists had been following the same line of reasoning. Here, under the direction of Dr. Walsh McDermott, another group of pitiful victims of tuberculosis were responding almost as miraculously. Delighted with their results, the two groups of researchers compared notes, carried on treating more cases and decided to say nothing to the outside world, until they were quite, quite certain.

But the news was medical dynamite. It was too startling to keep secret, and towards the end of February it leaked out. At a hastily summoned press conference the doctors had to tell reporters of their amazing findings. But they weren't happy. They knew that, even after (*Continued on page* 125)

a cook's quiz

***If you know all the answers, take twenty marks.
If you don't,
you'll find them on page 140***

1. Do you know what baking-powder is made of ?

2. Is it correct to use plain or self-raising flour in the following :
(*a*) pastry,
(*b*) sandwich cakes,
(*c*) batter,
(*d*) scones,
(*e*) sauce ?

3. Should one start meat in a
(*a*) cold,
(*b*) moderate,
(*c*) or hot oven ?

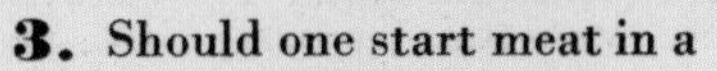

4. Should
(*a*) green vegetables,
(*b*) root vegetables,
(*c*) potatoes,
be started in hot or cold water ?

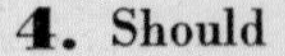

5. Is pressure cooking favourable or otherwise for the maximum retention of vitamins and mineral salts ?

6. Why is a hole usually made in the crust of a meat pie ?

7. Which is sweetest :
(*a*) cane sugar,
(*b*) honey,
(*c*) glucose ?

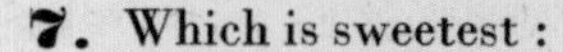

8. Should fruit be bottled in
(*a*) water,
(*b*) sugar syrup,
(*c*) golden syrup ?

CORRECT TEMPERATURE

FRUIT THAT SINKS

SUCCESS WITH YEAST

THE COOLEST PART

9. What makes a junket set ?

10. Why shouldn't you make cheese from soured pasteurized milk ?

11. What makes a sauce go lumpy ?

12. What causes a cake to sink ?

13. What causes fruit to sink in a cake ?

14. Do you know the secrets of success with yeast dough ?

15. How should one
(*a*) boil,
(*b*) hard boil
an egg ?

16. What foods should be kept in air-tight tins and which are best with slight ventilation ?

17. What is the coolest part of a refrigerator (other than the ice-box, of course) and what foods should be placed there ?

18. Why does jam sometimes go mouldy ?

19. When making jams and jellies, is it advisable to add sugar before or after cooking the fruit ?

20. Why is mustard for table use not served dry?

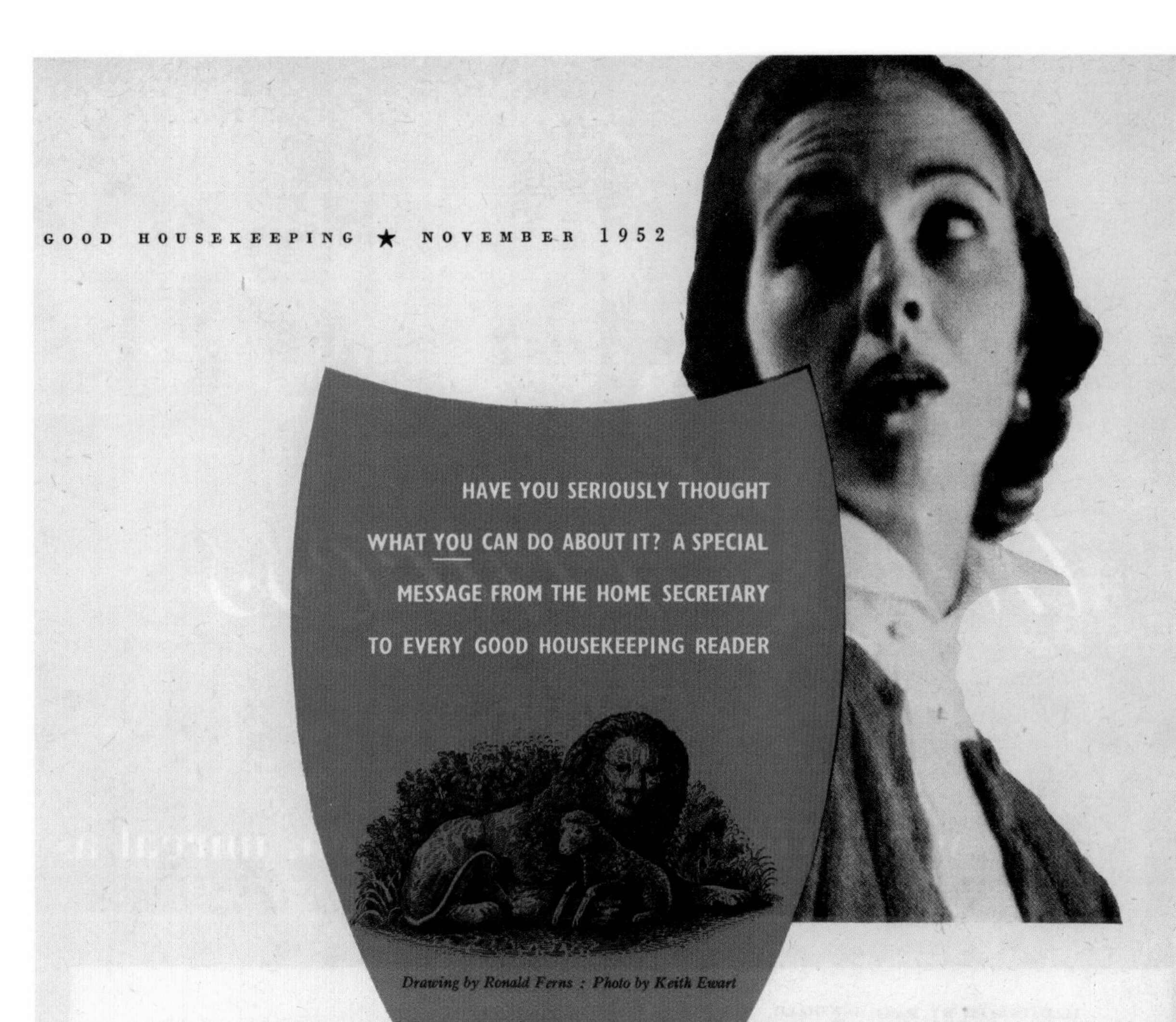

Drawing by Ronald Ferns : Photo by Keith Ewart

KEEPING THE PEACE

BY THE RIGHT HON. SIR DAVID MAXWELL FYFE, Q.C., M.P.

We all want peace, and no one longs for peace more than women with families. They have a stake in the future. They seek to assure themselves that all will be well for their children as they grow up.

Many unhappily know the consequences of failure to preserve peace—separation, evacuation, struggles to bring up families by themselves. They dread the possibility of it all happening over again and perhaps they try to shut out of their minds anything which reminds them of the dangers of war, even though it may be something which will, if faced, help to preserve peace.

The present Government, like their predecessors, are convinced that the best way to preserve peace is to be strong and to be prepared. The Government are, therefore, continuing to build up our Defence Services, the Fighting Services and, no less important, the Civil Defence Services. In this effort everyone's help is needed.

Is the effort really necessary? Anyone who reads the papers or listens to the news on the wireless must realize that we live in a difficult and a dangerous world. In Korea, Malaya, Indo-China, the Middle East, Berlin, there is either open warfare or tension and distrust. There is, therefore, a constant and grave threat to peace.

In that threat to peace, there may also be a threat to our way of life. We value freedom, freedom of speech, freedom of worship, freedom to elect our rulers or to dismiss them, freedom to choose our work, and we want to preserve those freedoms for ourselves and our children. But we know that there are other powers with different ideas, powers who want to impose their way of life on others, powers who are strong in numbers and resources. We believe that these powers will not attack us if we are strong. But if we are unprepared they may be tempted to seek an easy victory by a sudden knock-out blow.

If we are strong, we can stave off and perhaps banish the threat to peace and the threat to our way of life. That is why we must build up our defences. First of all the Fighting Services: they are the first and best deterrent to an aggressor. But almost (*Continued on page* **104**)

The Flattering Line

The woman interested in our supplement on the Age of Grace can see here how to choose clothes for their grace and distinction, for elegance imparted by a deceptive simplicity. For her, the almost stark severity of a tailored suit, the unerring perfection of cross-over styles, the long lines from shoulder to hem that carry the eye downward. Here, aided by Butterick patterns, these ideals have been achieved.

John French

BUTTERICK PATTERN NO. 5898. A gracious dress for afternoon wear, with a group of soft, unpressed pleats at one side. Short or three-quarter sleeves. In bust sizes 30 to 44 ins., price 2*s.* 9*d.*

BUTTERICK PATTERN NO. 5612 for a tailored linen suit with either long or short sleeves. The straight skirt has a centre back panel. It is available in bust sizes 30 to 44 ins., price 2*s.* 9*d.*

← BUTTERICK PATTERN NO. 6110. The long, flattering line in a simple button-through frock, with a skirt that is slightly flared. In bust sizes 30 to 44 ins., price 2*s.* 9*d.* The hats are from Gertrude Harris. For ordering instructions for patterns see page 151.

all's well at no.

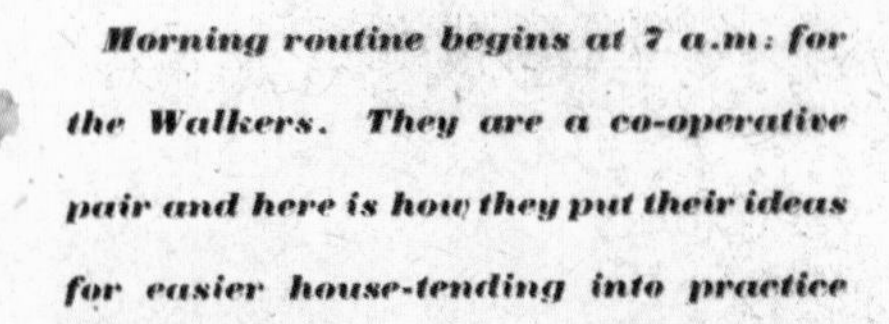

JOHN and Susan have a fairly strict arrangement about morning chores. By sticking to their own, they avoid muddle. John does the sitting-room grate; polishes the shoes; washes up the breakfast dishes and puts the garbage out. Susan gets the breakfast; packs up her lunch (as much as possible of the preparation of both breakfast and lunch is done the evening before and transparent polythene food-bags keep sandwiches, etc., beautifully fresh); makes the beds; dusts the bedroom and sitting-room and wipes round the basin, etc., in the bathroom.

Susan tries to get some special cleaning done in the evenings when she has only a simple meal to prepare. She vacuum-cleans the carpets one evening, polishes the furniture another and does kitchen cleaning on another. Every now and again she cleans the flat right through at the week-end. Washing and ironing are usually fitted in at week-ends. In this way she has a pleasantly-kept house and yet is free to spend most evenings as she and her husband wish. When unexpected visitors or some other interruption disrupt the schedule, John lends a hand with cleaning.

Here are some of the methods and equipment which the Walkers use to get through their house-tending with the least possible fuss.

The Housework In the sitting-room they have one of the new slow-burning grates. In coldest weather they keep it burning continuously, and because they are out so much have chosen one with a cover. It uses little fuel, does not throw out much heat when closed down, burns up briskly when required. John uses a covered box for the ashes to keep down dust, and spreads sacking to protect the rug.

Susan runs a sweeper over the carpet in the mornings. It's handier than taking out the vacuum cleaner every time, but a vacuum cleaner is invaluable for the "special cleaning." Her dusting mop has the lower half of the handle flexible for easy reaching under furniture. Susan finds a dusting glove very handy when she is doing the early morning chores.

Both John and Susan try to relieve the early morning rush by having a general tidy round before going to bed. They see that cushions are plumped, ash trays emptied, and newspapers put away last thing at night.

Susan has been ruthless about bric-a-brac. Some well-loved intricate pieces are displayed in a small corner cabinet. She has had a pair of beaten brass bowls buffed and lacquer-sprayed (much more successful than trying to do it herself). The lacquered surface does not need polishing but is rubbed up occasionally with furniture cream. Her cushion covers do not need very frequent

1

2 BUTTERICK PATTERN NO. 1637

three blouses to MAKE

1. A Paris-inspired blouse in white organdie, with a neatly fitting bodice and billowing sleeves that taper gradually to fit smoothly into the dropped armholes. Designed by the Needlework Room for you to make swiftly, easily, from Cut-to-Measure Pattern No. 122, cut expertly to your own exact size, price 6*s*. **2.** The perfect blouse with suits, a shirt blouse styled with long or short sleeves and a round or pointed collar. Butterick Pattern No. 6137, in bust sizes 30, 32, 34, 36 and 38 ins., price 2*s*. **3.** A simple cap-sleeved blouse with a row of buttons to fasten each shoulder. It is made from Butterick Pattern No. 6134, available in bust sizes 30, 32, 34, 36 and 38 ins., price 2*s*. You will find full instructions for ordering these patterns by post set out on page 119.

MARION HALL

3 BUTTERICK PATTERN NO. 6134

They rest informally: ceremony and pageant are to come

A seamstress (picture below) cuts the cloth for a peeress's robe—scarlet velvet trimmed with ermine. On the right, against a backdrop of banners, street decorations take shape

Keystone

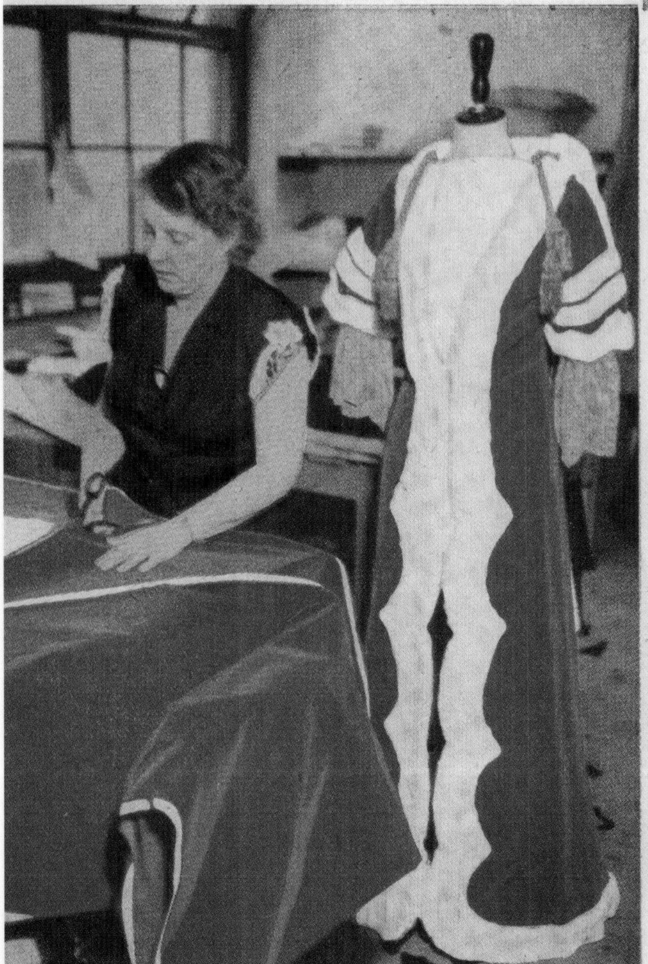

Chief Warder of the Tower of London, A. H. Cook, D.C.M., M.M., B.E.M., wears his state dress of scarlet and gold. His ceremonial mace carries a model in silver of the White Tower. Standing beside him, Yeoman Gaoler J. Ford wears the everyday blue uniform

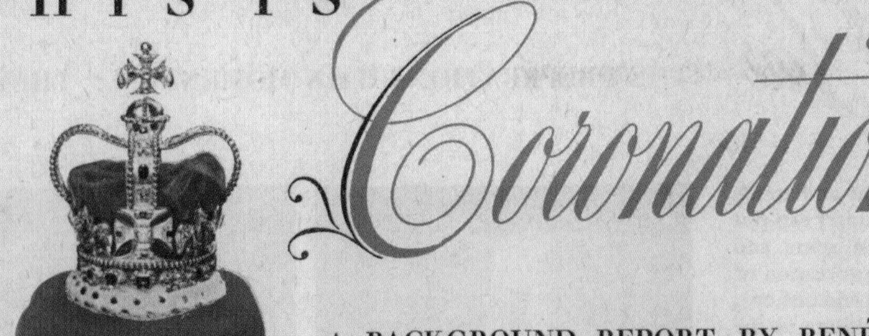

THIS IS *Coronation Year*

A BACKGROUND REPORT BY RENÉ LECLER

In the afternoon of February 12th last year, a few hours after the death of King George VI and just as the new Queen Elizabeth boarded a plane to return from East Africa to her capital, the seamstresses of a London firm of clothiers entered their vaulted stockroom under the great Covent Garden market. From long rows of cork-lined, black-japanned boxes, they took dozens of handsome robes worn by peers of the realm at the last Coronation in 1937, long trains of the richest crimson velvet edged with ermine, and began an inventory of the garments which would be hired out to peers.

Artists and craftsmen commissioned by the Royal Mint began to design new coins and medals. Royal heralds shook the mothballs off their rich crimson-and-gold coats. Swordmakers polished up their old blades. Officials of the Lord Chamberlain's department—which normally deals with the affairs of the Royal household—began to write the fateful word "Coronation" on their black-edged mourning notepaper.

This was no indecent hurry but rather the practical application of that ancient proclamation, "The King is Dead, Long Live the King." This time—on June 2nd, 1953—it will, of course, be a Queen, a young and fair one at that. The long tradition of a continuing, never-ending monarchy is once more being followed.

What is the Coronation? The holding of a jewelled crown over a young girl's head? A four-hour ceremony in Westminster Abbey, greatest

A. C. K. Ware

His is the main responsibility for all ceremonial: the Duke of Norfolk (above), the Earl Marshal. Left: Mr. J. Arnold Frere, Bluemantle Pursuivant; Sir Arthur Cochrane, Clarenceux King of Arms; Mr. Robin Mirrlees, Rouge Dragon Pursuivant; The Master of Sinclair, Portcullis Pursuivant —four of the thirteen officers of the College of Arms who will assist the Earl Marshal

HOMES TODAY

This is the first of a regular monthly series of features on home-planning and home-building. We begin with the group of three houses sketched on the opposite page . . .

A PLAN WITH 3 AIMS

This month we deal with the house on the left-hand side of the picture. To build a house at all is a big enough aim in these days of difficulty, but the designers of the first house discussed in this new feature have not contented themselves with merely scraping through the obstacles. They have triumphantly secured the three objects for which they had worked from the first.

These were. First: To produce a ground-floor room which would serve all the different needs of the family—meals, rest, reading, recreation (and, inevitably, homework!) in a single large compartment rather than in a series of little boxes each needing separate lighting and heating. At the same time these different functions had not to overlap or become confused.

Second: To make full use of a site which lies to the south of the road, and which slopes away to the south towards pleasant views. The site has no particular outlook to the north where other houses, higher up the hillside, limit its view.

The third aim was to build a house which will make a perfect setting for both old and new furnishings. Like so many, the owners have spent every penny on bricks and mortar, and must furnish with the carpets, chairs and curtains they already possess—even if it were not that many pieces are cherished heirlooms which could on no account be scrapped.

This house was finished a few weeks ago. Rather than give exact costs, etc., we feel it is of more general use to say that it complies with all Local Authority and Government requirements.

Room-by-room details of the house described here appear overleaf. Our Housing Editor will be glad to answer inquiries from readers interested in this house or wishing to discuss their own building problems

$1,000 TO SEE THE QUEEN

THEY BEGAN TO STUDY LUXURY BROCHURES BY THE SCORE

All of us, soaked in royalty from infancy, and with at least one Coronation behind us, can take this kind of thing in our stride. But to our friends Carol and Robert—those aren't their names—who come from a small town in one of the southern United States, it's quite different.

They've been to Britain before, once, and they already know it with the eager enthusiasm of the American who has ten days to see the country in, and realizes that there are 24 hours in each day and about 3,000 miles to an Atlantic crossing. Last time they were young and earnest, still undergraduates in approach, although both were quite a few years out of college. We used to tease them, then, because on the slightest provocation they'd whip out notebooks and ask searching questions about " conditions " in almost everything that came up casually. Now they're older and have a lot more money. And they look on this trip as a Vacation Extraordinary. Last time they were ready to be uncomfortable—in fact, they were such gluttons for misery that they stayed over into November to take pictures of a real London fog. This time, however, they're determined to be as plushy and expensive as possible. Their trip is unlikely to cost them less than £1,000 per head, and, at its most lavish, could cost more than double that figure.

So the Coronation, for them, is just the culminating point of a super-luxury holiday. " Coronation Cruise," sings the brochure they informatively sent us. " 36 glorious days—to Africa, Spain, Portugal, Ireland, Scotland, Sweden, Norway—and ENGLAND for the Coronation of Her Majesty Queen Elizabeth II."

They picked this particular trip in the Cunard Company's R.M.S. *Caronia* out of the piles of literature on Coronation Cruises which smothered them directly they betrayed the faintest interest—because it was the lushest, most costly, most luxurious, most once-in-a-lifetime piece of extravagance—and also because it was value for money.

Apart from the colossal *United States*, the 34,183-ton *Caronia* is the largest of the passenger liners built since the war—and she was designed specially as a dual-purpose ship, for cruising and for crossing the North Atlantic, so that she has the accent both on passenger entertainment and comfort and elegance—and on solidity. Carol and Robert can choose, for their own personal accommodation, between the extremes of a bedroom and sitting-room suite, where only the windows overlooking the sea remind them that they are in a ship at all—and an ordinary cabin with one bed and one upper berth. One will cost them per head $6,000 for the round trip—and the other $975—with various happy mediums in between. The prices won't cover tips, nor drinks, nor laundry and dry-cleaning, nor, of course, shopping in the ship's attractive shops—nor having their hair cut nor their faces done in the assorted salons.

It *will* cover, however, a bedside telephone in each room—there are 600 telephones altogether. And private baths or showers for each room, and air-conditioning in the public rooms—and an equable temperature throughout the ship whatever the weather—for the *Caronia's* hull is asbestos-insulated to be cool in the heat and warm in the cold.

So—from about 11 o'clock on the morning of May 5—when they slide away (*Continued on page* **107**)

They're coming from everywhere to see her; people of all nations and languages. Here we tell how two Americans feel about it—the money they're prepared to spend to be there, and what they'll get in return

BY DIANA AND MEIR GILLON

Drawings by Mary Dinsdale
Photos: Associated Press; A. W. Kerr, F.I.B.P., F.R.C.S.; Keystone

FLOORS

1. Electric polisher
2. Self-wringing mop prevents wet hands
3. Cylinder-type vacuum-cleaner
4. Waxer and polisher all in one
5. Polishing mop with rotating head

Make your *EQUIPMENT* *pay a dividend*

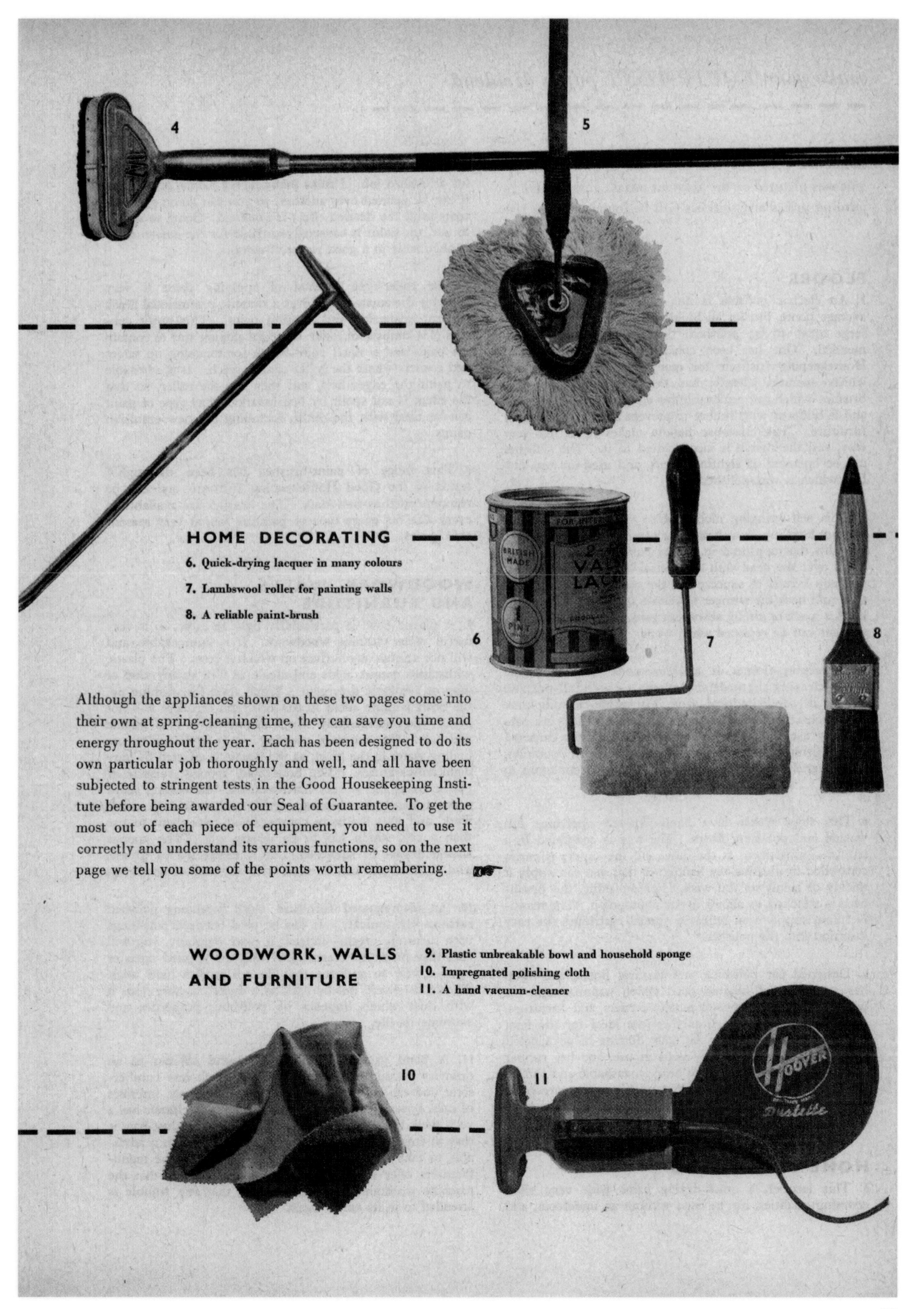

HOME DECORATING

6. Quick-drying lacquer in many colours

7. Lambswool roller for painting walls

8. A reliable paint-brush

Although the appliances shown on these two pages come into their own at spring-cleaning time, they can save you time and energy throughout the year. Each has been designed to do its own particular job thoroughly and well, and all have been subjected to stringent tests in the Good Housekeeping Institute before being awarded our Seal of Guarantee. To get the most out of each piece of equipment, you need to use it correctly and understand its various functions, so on the next page we tell you some of the points worth remembering.

WOODWORK, WALLS AND FURNITURE

9. Plastic unbreakable bowl and household sponge

10. Impregnated polishing cloth

11. A hand vacuum-cleaner

BY C. A. LEJEUNE

BBC VOICES THAT WILL BRING

The Greatest

O.B.* Ever

All about the most stupendous event in the annals of British Broadcasting—what you will see, what you will hear on the great day and round about it, with a personal introduction to celebrities from our own famous radio commentator

Now that the battle has been won for British viewers, and television is going to record a Coronation for the first time in history, it seems a matter of natural human curiosity to try and find out what the British Broadcasting Corporation intends to do with its opportunity. Or, if you prefer the word, monopoly. For whatever stories you may have heard (and I've heard plenty) about enterprising gentlemen from the other side of the Atlantic taking TV pictures of the Abbey ceremony, and then relaying them by a series of aeroplanes to America, they simply are not true.

It seemed to me that the proper person to ask for information was Cecil McGivern, who sits (when he has time to) in the biggest office in Lime Grove, and is Controller of Television Programmes. So I went and asked him. What, I said, are you primarily *aiming* at in your coverage of the Coronation? He replied that for the whole of Coronation week, or rather fortnight, TV programmes would have three basic aims. "Above all," he said, "they must be gay, exciting and happy. This may sound like a platitude, but we've always got to keep in mind the emphasis on *youth* in this Coronation.

"Secondly, we must satisfy the feeling that London is the centre of interest, and show people who can't get to London as much of its atmosphere as possible.

"Thirdly, we should remember that the occasion is going to be tremendously interesting to people outside England—the idea of this new Queen, this *child*, enthroned in a world of presidents and dictators, where there are few monarchies in existence. We mean to throw out a

fairly wide collecting-net; and set up a system by which we can capture and bring back, to show on celluloid later, some hint of the way the Dominions and Colonies, and the rest of the world, are reacting to this Coronation."

Whereas sound radio is concentrating on one week of Coronation programmes, the TV effort, on account of its shorter broadcasting hours, will be spread over three months. Periodically during the spring it has shown programmes building up the background to the Coronation; in which viewers have met, for instance, the fine needlewomen engaged on the embroidery of the Royal robes, and have watched the training and grooming of the horses that will take part in the Sovereign's Escort.

Another series that, as Mr. McGivern puts it, "pops in and out," is entitled "Young Elizabethans." This introduces viewers to a number of people under thirty years of age, who appear to show peculiar promise as scientists, inventors, technicians, planners. "Elizabeth is a young Queen, and she must be a forward-looking Queen. The series deals with the thinking-and-doing world, rather than with the entertainment world, and we have tried to find subjects who represent the spirit of the age. Where and who are these young people who are going to be so important to us when Queen Elizabeth is middle-aged? That's the question we have tried to answer. The programme, if I may put it that way, is a thing of the mind. Queen Elizabeth is a creature of the mind. She is serious. She *thinks*."

Although television has been preparing for the great day all through the spring, sketching in the background, orientating viewers' minds towards the Coronation ("but we must watch not to overdo it"), the main effort really starts on Sunday, May 24th, with a production of Clemence Dane's *Will Shakespeare*. The stage thus set, TV really, and in every sense of the phrase, goes to town. The programmes for the beginning of Coronation week will be mainly centred on London.

There will be a high proportion of outside broadcasts, showing the illuminations, the decorations, the firework displays, and the scenes in the streets. In the studios, Sir Hugh Casson will talk about decorating London. Philip Harben will invent and cook a special Coronation dish. A special Coronation square-dance has been composed, and will be demonstrated; the gimmick being to prove that London might be a gay and jolly place in the new Elizabethan Age.

Veteran composer Vaughan Williams once wrote a Masque called *The Bridal Day*. This (*Continued on page* **152**)

EAT WELL AND

KEEP WELL

Good Housekeeping presents a practical guide to good and healthy eating

Our bodies are made from the food we eat—a good enough reason for eating sensibly. Our Institute dietitian has planned this section to help those who want to know and understand the basic facts

Putting the right food at the right time on the table—that is every woman's aim. But there is a world of significance in that word "right." There are still shortages to contend with; there are likes and dislikes, of course, as is only too well known; there is the attractiveness associated with colour schemes in food to be considered; then there is the dragon of cost which inevitably rears its head to affect one's choice. Small wonder that health, which brings beauty of skin and body in its train, is sometimes regarded insufficiently by the most conscientious housewife. Of course, there are people who greet the suggestion that food may make or mar health with scepticism, but it is an unalterable fact that the human body is, and can only be, formed from the food we eat. Some may concede that children, with their growing bodies, may well be affected by food, but what about adults? Isn't it true that their bodies are as well and truly laid as foundation-stones? Research negatives this supposition: much of the structure of the body is continually changing, even in a matter of hours.

But even granted the will to eat more healthily, we feel many women shrink from the idea of having to pay strict attention to vitamins, calories and so on. They don't want to embark on a calculated diet, but they need working knowledge, quickly acquired, to enable them to provide balanced meals. So here it is: Good Housekeeping's own guide to healthier eating.

What should one eat?

In order to plan healthy meals, you must know which foods are important. The following list is a nucleus round which you can build the day's menu. Each of these foods should, ideally, be eaten *every* day.

1. **1 pint of milk.**
2. **2 servings of vegetables (e.g. 1 root and 1 green vegetable, or 1 root vegetable and a salad).**
3. **1 serving of fruit containing Vitamin C (e.g. grapefruit, oranges, tomatoes, soft summer fruits).**
4. **1 serving of meat, fish or cheese.**
5. **An egg.**
6. **1 serving of whole grain cereal (e.g. wholemeal or national bread) with butter or vitaminized margarine.**

Milk Why is milk so important? Sores and cracks at the corner of the mouth and sore tongues can result from drinking too little milk; colds may be caught more easily; rickets and bad teeth may occur in the young, "rheumaticky" pains and brittleness of bones in the old. On top of this, milk can give us much of the protein which is one of the "musts" for children. Its value is less obvious in grown-ups, but a vague off-colour feeling or anæmia may be the result of too little milk and other protein foods.

Vegetables The next item may cause many to exclaim incredulously, "*Two* servings of vegetables! Surely not!" But spots on the skin and a general feeling of slackness come in the train of carelessness on this point. Root vegetables, especially carrots, may help milk in protection against catching colds.

Fruit Few will need encouragement on the third item, at least in summer, when the soft fruits are in season. In winter, oranges and grapefruit are expensive. Yet these fruits come next in importance to potatoes in supplying us with the invigorating Vitamin C. As potatoes lose their vitamins during winter storage, these fruits gain in value, being of maximum importance in the early months of the year.

Meat, fish or cheese One reason for Item 4 is obvious to most people. With too little protein, children are small and puny, grown-ups may develop anæmia. But there are other reasons too, why nutritionists rank meat high, too detailed to mention here.

An egg This contributes a useful amount of two vitamins and iron, and, of course, protein.

Whole grain cereals Many arguments rage around their value as compared with their white sisters. Briefly, they contain more protein, vitamins and iron, but less calcium, and for some people are less digestible.

Most people are "over-convinced" of the need for butter or margarine. They do come well up in the list of providers of Vitamin A and they are invaluable for tempting and satisfying the appetite. But it is not yet known for certain whether fats form an indispensable part of one's diet.

(Continued overleaf)

Keith Ewart

● Get your teeth into this simple statement: The state of the nation's dental health has never been worse than it is today. For out of every hundred people in this country approximately only two have perfect teeth and gums. We are a nation without dental pride; we are a nation bleakly disinterested in oral hygiene; we are a nation which apparently acts on the principle that dentists should not be *seen* and much less *heard*.

Caries—decay of the teeth—is the most prevalent disease in Britain today. Yet dental disease, of all diseases, is one of the few where the co-operation of the patient can play a vital part in its prevention. In most diseases the preventive measures which can be taken by the sufferer are limited. Where caries is concerned it is a different story.

There are three reasons why nearly everyone in Britain has some form of dental decay. We eat the wrong diet. We do not take sufficient care of our mouths. Our visits to the dentist are too infrequent. There are three simple courses of action, ignored by most of us which, if universally adopted, would improve the state of the nation's dental health immeasurably.

First, regular visits to the dentist every six months. The fact that you or the children have not had toothache is no reason for putting off the appointment. An aching tooth is not Nature's first warning that something is wrong—it is more likely to be her last call for action.

Secondly, use your toothbrush the right way, and teach your children to do so too. Remember, it is even more important to brush the gums than the teeth, for more teeth are lost through diseased gums than through decay. That is why the dental profession always insist you should handle the toothbrush so that it quickens the blood circulation of the gums. So brush from the gums to the tip of the tooth with a sweeping movement. This gets the bristles between the sides of the tooth, and it also helps to prevent the gum from receding from the base of the tooth. Clean your mouth this way night and morning and when possible after every meal.

Third, diet is important. An adequate, well-balanced diet, particularly for expectant mothers and growing children, is an essential for the proper growth of the mouth and for the rest of the body. Hard foods which require chewing—crusts, apples, raw celery and carrots—clean the teeth and keep the gums healthy. So always finish a meal with one of them, and so help to clean away the remains of the sweet, sticky foods which cause decay.

For a moment let statistics spotlight the national picture. Examining a cross-section of the public numbering one hundred people, you would find that 40 people would have complete or partial dentures; 16 would need extractions; and 42 would be in need of fillings or other treatment. With children the figures are much worse—worse because the young represent a growing generation ignorant of oral hygiene, who, unless something is done, will pass on that ignorance to the next generation. Ninety-five per cent. at least of the children in this country have decayed teeth. Latest figures show that of children between the ages of six to ten years, 40 out of every thousand have had to have deciduous teeth (first teeth) extracted, and that dentures have been supplied to slightly over eight children out of every thousand between the ages of 16–17. This is not only appalling, it is tragic.

The extraction of deciduous teeth is to be deplored, for, contrary to popular belief, the fact that the child will naturally lose them does not mean that they have no value or that their loss is unimportant. Deciduous teeth are essential for adequate chewing of food. If they are extracted because of decay, overcrowding of the permanent teeth may result, which can in turn lead to the extraction of sound permanent teeth.

So, broadly speaking, this is the state of the nation's dental health today. And the remedy is in your hands—particularly for your children. Perhaps you are thinking that all responsibility has been laid at your feet. What about the dentist? What can he do? What are the dentists doing about the state of the nation's teeth?

☛ ***Straight talk from a dentist on his own subject : a challenging disclosure of blunt facts about a vital aspect of national health***

DO YOU KNOW THAT:

★ **OUT OF 100 ADULTS**
40 have false teeth,
16 need extractions,
42 need fillings or other treatment?

★ **ONLY TWO PER CENT.** *of the adult population of this country have perfect teeth?*

★ **95 OUT OF 100 CHILDREN** *have decayed teeth?*

and the Nation

BY A DENTAL SURGEON

New methods of treatment are constantly being evolved. New types of fillings such as plastic fillings are being used which dentists believe to be better than the old silicate cement ones. Also, they can be made quite undetectable and so restore the natural beauty of the tooth. With modern treatment there need be little discomfort, for today dentists can work on a tooth under a cooling spray of water, and many of them use local injections for working on a cavity. Also careful scaling removes deposits from the teeth and prevents irritation to the gums. Such treatments as these are available under the National Health Service.

This, briefly, is what the dentists are doing to deal with the results of dental disease, but on the other hand research workers all over the world are seeking for its causes, and tremendous efforts are being made towards prevention rather than cure.

Yet what the dentists have to contend with, what they have daily to fight against, as pernicious perhaps as the evils of wrong diet, and patients who stay away from their doors, are the countless fallacies and prejudices about teeth which are positively endemic in this country. If these fallacies and prejudices can be broken down, a real start can be made towards the goal of healthy teeth and gums.

Where shall we begin? I am going to take the advice of the King in the trial scene in *Alice in Wonderland*. He said, "Begin at the beginning, and go on till the end; then stop."

The beginning of the story of oral hygiene begins naturally with the unborn child and his mother. There are today an absurd number of old wives' tales concerning teeth during pregnancy.

There was the young wife who made an appointment with her dentist and told him, "I thought I had better come along and have a check-up. You see, my doctor has just told me that I am going to have a baby. So I think you'd better see me right away in case I have got a tooth which ought to come out, because I couldn't have gas or an injection once pregnancy is advanced, could I?"

This, of course, was nonsense. Pregnancy in no way prevents the use of anæsthetics or injections, nor does it result, as some women believe, in the embryo taking calcium from the mother's teeth and thereby causing decay, nor does it necessarily result in an unpleasant mouth condition, nor must the mother expect to lose one tooth for every child she has.

This young wife had been listening to the tales of old wives—who, it seems, delight in bombarding the young mother-to-be with absurd yarns like a chorus of Mrs. Gamps. It is true, however, that the gums of pregnant women tend to be more vascular and soft and therefore more susceptible to irritants. This, then, predisposes to gum disease and, if untreated, to periodontal disease—pyorrhœa, for example. During pregnancy it is of supreme importance to see your dentist regularly, and to take particular care that teeth and gums are properly brushed.

Where you do get a condition known as pregnancy gingivitis—extensive bleeding and swelling of the tissues indicate this—it is usually due to some systemic disorder. It is not common.

Any treatment needed for your teeth during pregnancy should be done in plenty of time before confinement. After the child is born the new mother literally and metaphorically has her hands full. The first few months of motherhood are both absorbing and physically demanding—a visit to the dentist is the very last thing to be put down on her list of commitments. It is understandable now how important are those pre-natal visits to the dentist, and how also the care of your teeth and gums during the waiting period is largely a matter of partnership between you and your dentist. If you do not practise oral hygiene in the home, his practice in the surgery is sabotaged to a considerable degree.

This, then, is the beginning of the story of oral hygiene. Your child is born and by the time he is two years old you should start teaching him to clean teeth and gums with a soft toothbrush, and by the time he is three he should make his first visit to the dentist and be cleaning his own teeth.

The fact that he has not complained of toothache is no (*Continued on page* **108**)

MASTER THIS IMPORTANT SECRET, AND YOU'LL

Do you know what doctors the world over are discovering is one of the chief causes of illness? It's tension. They have found that about half their patients describe symptoms for which no exact diagnosis can be made. They simply complain that they do not feel quite well, are troubled with nerves, persistent fatigue, constant headache, backache or vague bodily pains. Yet even careful clinical examination reveals no definite disease. The doctor can only give the assurance that there is nothing organically wrong, prescribe a tonic and suggest a holiday. " Relax and take things more easily," is usually his parting advice.

Perhaps you, yourself, have been to your doctor in circumstances like that. If, after a proper examination, you were assured nothing was wrong organically, and your doctor gave you the sort of advice I have indicated, I suggest that you will probably derive great benefit from teaching yourself the gentle art of relaxation.

Just what is relaxation? A precise definition is not easy, but try to call to mind some occasion on which you, yourself, *did* feel completely relaxed. It was probably a day when things had gone well. You had achieved what you had planned to do—whether it was turning out the linen cupboard or just doing the weekly wash—you were satisfied with what you had done, and had time to sit afterwards and read or knit without the nagging thought that you must hurry on to the next job. Body and mind were both at ease, for relaxation is a mind-body relationship. You cannot relax physically if your mind is worrying.

Reasonable bodily exercise should lead to a feeling of relaxation, not to an awareness of being physically overtired. If, after a morning's cooking or cleaning, all your muscles ache when you come to sit down, then the probability is that you have been tense as you were working, thereby over-tiring your muscles and joints by wrong usage. Let me give a more concrete example.

Can you remember when you first started to drive? Can you recall how you gripped the wheel as if your life depended on it, your body tense? Turning an easy corner demanded a tremendous effort and you came in from your lesson or drive feeling stiff and sore all over. And now, if you are a good driver, what is the difference? The lightest pressure serves to control the car; with the minimum of movement, and therefore of effort, you can negotiate the sharpest corner. In fact, you are relaxed.

Next time you are worried or angry, look at yourself in the mirror. That frown, those creases round your eyes, the rigid line of your mouth and jaw, are all caused by tension, and tension is the exact opposite of relaxation. Of course some people find it much easier to relax than others. The easy-going person who takes life as it comes is basically more relaxed than her quick-tempered, over-anxious sister. Yet the most restful-looking person has tensions, and underneath a veneer of " couldn't care less " there often lies a worrying personality.

But you can teach yourself to relax if you will give your mind to it. But you must be prepared to set aside two quarters of an hour daily for practice, and you *must* go where you are not going to be disturbed.

The best place is your bed. Lie on it and place a pillow so that it is clear of your shoulders but supporting your head. This is the basic position and it is vital that you should get it right. When you are sure that your head and shoulders are comfortable

CONDUCTED BY ETHNE DAVIES

BE HEALTHIER, HAPPIER, AND LIVE LONGER

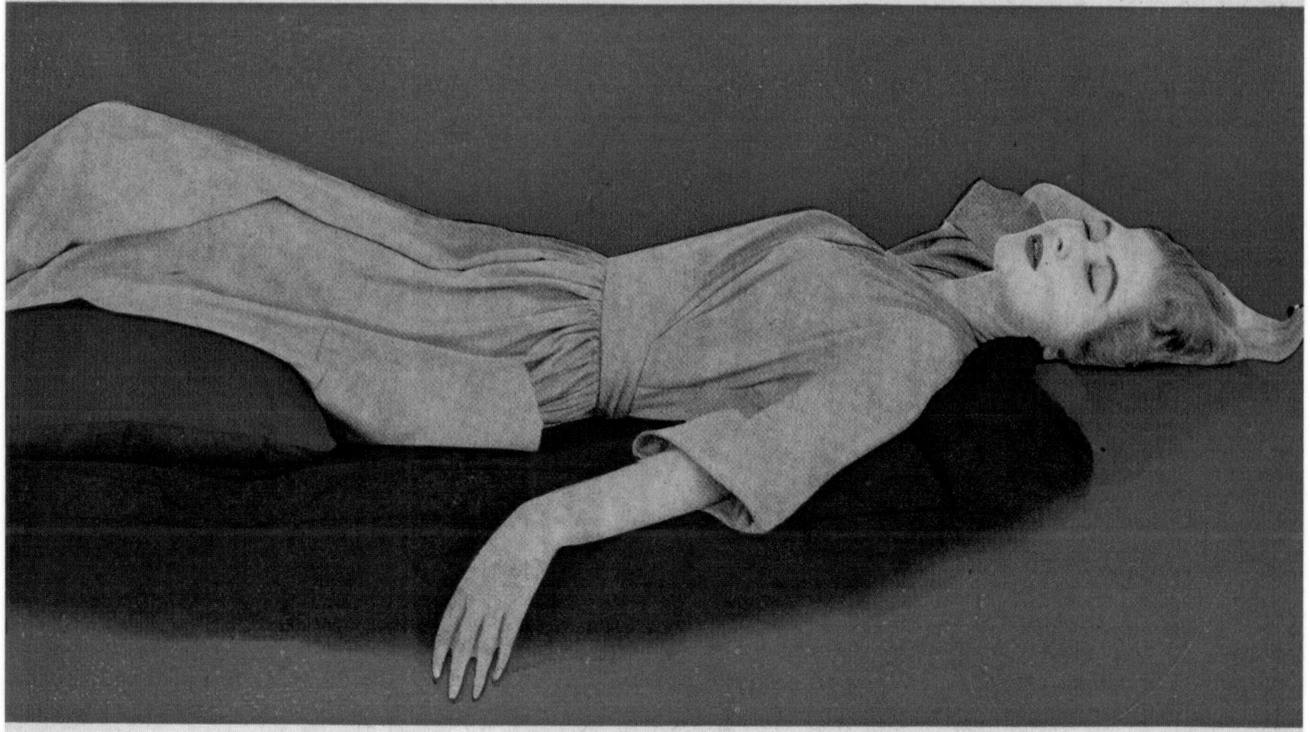

Housecoat by Horrocks from Harvey Nichols — Keith Ewart

put another pillow under your knees so that they are slightly bent.

The next step is to get the sensation of being relaxed. This is best done by contrast. Stretch your arms and legs down as far as you can, clench your fists, screw up your face. Now let go. Can you feel the difference? *Let go.* Those are key words. Repeat this experiment several times, until you are sure you appreciate what a moment of relaxation feels like.

Next turn your thoughts to deeper breaths. Try breathing in and out as you read these words in order to get the rhythm. Breathe in—two—three—four—and breathe out—two—three—four. Count to yourself as you breathe. When you are doing this easily and smoothly with no breaks or gasps, go on to the next step. Start thinking about your left arm. Concentrate on the section from the shoulder to the elbow. Just let the muscles go quite loose and slack. Imagine that your arm is getting heavier and heavier. Let it sink into the bed. Now from the elbow to the wrist; let it go, let it relax. Imagine the muscles getting quite soft and flabby. (Actually this is exactly what is happening.) Now from the wrist right down to the tips of the fingers, every single finger, relax, relax. See in your mind the whole arm again—shoulder to elbow, elbow to wrist, wrist to the finger-tips—completely relaxed. Did you feel a slight twitch in your arm? That means that you are already learning to relax. Now turn your attention to your right arm. Follow the same technique. Shoulder to elbow, elbow to wrist, wrist to finger-tips. Both your arms should now feel heavy. Tell yourself that they would be difficult to lift. But do not try to lift them, just turn to your legs.

Left leg first. Relax, relax; from the hip to the knee (just imagine those muscles quite soft and flabby); knee to ankle (your leg is too heavy to lift now); ankle to the tips of the toes (let your foot roll out sideways if it wants to); you are not going to bother about it. And now over to your right leg.

Let your arms and legs lie quietly relaxed, and start to think about your back. Imagine that you are sinking through the bed. Once again let your whole body become heavier. Relax your backbone in sections from your neck to your tail. There is no need to keep a straight back now; just let it sag. Now the front of your body. Make sure once again that you are taking those slightly deeper breaths. Now try and let your ribs fall in and your abdominal muscles go absolutely loose. Imagine the front of you so relaxed that it just collapses and touches your backbone.

And now your head. It, too, will become very heavy and relaxed if you imagine it to be falling through the bed. Try this and see what happens. Let it go; let your shoulders and neck muscles go too. Let them relax, and then relax some more.

Lastly, your face. This is very important, for when you can relax, lines and wrinkles automatically smooth themselves away. At the start open your mouth gently and then close it until your lips are just touching. Open your eyes and then gently close them too. Now let go all the tension round eyes and mouth. Let your face become expressionless; nobody is looking at you. There is no need to be bright or alert. Let your whole face fall into repose.

Now for the final, most difficult part (*Continued on page* **103**)

BY NOEL STORR

ABOUT PASTA

You can ring the changes with this Italian speciality, the most versatile food in all the world

Anyone who has kept house in Europe or has had a holiday on the Continent is likely to be familiar with Italian pasta in one or more of its many forms. Other European countries have their own specialities, but Italy is the land of its birth and the country where it forms the staple diet of the people, especially the peasants. It is eaten plain as a preliminary course, or combined with meat and fish in an almost endless variety of main dishes.

Pasta is usually made from wheat. The wheat is washed and ground into coarse meal, the husk and other very rough parts being removed. This pure wheat flour is then mixed with water to an elastic dough and is made into an enormous variety of shapes and sizes. After being cut or twisted into the desired shape, the pasta is dried until quite hard and crisp. It is still a common sight in Italy to see strings of macaroni or spaghetti hanging in the sun to dry.

Here is a guide to the different kinds of Italian pasta shown in the photograph on these pages: (1) Conchiglie; (2) Farfalle; (3) Cappellini; (4) Alfabeto; (5) Tagliatelle; (6) Maccheroni; (7) Spaghetti; (8) Cannelloni; (9) Ravioli; (10) Taglialini; (11) Vermicelli; (12) Lasagne

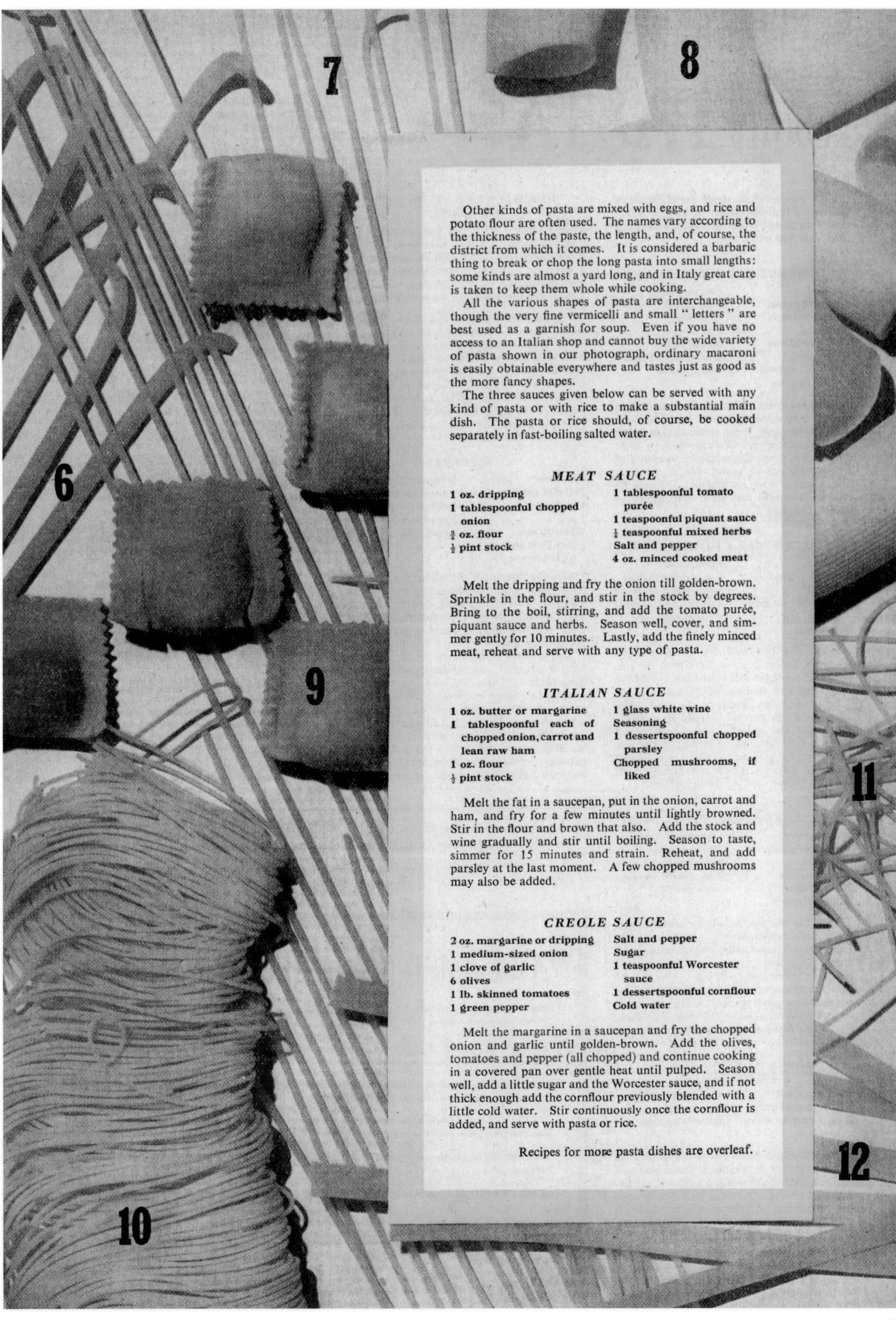

Other kinds of pasta are mixed with eggs, and rice and potato flour are often used. The names vary according to the thickness of the paste, the length, and, of course, the district from which it comes. It is considered a barbaric thing to break or chop the long pasta into small lengths: some kinds are almost a yard long, and in Italy great care is taken to keep them whole while cooking.

All the various shapes of pasta are interchangeable, though the very fine vermicelli and small " letters " are best used as a garnish for soup. Even if you have no access to an Italian shop and cannot buy the wide variety of pasta shown in our photograph, ordinary macaroni is easily obtainable everywhere and tastes just as good as the more fancy shapes.

The three sauces given below can be served with any kind of pasta or with rice to make a substantial main dish. The pasta or rice should, of course, be cooked separately in fast-boiling salted water.

MEAT SAUCE

1 oz. dripping
1 tablespoonful chopped onion
¾ oz. flour
½ pint stock
1 tablespoonful tomato purée
1 teaspoonful piquant sauce
¼ teaspoonful mixed herbs
Salt and pepper
4 oz. minced cooked meat

Melt the dripping and fry the onion till golden-brown. Sprinkle in the flour, and stir in the stock by degrees. Bring to the boil, stirring, and add the tomato purée, piquant sauce and herbs. Season well, cover, and simmer gently for 10 minutes. Lastly, add the finely minced meat, reheat and serve with any type of pasta.

ITALIAN SAUCE

1 oz. butter or margarine
1 tablespoonful each of chopped onion, carrot and lean raw ham
1 oz. flour
½ pint stock
1 glass white wine
Seasoning
1 dessertspoonful chopped parsley
Chopped mushrooms, if liked

Melt the fat in a saucepan, put in the onion, carrot and ham, and fry for a few minutes until lightly browned. Stir in the flour and brown that also. Add the stock and wine gradually and stir until boiling. Season to taste, simmer for 15 minutes and strain. Reheat, and add parsley at the last moment. A few chopped mushrooms may also be added.

CREOLE SAUCE

2 oz. margarine or dripping
1 medium-sized onion
1 clove of garlic
6 olives
1 lb. skinned tomatoes
1 green pepper
Salt and pepper
Sugar
1 teaspoonful Worcester sauce
1 dessertspoonful cornflour
Cold water

Melt the margarine in a saucepan and fry the chopped onion and garlic until golden-brown. Add the olives, tomatoes and pepper (all chopped) and continue cooking in a covered pan over gentle heat until pulped. Season well, add a little sugar and the Worcester sauce, and if not thick enough add the cornflour previously blended with a little cold water. Stir continuously once the cornflour is added, and serve with pasta or rice.

Recipes for more pasta dishes are overleaf.

BY NORA ARIS

how Safe are OUR

To be happy, normal and free from fear—that is their right. How can we protect them from a social menace of increasing gravity?

A friend of mine rang me up not very long ago and asked if she could come and talk to me—she was in trouble and badly needed help in a very personal matter. I had always thought of her as an intelligent, level-headed woman with a charming and happy family and I was surprised at the note of distressed urgency in her voice.

She came round straight away and wasted no time in coming to the point. It seemed that her ten-year-old daughter had been walking with the dog, in the late afternoon, in the copse half-a-mile from home. A stranger, a man about thirty, quite well dressed and well spoken according to Jennifer's account, had stopped and admired the dog in the most natural way, then got into conversation with the child. Finally, on the pretext of finding some rare wild flower, the man, still spinning stories, had persuaded Jennifer to tie the dog to a tree, had taken her into the thickest part of the copse and there had assaulted her.

I asked how the story had come out. When Jennifer had come home rather late, I was told, she looked flushed, she was quiet, and, unlike her usual sweet, open self, she was evasive about her doings. Quite unsuspecting at first, her mother had questioned her further and the whole story came out. The man had throughout used fair words, he had not been violent or threatening, but he had bribed and cajoled the child (" We have a little secret between ourselves, and secrets are fun, aren't they? ") to say nothing at home and to meet him the next day.

Naturally I wanted to know what was Jennifer's state of mind after this experience. She seemed more bewildered than actually frightened or upset, her mother said, and it was this non-committal, almost shut-in attitude of her little daughter's which alarmed my friend so much. " I have always answered her questions truthfully," she said pathetically. " I thought she understood. And I have always made it such a strong point that she should never talk to strangers. How could this have happened? " Here was my friend, usually so competent and so sure that she understood her children, face to face with a wholly unexpected problem and unprepared for her daughter's reaction to it.

Until a story such as this comes right home to us, we hardly believe it. It is a newspaper story, not the kind of thing that happens in our own circle. Yet I have come increasingly to believe that there are very few families which have not had some experience of unwelcome advances from strangers.

Perhaps the mother looks back to the night when, coming home from a late meeting during the war, she was followed and accosted in the lampless street. The grown-up daughter remembers, half-ashamed, the young man from whom she accepted a lift while she was hiking, and who threatened to become more than " fresh "; and there was the time when young Ann came home and remarked to her mother in shocked tones, " Mummy, there is a man round by the pillar-box. I think he must want to go to the lavatory." Not one of these had come to serious harm, but there are others who have met real trouble, both mental and physical.

It is everybody's problem, but it is not a single problem, and because there are so many questions to be considered and the answers need so much wisdom and experience, I asked for the help of a number of different people, some with professional experience of sex crimes, some with exceptionally wide knowledge of girls and some who are mothers of adolescent daughters.

Sex crimes are as old as human nature and it would be foolish to conclude that we have a monopoly of evil practices today, but in all soberness the criminal statistics force us to realize that crimes against girls have markedly increased of late. In an office lined with books on social hygiene and in an atmosphere of departmental committee reports, I talked to Miss Chave Collisson, general secretary of the Association for Social and Moral Hygiene. She showed me figures which cannot fail to impress. In 1945 the number of indictable sexual offences tried in the magistrates' courts was 1,363 and in 1951, the latest year for which official figures are available, the number was 2,216. During these same six years there was a steady rise in the cases of defilement of girls under sixteen.

What reasons can we find for these disturbing facts? Undoubtedly the effect of two world wars has been to shake and disrupt the stability of our social life. But what of the freedom which the girls of today enjoy? Does it loosen restraint and provide freer opportunities to unstable men?

No time and practically no place is entirely free of this type of risk—Jennifer's experience near her own home in the afternoon was by no means uncommon—but undoubtedly the most dangerous (*Continued on page* **158**)

Geoffrey Gilbert

DAUGHTERS?

Slim dress in kitten soft charcoal angora. Keep the striped silk vest or lift it out and trim to please. London Town about 7½ gns. at Galeries Lafayette, Regent St., W.1, and Alexander Henderson, Glasgow. Decanter, glasses and tray by Liberty

If it's a family affair—lots to do, no time to change—these dresses will solve your problems

. . . AND THE INSTITUTE SAYS

● For a Christmas gathering at home, when you have to work as well as play, planning is essential: planning your rooms, so that they look different from their everyday selves; thinking out the food and drink in advance and preparing as much of it as possible beforehand; planning lighting and heating; providing games and entertainment.

Cold sweets, such as soufflés and jellies, are best made the day before the party, so that there is ample time for them to set. If you want some new ideas, the Good Housekeeping booklet, *Cold Cookery* (price 1s. 6d. — see page 128)

Another versatile dress this time in heavy silk grosgrain with bolero corselet bodice and deep décolletage. By London Town, price approx 13 gns., at Selfridges, Oxford St., W.1, and Catherine Martineau, Birmingham

gives full instructions for preparing a cold buffet. Food that will be served hot, such as patties and bouchées, should also be made the day before; they can then be quickly heated up in the oven when needed.

Make sandwiches on the morning of the party; they will stay perfectly fresh if wrapped up in polythene bags. Cold cups and punches should be prepared early in the day and left in the refrigerator to chill thoroughly. Make fancy ice-cubes by putting small pieces of fruit, mint leaves, etc., in the freezing trays when you fill them.

Hair-drying at home is quick and easy with the Pifco hair-drier which can be adjusted to give varying heats

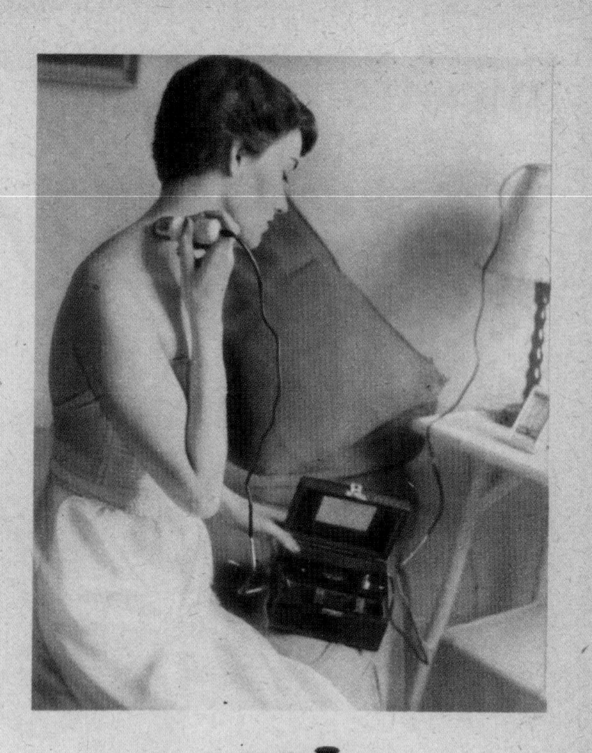

FOR PERSONAL SERVICE

LIVING electrically is not just a matter of using a refrigerator or a vacuum-cleaner, but also one of letting it do for you personally what it can do best and most quickly. It can provide the kind of service once given by personal maids and valets. A hair-drier, for instance, saves the fatigue of rubbing and the discomfort of feeling damp in winter. For a man, an electric razor often spells the end of early-morning misery.

Electricity can boost your morale and health with the use of vibratory massagers and sun lamps. And when the nights are cold electricity will help again by giving you the electric hot-water bottle.

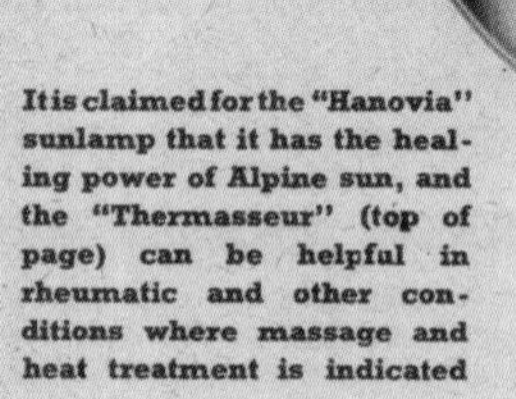

It is claimed for the "Hanovia" sunlamp that it has the healing power of Alpine sun, and the "Thermasseur" (top of page) can be helpful in rheumatic and other conditions where massage and heat treatment is indicated

PRICES OF EQUIPMENT ILLUSTRATED
"Thermasseur": £5 5s.
Pifco hair-drier: £3 14s. 6d.
Hanovia model 6 sun lamp: £25
"Belclere" hearing aid: £12 12s. to £37 16s.
Pifco "Mirrolite" shaving mirror: 19s. 11d.
Remington 60 razor: £9 19s.

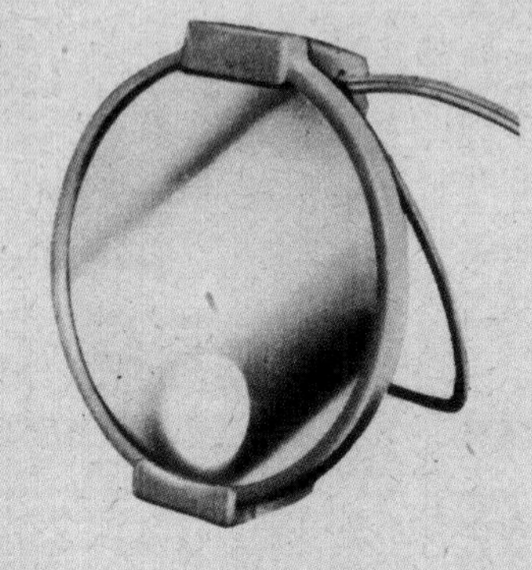

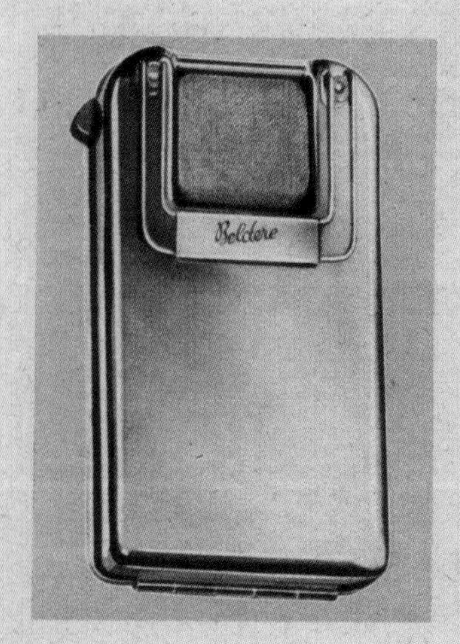

The "Belclere" hearing aid (left) works from a battery and is made by John Bell and Croydon. Pifco's magnifying shaving mirror has a small light enclosed to give a more honest reflection, and the Remington 60 electric razor is effortless in action, simple to operate and easily cleaned

At the far left is the Goblin "Teasmade" which will waken you with a hot, freshly made pot of tea, and (left) the Falks coffee percolator which, because of its automatic control, can be set to keep coffee hot without boiling for as long as desired

ELECTRICITY ABOUT THE HOUSE

Smith electric alarm clock in blue or green case with a colourful pictorial dial

HALF a century ago, people thought that electric lighting in homes was a miracle. Today, electricity is the maid-of-all work around the house. Month by month, year by year, it appears in all kinds of new forms to perform simple or highly complicated tasks.

Take, for instance, the question of getting up in the morning: electricity will take the rough edge out of that by making a cup of tea at your bedside before you wake up; if you come in late at night it will keep your food warm on the hot plate; if you want to make sure that the baby is not crying unheard in another room, the electrical home-broadcaster now marketed will relay his slightest whimper to you wherever you are in the house; and if you want to go into the baby's room without the click of the switch waking him up, all you have to do is to buy one of the new "silent switches": you can "feel the click" when pulling its cord, but you cannot hear it.

If you are a little hard of hearing and may fail to hear the front door bell ring, this is your answer: a luminous call system which will flash a small light or unmask a white panel in front of you when the bell is pushed.

If you are the forgetful type or simply happy-go-lucky, the properly planned use of electrical time-control switches around your house will leave you with a clear conscience. The time switch will start or stop cookers, heaters and every other appliance controlled by electricity.

Think of what electricity can do for you: it makes your toast, keeps your tropical fish happy in their tank, gives you hot coffee, tells you the time, works your sewing-machine and your radiogram and television, and announces the arrival of your visitors with a musical note at the front door. There is almost no limit to what electricity can do for you if you will let it.

Living is easier with these: Hawkins' "Hostess Trolley" (above) which will keep food hot, can be used as a table, and has plugs for a toaster and percolator; the Hotpoint upright toaster, with glass side-panels and easy "turn-over" action; and the G.E.C. Home Broadcaster (below) which will superimpose any sounds from the nursery over the wireless programme

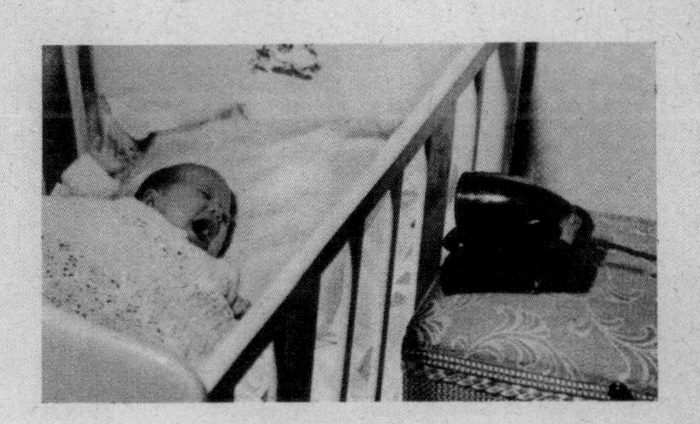

'Formica' is here.. there.. and

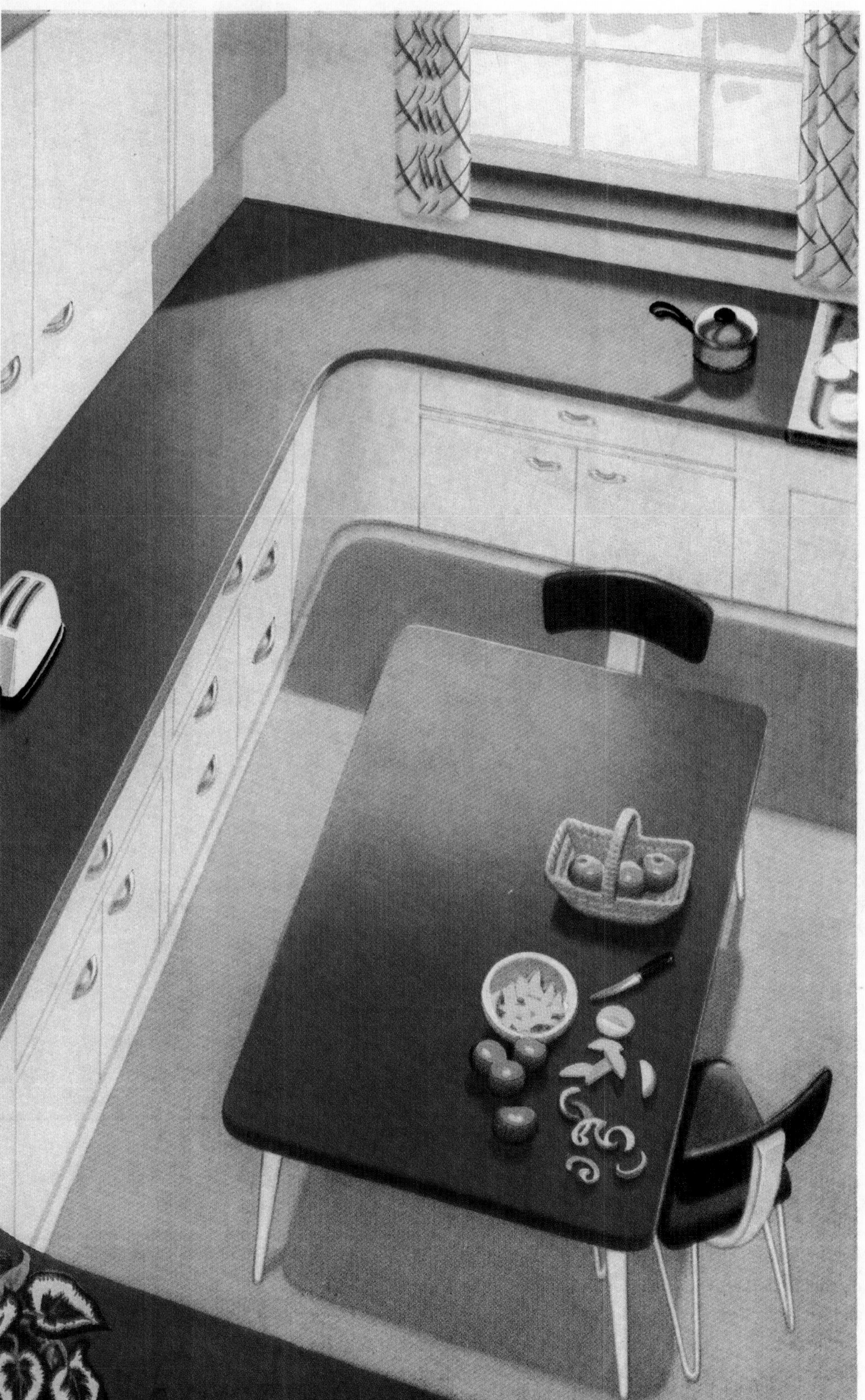

DRESSING TABLES *with this work-saving finish are never marked by creams, lotions, perfumes. No more rubbing and polishing!*

NURSERY FURNITURE *is a* 'FORMICA' *inspiration. Grubby finger marks, spilt foods and drinks just wipe off.* 'FORMICA' *thrives on hard wear.*

TEA-TROLLEYS, *coffee-tables, book cases in beautiful* 'FORMICA' *wood-grains bring new leisure and luxury into your lounge.*

LIFE WITH 'FORMICA' is bliss for busy wives. You breeze through the chores when this jewel-bright clean-at-a-wipe laminated plastic comes into your home. A wipe with a damp cloth makes it glow. Scrubbing and polishing are out! No wonder you see this friendly surface in practically every room in modern homes.

everywhere in easy-to-run homes

IS YOUR KITCHEN a *happy* place? Is it as bright and colourful and easy to work in as it might be? Think what a difference 'FORMICA' surfaces would make. There's half the work and twice the pride wherever this satin-smooth surface goes. No worries about stains or dirty marks, no scrubbing and polishing. 'FORMICA' *wipes* clean, saves you minutes at every turn and goes on doing it for a *lifetime!* It is just as big a help in every room in the house. It saves you work and worry in your lounge, dining room, and bedrooms as well as in your kitchen and larder.

COSTS LESS THAN YOU THINK Can you afford it? Yes! It looks wildly expensive, but is very reasonable in cost and lasts so long that it is a truly thrifty investment. You can make a start on your 'FORMICA' dream kitchen for much less than you might expect. And once you have it, it's yours for life. That is why you'll be wise to see you get the real thing. No other laminated plastic is quite as tough, as thick, as resistant to stains and wear. So when you buy, look for the label on every piece. Ask for 'FORMICA', pronounced as in 'for MY kitchen'. *Look for this label.*

WAYS AND MEANS Many stores can show you a whole range of furniture with this satiny finish—anything from a tea-tray to a dressing table—in a variety of colours and patterns. If you would like to have existing surfaces refinished by an expert 'FORMICA' fabricator, write to us and we will put you in touch with a first-class craftsman in your district. If you would like to do the job yourself go to a good ironmonger's and see the selection of 'FORMICA' panels. Many dealers will now supply panels cut to any size and shape you require.

DO IT YOURSELF—AND SURPRISE YOURSELF! You can make your home a show place with less effort and less outlay than you would credit—if you or your husband are reasonably handy. Just get your 'FORMICA' panels and a tin of the right adhesive (ask for EVO-STIK). You can transform a 3 ft. by 2 ft. table for £2—the cost of a panel that size in the popular 'Linette' pattern and a tin of the adhesive. Non-standard sizes average 6/6d. a square foot. Measure the surfaces you want to cover—the ones that get hard wear and need frequent cleaning. See the patterns and colours at your dealers. Ask for the helpful 'Do-it-yourself' leaflet and you are ready to start!

FREE LEAFLETS: Write for 'FORMICA' leaflets to Thomas De La Rue & Co. Ltd. (Plastics Division), Dept. Q.11, 84-86 Regent Street, London, W.1. Regent 2901.

Do you realise how easily it can be yours?

CLEAN SWEEP: *For £100 or so you can have your present kitchen transformed. A completely new super kitchen costs rather more.*

EASY STAGES: *Why not make a start now with a new 'FORMICA' topped kitchen table and add other pieces as you can afford them?*

DO-IT-YOURSELF: *See the range of ready-cut 'FORMICA' panels at any good hardware store. They cost from 33/- for a panel 3 ft. by 2 ft.*

the surface with a smile

'FORMICA' is a registered trade mark, and Thomas De La Rue & Co. Ltd. is the registered user.

What they teach you at

Constance Spry, Principal of Winkfield Place school

● When does a teenage girl become a lady? At what age does she learn dress-sense, savoir-faire or home management?

The answer, according to Constance Spry, the world-famous authority on flowers, is between the ages of seventeen and twenty. At seventeen a girl leaves the blushing gaucherie of adolescence behind her, and by the time she is twenty she has acquired as much *natural* poise as she will ever gain. In between these ages a girl must be helped, encouraged and led along the right path to easy and gracious living. Constance Spry knows something about all this: in the past seven years over three hundred and fifty girls from Britain and all parts of the world have been taught " how to live " by this versatile woman.

At Winkfield Place, a beautiful 18th-century mansion set on the edge of Windsor Forest, Mrs. Spry runs a school for the hostesses of tomorrow. It is not a finishing school in the proper sense of the term, for Winkfield girls do not learn deportment, or diction, or how to curtsy—though many débutantes have been pupils there. Neither is it a domestic science college, because its training is not specialized enough for the girl who wants to make this her career.

Yet it teaches her the things which every woman should know—though by no means every woman does—how to plan the furnishings of her future home, the basic principles of cookery, how to arrange flowers in the house, how to run up a simple dress. She learns something about budgeting and secretarial work, about the organization of a party and even about taking the spirit stains off her furniture after the guests have left. . . .

All this takes place in an atmosphere so far removed from that of St. Trinian's High as to be in another world. Winkfield Place is a country house adapted for community living; it stands in twenty-one acres of wooded Berkshire countryside, with a (*Continued on page* **144**)

Left: Flower arrangement is naturally one of the school's specialities. Two girls add the final touch to a joint composition. Right: a student in the dressmaking class tries on a wedding gown she is making for her sister

WINKFIELD PLACE

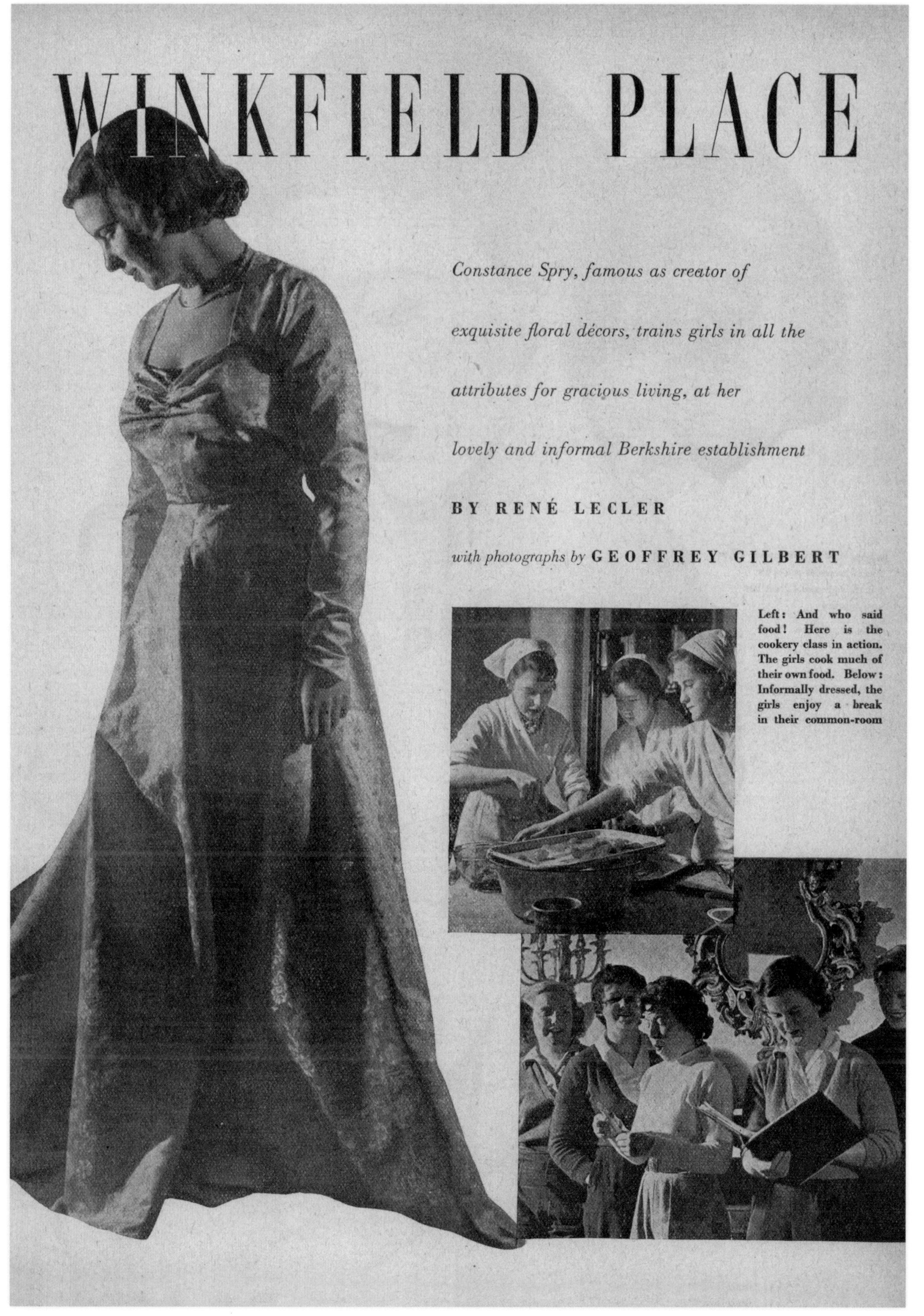

Constance Spry, famous as creator of exquisite floral décors, trains girls in all the attributes for gracious living, at her lovely and informal Berkshire establishment

BY RENÉ LECLER

with photographs by GEOFFREY GILBERT

Left: And who said food! Here is the cookery class in action. The girls cook much of their own food. Below: Informally dressed, the girls enjoy a break in their common-room

David Ogilvy, ex-R.A.F. pilot, is Chief Instructor

City men and secretaries, stockbrokers and taximen, they're all in it together— and you, too, could fly if you wanted to

Week-end

BY RENÉ LECLER
with photographs by
GEOFFREY GILBERT

As we stood on the grassy edge of Elstree Aerodrome, a tiny, blue-and-white Auster two-seater came in out of the sun and landed on the tarmac. It taxied slowly, waddling across the field and with its propeller still flashing came to a stop by the petrol pump. A girl stepped down from the cabin, turned to the attendant and said: " Fill her up, please, Joe."

We looked inside the cabin. Nobody else. She had landed, out of the blue, all by herself. It seems that at the Elstree Flying Club this is the sort of thing that girls will do. Then she went home on her bicycle.

Her name was Rita May Davis and her age twenty-two. Her only other connection with the air world: a job in the drawing office of an aircraft firm. Apart from this, Rita is a pretty average London girl, and when her father, a stockbroker, once said: " Why don't you take up something interesting. . . . Like flying, for instance?" Rita replied: " Why not? "

Her flying career has been interesting and exciting too, like the time when, on a cross-country flight to Leighton Buzzard, she took only one quarter-inch-to-the-mile map with her and forgot the next sheet. Winds carried her a bit off course and she literally flew off the map. For a while she circled around, looking for railway lines, cross-roads and other landmarks. But the world from 2,000 feet up does not look quite the same, and so, when Rita saw an airfield, she did not hesitate. She landed straight away and, finding a kindly official, asked where she was. The only trouble was that this airfield, belonging to the Royal College of Aeronautics, was officially closed. (*Continued on page* **77**)

Off to Paris for the week-end, and no bookings in advance needed. Mrs. Walter Bowles with her daughter in their private plane

Mr. C. Nash, who heads a group of flying taxi-drivers, says flying isn't as expensive as beer, cigarettes or television, and a great deal more fun

Gay Allen, London secretary, the Club's youngest experienced pilot, had her first lesson on the eve of her eighteenth birthday

Twenty-two-year-old Rita May Davis lands from her plane and goes home to Kingsbury on her bicycle. Her second favourite hobby, raffia-work, she shares with her younger sister (see small picture right)

YOU CAN'T WEAR A

But you can—and do—wear materials made from a wide range of them. This is what you can—

A fibre is just an inconsequential-looking little wisp. It must be made into yarn, then fabric, then clothes before you can wear it. But if you know the fibre's properties, you'll have some idea of what to expect of the garment.

Natural Fibres

For thousands of years cloth has been woven from the fibres that come from plants and animals. Fabrics woven from them now have new uses, new appearances.

COTTON is still well up on the list for popularity—and with good reason. It is comfortably absorbent and easy to launder. Cotton is strong and can be woven into a wide variety of fabrics. It can be dyed in many fast colours and finished to give crease resistance, water repellency, shrinkage control, or an embossed surface.

LINEN has a high degree of absorbency, dries quickly and is cooler than cotton of similar weight and weave. Linen is more expensive than cotton and cannot be made in as many weaves or dyed as easily. It creases readily, but today dress-linen is usually given a crease-resistant finish. It doesn't soil easily, and its appearance is actually improved by washing.

SILK fabric has a smooth, lustrous appearance and drapes beautifully. Silk fibre is very fine: and though silk fabrics may seem fragile, they are quite strong and elastic. Silk, though absorbent, does not conduct heat away from the body and is therefore a warmer fabric than cotton or linen, of the same construction. Resistance to sunlight and perspiration is not especially good, particularly in the case of weighted silks. The latter is therefore more appropriate for more dressy occasions and is better cleaned than washed.

WOOL today is a year-round fibre. It can be woven or knitted into very sheer and light-weight fabrics suitable for summer dress or sportswear, as well as into heavier winter-weights. Wool has great elasticity. Fabrics drape gracefully, hold their shape, and have natural crease-resisting properties. They are vulnerable to moths but in many cases are given special moth-resistant treatment.

Synthetic Fibres

Most of these are of fairly recent vintage. Their basic materials are coal, water, petroleum, natural gases, and various chemicals, as well as wood and groundnuts.

RAYON, the first of the man-made fibres, makes a cool fabric, although spun rayon, produced by cutting the long continuous filaments into short lengths and then spinning to form a twisted yarn, is warmer and fuller. Because of its special characteristics, fine yarn made from this fibre can be woven into good crêpes. Some rayons are washable. Today many are treated with special finishes so that they retain their crispness and fit. Wash and wear qualities are high if rough handling is avoided when washing and a cool iron is used.

NYLON is the strongest of all fibres. Its long-wearing qualities and easy launderability are outstanding. Knit tricots and woven sheers require little if any ironing: shrinkage is held to a minimum. Nylon has good elasticity and is therefore popularly used for hosiery. Because of the nature of the fibre, fabrics can be durably pleated by the application of heat during manufacture. Nylon is not very absorbent and, therefore, not particularly cool unless of open weave.

TERYLENE is a relatively new synthetic fibre invented in Britain in the early 1940s. There are two forms, the one a filament yarn similar in many respects to silk, and the other a staple fibre which has wool-like characteristics. Skirts and men's suits, the former containing 50 per cent Terylene and 50 per cent wool, are already available as well as a wide range of dress, lingerie and fur fabrics. Although Terylene is resistant to stretching, it is a resilient fibre and comfortable to wear: it is also resistant to creasing, does not shrink, dries quickly, only wants occasional ironing and is also moth-proof and hard-wearing.

ARDIL is another British-made fibre and, even before the war, a few Ardil and wool suits were made and indeed are still being worn. (Presumably these are men's suits.) Ardil is a protein fibre and in this respect resembles the natural animal fibres, wool and silk. Actually, however, it is made from groundnuts after removal of the oil. Like wool it is a warm fibre but unlike wool the fibre has a

FIBRE

and cannot—expect of each

smooth surface. It does not felt or shrink and it is resistant to insect attack. There is little doubt more Ardil will be seen about in the not-too-distant future. Already it is being used, mixed with wool, for all kinds of fabrics, blankets, carpets, etc. These are almost indistinguishable from all-wool materials and are less costly. In the finer weave fabrics Ardil can give the same effect as would otherwise only be achieved with the finer, expensive qualities of wool. Ardil can be mixed with cotton, nylon and rayon, to contribute warmth and comfortable soft feel, making blended fabrics suitable for a variety of purposes, including warm dressing-gowns, etc.

BLENDS of two or more different fibres are, we think, the fabrics of the future. Manufacturers are continually working to give you fabrics that are easy to care for, long-wearing and inexpensive.

Synthetics are used with each other because, though all have individual properties, they have them in varying degrees. When used in the correct proportions, the most desirable features of each fibre can be incorporated.

Synthetics are used with natural fibres because, although man-made fibres are remarkable in several respects, some of their properties are less desirable than those found in natural fibres. For example, no new fibre is comparable to wool in springiness, or to silk in soft drapability, or to linen in absorbency. By blending it is possible to produce a fabric with the good features of both, and often at lower cost.

A Terylene and wool blend is logically and ideally suitable for sportswear, the fabric and pleats withstanding washing and wear. "Hanging" instructions to safeguard pleats are given with this skirt by Windsmoor

BY LYN ARNOLD

How to get on WOMAN'S HOUR

You've heard others do it, so why shouldn't you try?

This article weighs up your chances of getting there

Here are the faces behind some of the familiar voices you hear on "Woman's Hour"

Photos: BBC

Mary Ferguson

Commander William Ibbett

Ruth Drew

It has probably crossed your mind as you listen to *Woman's Hour* that a lot of the speakers (in fact, at least five a week) are unpractised, amateur broadcasters: ordinary housewives, Mrs. Smiths like you. You have possibly wondered in a vague sort of way " Well, if they can do it, after all, why can't I? "

Well, after all, why not?

How are those Mrs. Smiths chosen?

Some are approached direct by the BBC. The editors want, say, a seller of gloves, shoes, handbags to tell listeners how to make the best buys in a series of talks on dress accessories. They will make the contact through the personnel manager of a big store, and that Mrs. Smith—who, though she never before saw a microphone, is, in her own line, something of an expert—goes on the air without herself lifting a finger.

Perhaps the editors plan a dozen talks like the recent Budget series, for which they will need a dozen Mrs. Smiths of varying type and income-level. Some will be chosen because it happens they " know someone who knows someone who knows someone." Editors and producers of programmes like this must obviously make and keep the widest possible personal contacts. But other Mrs. Smiths come " out of the files." Anyone who is microphone-tested, and does quite well, but whose talk somehow isn't right, is " kept in mind " by means of an intricate filing system. And when the day comes that a Mrs. Smith, forty years old, with three children, one part-time domestic help, and a chartered accountant husband is required, the files will produce her, just like that. So previously " failed " Mrs. Smiths need not give up hope!

Some write to *Woman's Hour* (four or five hundred letters arrive each week) to say " I enjoyed Wednesday's talk so much " or " I so profoundly disagreed with it " that " I felt I must write to say . . ." And in that letter the editors " see " a talk from a Mrs. Smith who probably never intended one. Some of the best talks, I'm told, arise this way—perhaps because amateur writers often write best when their aim is simply to get something off their chests, and they haven't got one eye fixed on a possible audience.

But most Mrs. Smiths start off by writing a script. They *all* get looked at. If any Mrs. Smith at this moment burns with resentment " because, my dear, I'm sure they don't *read* the stuff! " she should bear in mind the true tale of a lady who, getting her manuscript back from a magazine, wrote in fury: " I know you've not read it, to test you I stuck pages 16 and 17 together. They've come back stuck! " The editor promptly replied: " Dear Madam, if you will unstick the pages, you will see that I took the liberty of pencilling my initials there before re-sticking them!"

All scripts get read—but seventy-five per cent fall down at first reading. This may not necessarily be (though it probably is!) because the talk's bad. When two talks are of roughly equal merit, one may be rejected and one be broadcast, because the first covered a subject dealt with last week, while the second happened to fit in with programme needs. For instance: Suppose a Mrs. Smith wrote " A Patient's Views on Nurses," and another Mrs. Smith had just sent in " Patients, by a Nurse." Neither talk would have stood alone; together, they might make an interesting feature.

But, broadly speaking, your talk will race back to you if it's all about quaint old recipes, how you turned out the attic, what you found in grandmother's workbox; if it's a schoolgirl-essay or schoolmistress- (*Continued on page* **193**)

The Ford Popular, though quite an inexpensive car, has a surprisingly roomy boot—a great convenience at holiday time

BY JEAN WAKEMAN

With driving no longer a masculine monopoly, motor manufacturers are bidding more and more for feminine favour

What a WOMAN *looks for in a car*

A bloodless revolution is taking place in the motoring world. Have you noticed it? Sooner or later you will, for it is going to affect us all. After years of monopoly and good-humoured sarcasm, men are at last beginning to realize that women have ideas worth considering about cars. Sound, too, most of them. In fact, the time has arrived when special attention is being given to our requirements, and cars are now being made just as much for you and me as for our menfolk.

It seems a good moment, therefore, in this Motor Show month, to give you some idea of the features to look for in a car if you are thinking of buying one yourself, or if your family is going to have a car. And, if neither of these nice things is to happen, save this knowledge till you need it, for, who knows, second-hand cars are getting cheaper all the time.

This year, more than ever before, our tastes are being catered for by the manufacturers, and you will not need to go far at Earl's Court to see this for yourself. Wives as well as husbands drive the family car, and many women have their own. Add to this the fact that a woman influences a man's choice considerably, and you will appreciate how important it is that you should be able to make a wise choice.

First, we must assume that you and your husband have an idea of how much you can afford to pay for your car. Whatever that may be, remember that the smaller the engine the cheaper the running costs. Indeed, unless you have to do high daily mileages, a small car is a wise investment, for many reasons. Parking—that modern bugbear—is much easier, the car is lighter to handle and the petrol consumption is lower.

The most important thing about a car is its engine. Over that, your choice will depend on the money you propose to spend, so it is not my purpose now to give advice on that subject, but to concentrate on other features. First, especially if you are going to drive the car yourself, choose one that can be easily handled and manœuvred. If you are like me, you will insist on a simple gear-change. For that reason I like the fashionable idea of a gear lever on the steering column, though many people think this is not necessarily a good feature. But this is a matter really of personal taste, and I stick to mine persistently.

Let us scotch, too, that long-standing notion that women don't know, and don't care, what is under (*Continued on page* **234**)

The small 2 CV Citroen has a good notion—the boot when packed from outside can be reached from inside

The latest Morris Oxford has an easy gear-change, neat instrument panel, bench-type front seat and a parcels shelf

A Vauxhall with the latest alligator-type bonnet, operated by a spring. It will swing and remain open

THE INSTITUTE

Chaloner Woods

The eventful story of the Institute's growth and

of thirty revolutionary years in home management

KEEPS PACE

THIRTY YEARS AGO this country was at a turning point in its social history. Even the most optimistic housewives were accepting the fact that the unprecedented shortage of domestic labour caused by World War I would remain a feature of the Britsh way of life even in peace, with one general maid permanently taking the place of the elaborate staffs of their mother's day.

The age of black lead

It was indeed a sobering reflection. For running a house in those days, even with an efficient maid, was a heavy 12-hour-a-day task, involving scores of regular chores of which the younger generation today at any rate has little inkling. There was black-leading the kitchen range, for instance, and stoking it regularly every hour or so; cleaning the knives with brick-dust, hearthstoning the white front step; scrubbing the wooden kitchen table; and, in many country districts, tending the oil lamps.

Kitchens were depressing places, often designed without thought of daylight and ventilation. The equipment in them usually consisted of stove, sink, open dresser (a shocking dust-collector), and the tyrant kitchen range which often gave only a poor hot-water service. These meagre amenities had usually been fortuitously sited by the builder with little thought for the convenience of the user or the order of the work to be done.

Domestic tools of then and now. Top: modern Goblin vacuum-cleaner with (just below) its forerunner, which also was a boon yet to come in 1924. Below: the sort of gas-stove that was widely in use 30 years ago

The beginnings of labour-saving

Electricity and gas—those twin universal servants—had only just begun to reveal their great potentialities. There were gas cookers certainly—but without the gleaming porcelain enamel, durable chromium or thermostatic controls of today. An enterprising vanguard of housewives were trying out the first vacuum cleaners, but in most homes turning out a room still meant swathing all heavy furniture in voluminous dust-sheets and carrying everything portable outside while brushes and brooms got to work.

Wash-day was a weekly nightmare, with hard hand-rubbing the usual order of the day. Not only were nylons, seersuckers and crease-resisting fabrics unknown, but labour-saving equipment was almost non-existent. A few hand-operated, rather cumbersome washing-machines had certainly made an appearance, but their use demanded constant personal effort. Washing was followed by boiling, blueing and starching, for much of the family wash consisted of white cottons and linens. Finally came a tremendous amount of ironing,

---

←

The Institute at work today. Top left: cooking equipment under test. The accuracy of the oven settings is checked with a thermocouple; the electric mixer tried out for cake-making. Top right: Miss Garbutt, Principal of Good Housekeeping Institute, signs a completed report. Below left: a vacuum-cleaner, after practical test, is stripped and construction checked. Below right: laundry equipment under test. The temperature of the iron settings is checked; the wringer of the washing-machine tried for ease and efficiency of operation

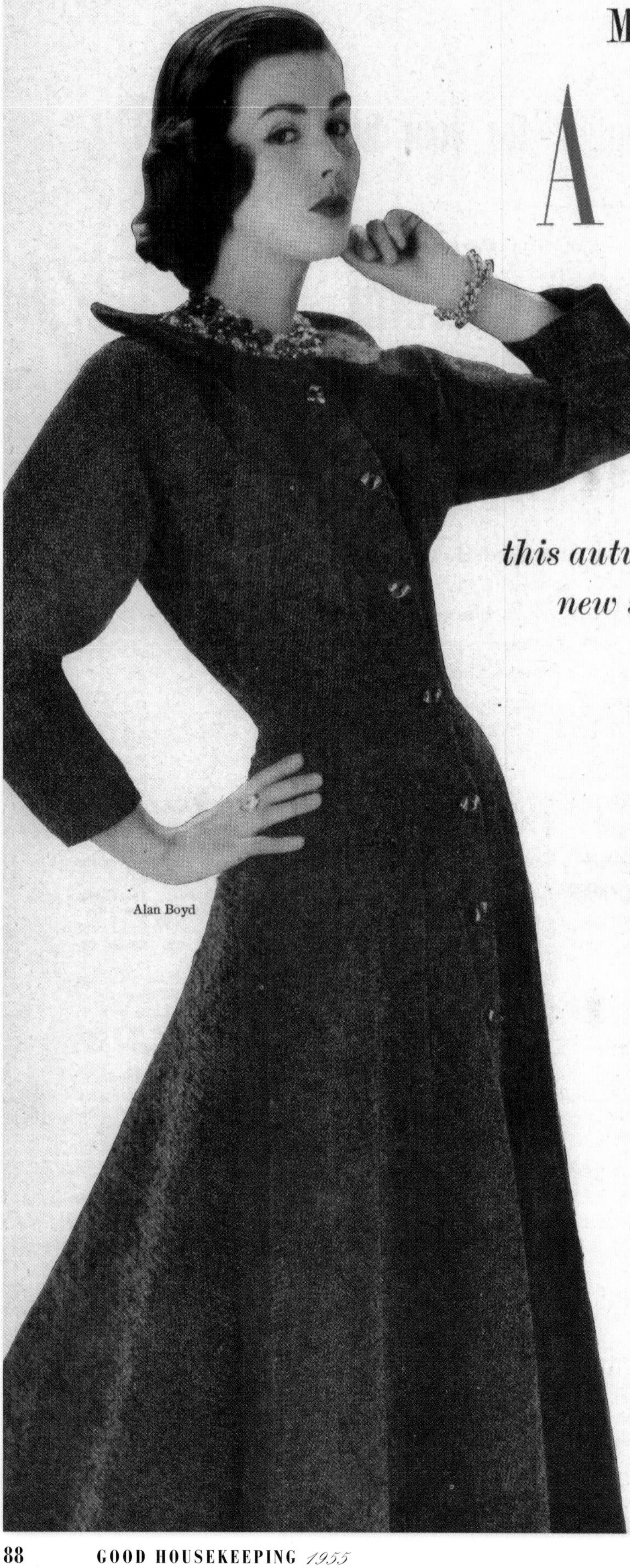

MAKE YOURSELF A Hostess Dress

Home sewing is news this autumn. We start an important new series on character clothes

Alan Boyd

● We have chosen this month a Simplicity printed pattern which would be a blessing to any wardrobe. And to prove our point that home dressmaking means more clothes in your wardrobe, we have sketched for you to see one of the many variations of this pattern and show you several fabric alternatives in colour.

This feminine soft-line design we have made up in the new luxury-feeling chenille tweed, but it can be different for every woman who wears it. The one pattern includes instructions for making a snug high neckline, a sophisticated scooped out neckline (we chose this), or a plain V neckline. The sleeves can be cut short, full length or three-quarter length, so that you can choose your style or your fabric to suit your personality. But this hostess gown would look enchanting, too, as a shortie, the hemline cut to ordinary day length.

Add an irresistible distinctive touch in the glitter of buttons, a froth of white at the neckline, the sparkle of jewellery. If warmth is your particular need, there are several bright wools from which to choose. If you want glamour and warmth combined, Jacqlinta, the wool tweed with the gold Lurex glitter thread interwoven, or chenille tweed with its velvety thread, should meet your requirements.

This hostess dress adds distinction to warmth.
Material is the new chenille tweed (see opposite page).
Simplicity printed pattern No. 4924
in bust sizes 30 to 42 inches. Price 2*s*.
To order by post, see page 160

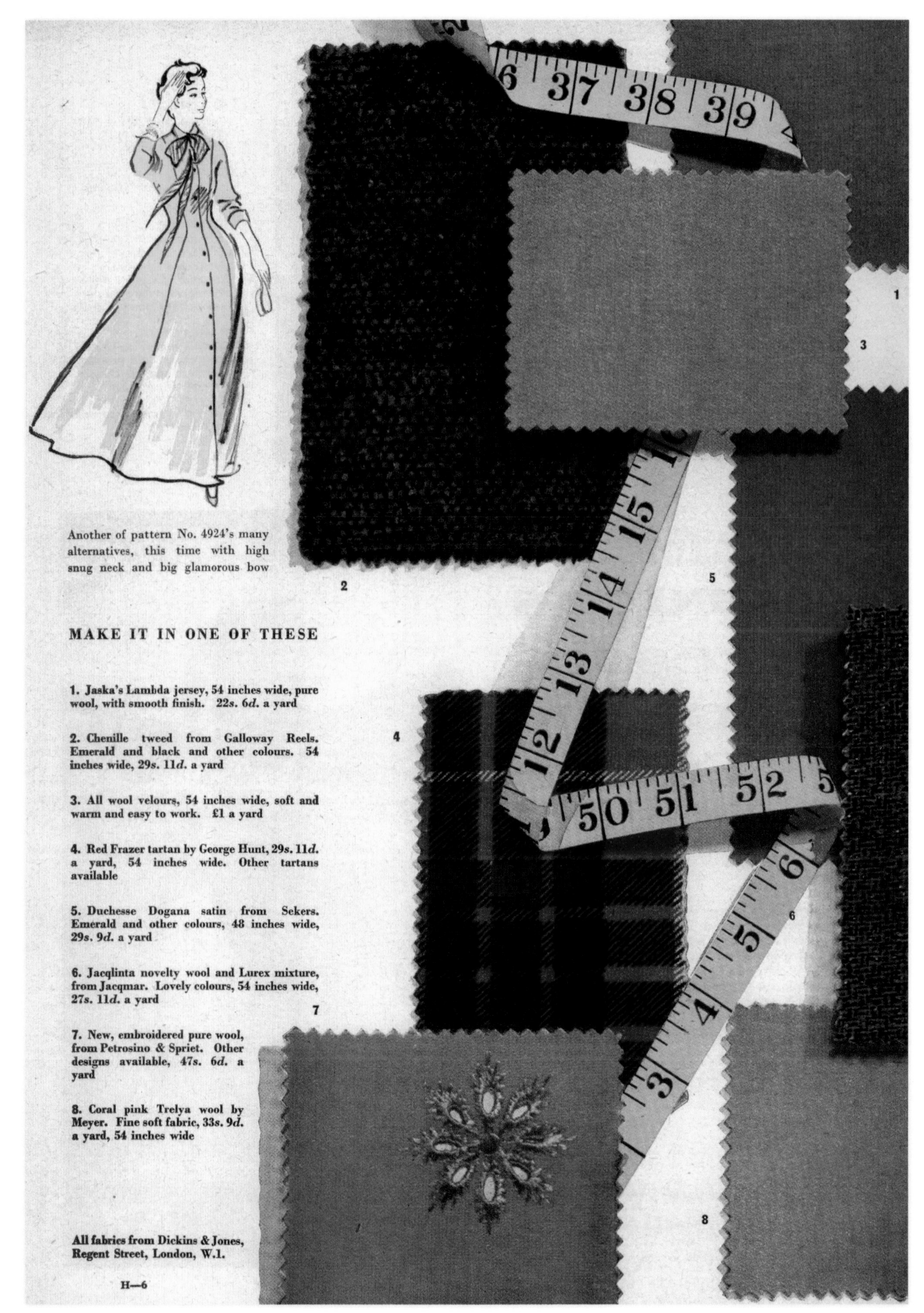

Another of pattern No. 4924's many alternatives, this time with high snug neck and big glamorous bow

MAKE IT IN ONE OF THESE

1. Jaska's Lambda jersey, 54 inches wide, pure wool, with smooth finish. 22*s*. 6*d*. a yard

2. Chenille tweed from Galloway Reels. Emerald and black and other colours. 54 inches wide, 29*s*. 11*d*. a yard

3. All wool velours, 54 inches wide, soft and warm and easy to work. £1 a yard

4. Red Frazer tartan by George Hunt, 29*s*. 11*d*. a yard, 54 inches wide. Other tartans available

5. Duchesse Dogana satin from Sekers. Emerald and other colours, 48 inches wide, 29*s*. 9*d*. a yard

6. Jacqlinta novelty wool and Lurex mixture, from Jacqmar. Lovely colours, 54 inches wide, 27*s*. 11*d*. a yard

7. New, embroidered pure wool, from Petrosino & Spriet. Other designs available, 47*s*. 6*d*. a yard

8. Coral pink Trelya wool by Meyer. Fine soft fabric, 33*s*. 9*d*. a yard, 54 inches wide

All fabrics from Dickins & Jones, Regent Street, London, W.1.

H—6

INTO THE SHOPS

Prices given in this supplement have been checked carefully but should be confirmed before purchases are made

within one year

Over and above the familiar services expected from any fuel—heating, lighting and cooking—electricity has an almost bewildering range of applications.

This year you can buy electric driers which will dry your week's wash in under two hours; electric scissors which make short work of cutting-out patterns; time-switch controls which automatically turn cookers on and off, washing-machines and food mixers.

You can leave electricity to act as a baby-sitter. You can mix a cake or squeeze an orange in a matter of seconds.

Electricity will polish a floor, trim a hedge, hoe an herbaceous border. It will keep food warm, make ice-cream, dispose of your garbage and wash up your dishes.

You can turn to it for television and radio, shave by it, warm your bed with it, and press your clothes with it.

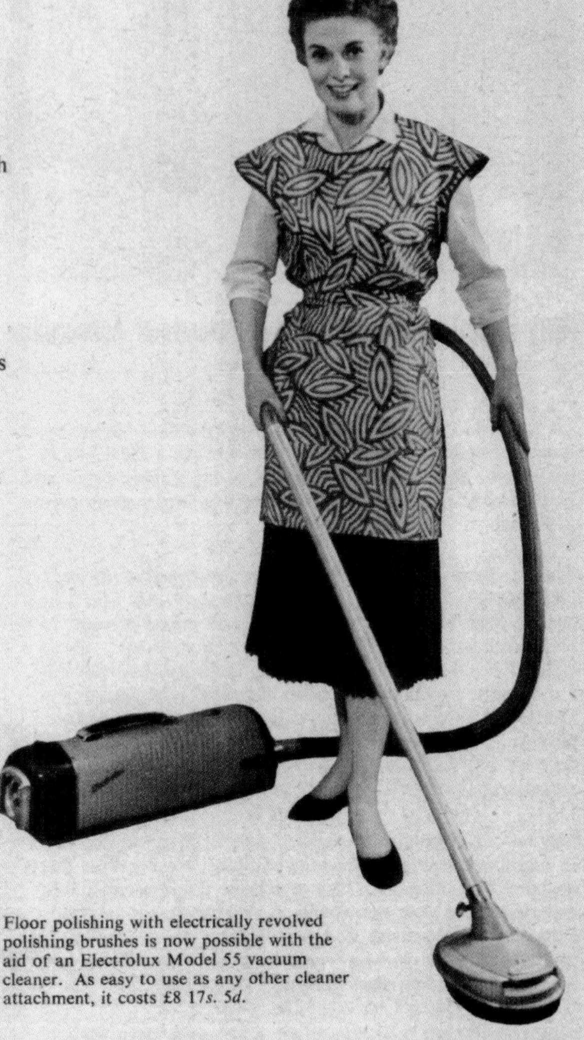

Floor polishing with electrically revolved polishing brushes is now possible with the aid of an Electrolux Model 55 vacuum cleaner. As easy to use as any other cleaner attachment, it costs £8 17*s.* 5*d.*

Space for bottles, door shelves, and an entirely separate compartment with its own heater for keeping butter at a spreading temperature are features to be found in many of this year's refrigerators. The 7 cubic feet Coldrator costs 128 guineas.

Sewing on buttons, embroidering, zig-zag sewing, and numerous specialized finishing stitches are done automatically by the latest zig-zag sewing-machines. The Jones costs £88 11*s*. 6*d*.

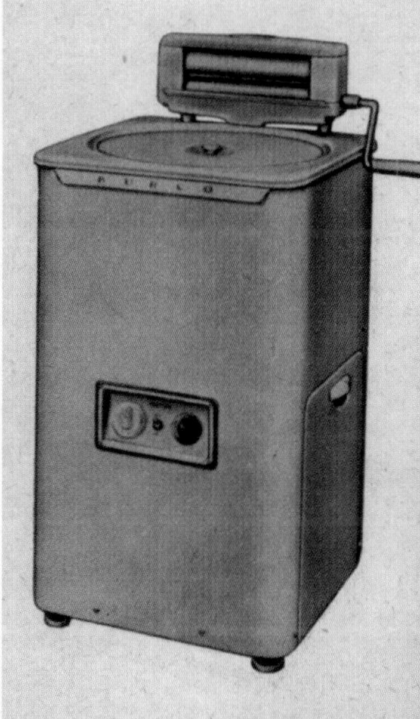

Boiling, as well as washing, clothes is a service given by many of this year's washing-machines. The Burco costs £48 5*s*. 8*d*.

As well as drying laundry to ironing dampness in a matter of seconds, a heated tumbler drier will dry blankets from wet to bone dry in 90 minutes. The English Electric tumbler drier costs £69 10*s*.

No matter how loud your radio or television is, or how far away the nursery, you can use this Cri-Call baby alarm to hear every sound that the baby makes. It costs £7 19*s*. complete.

Soothing pains and bruises, infra-red ray lamps are in use in sportsmen's dressing-rooms all over the country. The Infraphil is a neat portable unit which costs 5 guineas.

Warm air in winter and cool air in summer can be provided by electric fan heaters. The Cotswold, with a loading of 1,500 watts, will heat a room of average size (10 feet by 12 feet) and costs £7 17*s*.

Automatic washing, rinsing and drying of dishes for a household of four is achieved in about six minutes by an electric dish-washer. The Ada-Maid costs £68 16*s*.

Continued on page 144

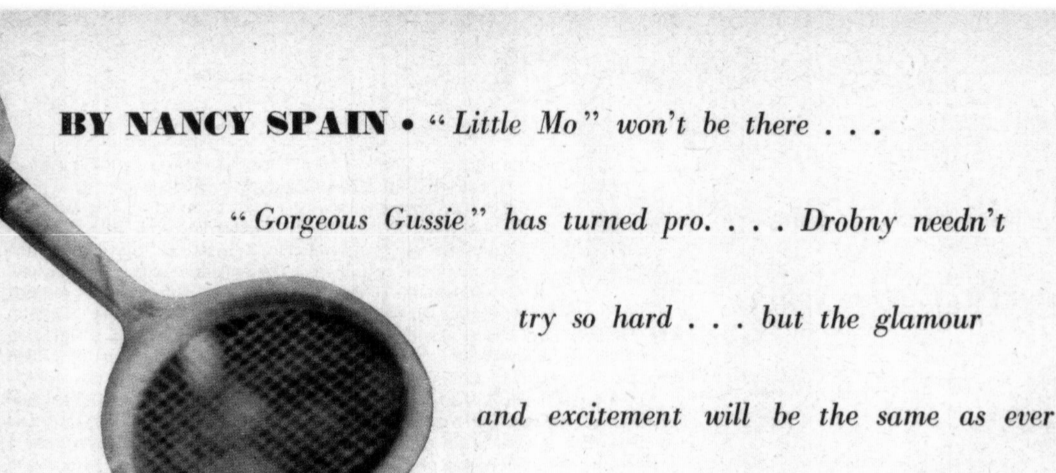

BY NANCY SPAIN • *"Little Mo" won't be there . . . "Gorgeous Gussie" has turned pro. . . . Drobny needn't try so hard . . . but the glamour and excitement will be the same as ever*

Royal Wimbledon

Good-looking Victor Seixas on his way to winning the Men's Championship in Coronation year

THERE are plenty of tennis tournaments in the world: at Forest Hills, Beverly Hills, Monte Carlo, Paris. But there is only one Wimbledon. Royal Wimbledon. The American players are the first to admit it. "Your Royal Wimbledon is just tennis heaven, that's all," says "Teach" Tennant, the greatest woman coach the world has ever seen. "The whole of my tennis career seemed worth while as I stood there shaking hands with Queen Mary," says Helen Jacobs. "It was the greatest moment of my life," agrees Alice Marble, another former champion from the U.S.A.

Why is this so? What is it that Wimbledon has that other tournaments have not? It has the Championships of the World on Grass, of course. But then *other* countries have *other* world championships: on hard courts, rubble courts and wood in U.S.A., France and Belgium respectively. So that is not it.

Myself, I am convinced that Wimbledon is "special" simply because it *is* Royal. Kings and queens have always played there, at the All England Club. King Manoel of Portugal used to play every morning in the summer: and on the day of his death was actually booked for a court at 10 a.m. King Alfonso XIII of Spain, too, and King Gustav of Sweden (the former a "reckless" player, the latter an enthusiastic "lobber") were also very keen. And this invested the famous club courts with the glamour of Royalty. Then, of course, our own beloved Royal Family have bestowed their patronage on the Championships themselves. One year (1946) when Queen Elizabeth the Queen Mother was presenting the men's singles cups she remarked, "Oh, bother! I never looked to see what was engraved on the cup," and promptly took it back from the winner to examine it. A charmingly spontaneous gesture, absolutely typical of her. And typical, too, of Wimbledon.

It was impossible not to be moved when Queen Mary came into the Royal Box. Players would stop in the middle of a rally and bow. The spectators would rise, often they would cheer, spontaneously. One year Her Majesty had to ask that the crowds should *not* demonstrate their affection. She said it put the players off . . .

Queen Mary was very, very keen on watching the tennis. She would sit out long and exhausting matches. Sometimes she stayed for four hours, only moving to the back of the Royal Box when the setting sun

A thrilling moment of many past years—the arrival of Queen Mary at Wimbledon

" Little Mo " Connolly, in 1954, winning the Women's singles for the third time while still in her teens

Fashions on the court sometimes provide minor but colourful sensations

Photos: Picture Post, I.N.P., L.N.A., Keystone, A.P., Mirrorpic

The late King, as Duke of York, playing at Wimbledon in 1926

Below, Jaroslav Drobny, popular and gallant winner in 1954, receives his trophy from the Duchess of Kent

The idol of the 'twenties—the fabulous Suzanne Lenglen

shone directly into her eyes and proved too much for her sunshade. One very hot day she even lent her fan to Mrs. Gerke, wife of the First Secretary in the Czechoslovakian Legation, saying, as Mrs. Gerke fanned herself with a newspaper, " My fan will be better for you, my dear." Queen Mary's enthusiasm for lawn tennis definitely dated from the happy engagement of King George VI and the Queen Mother (then Duke and Duchess of York). Many happy snapshots exist, taken on the tennis court at the time. And in one unforgettable year (1926) the Duke of York himself played at Wimbledon. He won the Men's Open Doubles at the R.A.F. Tournament with Sir Louis Greig and so qualified to play in the first rounds of the Wimbledon Men's Doubles.

Their match was announced for Court Number One, when a crowd of 3,000 saw them lose to H. Roper Barrett and A. W. Gore, a former champion pair, 6–2, 6–3, 6–1. The Duke of York had bad luck in the draw. Sir Louis and he were a strong pair and if they had not immediately encountered Gore's hard hitting and Roper Barrett's puzzling little " soft balls " they might well have got through a round or two. The Duke of York was a strong left-handed player with an excellent forehand drive and " a jolly good serve." A friend who often played against him said, " Until Roper Barrett remembered that His Majesty was a southpaw and began to exploit his backhand weakness, His Majesty often caught him on the wrong foot with his top-spin drives."

Strangely enough, this historic game went almost unnoticed. For this was the awful day *(Continued on page* **219***)*

STRICTLY FOR WIVES: *The Secrets of Having*

A WELL-DRESSED HUSBAND

How do you do?

The Editor has asked me if I would care to write an article pleading with wives to do something about the "sartorial inadequacies" of their husbands. I have looked up the words in the dictionary and given the matter much thought. A sense of duty to my fellow men compels me to accept the invitation. But I know very well that my advice may be strongly criticized, mainly because I, obviously, have a larger wardrobe than the average male.

So first let me correct a fallacy. Never think that the amount of a chap's income (or the facility with which he can talk his tailor into extending credit) has anything to do with it. It is not the number of his suits that will win him an Oscar for being well-dressed. The people who can afford to buy the finest race-horses in the world don't necessarily win the races. Or, to give a more practical example, look at the clothes of the wealthy men whose pictures you see in the daily papers—industrial magnates, cabinet ministers, millionaire land-owners, pool promoters. Well, you see what I mean.

To show you that it is more important for a man to know *how* to wear clothes than to spend a great deal of money on them, I have had myself photographed twice in a favourite suit of mine. It is of tropical-weight cloth and I bought it ready-made in New York for twenty-four dollars (£8). This type of suit is worn a great deal in New York during the summer. So in one picture I show it as I frequently saw it being worn there, and in the other as I wear it. A note of comedy seems to have asserted itself but it does not, I'm certain, obscure the fact that one view looks a little odd and the other—I think—rather smart.

And there, ladies, is point number one for you. Arouse in the breast of the male that fundamental urge "to look his best." After all, the pea-hen knows how to do it, so I'm quite sure you can.

But will you? I regret to say it, but I believe that one reason for the apparent lack of masculine pride in dress is that men, sensitive and dependent creatures, don't get all the encouragement they need from their women-folk. Many a budding interest has been withered with a word before it could flower. "I should choose a blue serge again if I were you, Herbert. It's so *useful* . . ." And bang go his hopes for the lovat green he'd set his heart on.

I have my theory about this. The Englishman—as we know—has a reputation for his conservative outlook on dress, but it is a reputation which has been built up from the middle of the last century, influenced, perhaps, by Queen Victoria's prolonged period of mourning. During that time men's clothes were stabilized not only in colour but also in cut, and have, except for very small subtleties, remained the same up to the present day.

Before that, there was a time when men were certainly the more colourfully garbed of the sexes, but women, never slow to take advantage of an opportunity, seized their chance to jump into the lead. And since then they have been enjoying themselves enormously—changing their fashions from one letter of the alphabet to another every year.

But the fine old male spirit isn't dead entirely. Any day of the year you may see a group of men in front of a shop window, gazing wistfully and sheepishly at an array of gaily-coloured socks or sporting-looking headgear. I believe that the old spirit *can* be revived—but it may take time. There was the case of my brother's hat.

The other day I went down to see him in his office in the city, and he suggested that we might go out to lunch. I accepted because he is my eldest brother, and I felt pretty certain that he would pay the bill. As we walked out into the street, I was delighted to notice that he put on a dark green trilby hat. I had always seen him before in a bowler, which did not suit him at all. A green hat may sound a little "Chelsea" but actually it looked extremely respectable. But the main point is that it suited him. I wasn't slow to point out this great improvement.

"Yes," he said. "I realized about six months ago that a bowler hat didn't suit me, and I also realized that I shouldn't be offending anybody by wearing a green trilby."

It's not what it costs but how it's worn that matters

BY TERRY-THOMAS

I couldn't help thinking that it was a terrible pity it had taken him about thirty years to find that out.

I am not going to suggest for one moment that your husband should not wear a bowler hat if it suits him. I am also quite aware that some employers may take exception to a green trilby, though if they do they must be related to my first boss. He objected to the fact that I always carried a Malacca cane and wore a dark red carnation (if you wonder how I could afford a daily carnation the answer is I couldn't). Anyway, as I was leaving the office one evening he said, " Tell me, boy, what do you think you are—a managing director? " I'm pleased I gave him the right answer. Otherwise I might still be working in the same office.

The trouble with many husbands, let's face it, is that they are not very discriminating. A swift glance at any bunch of them will often give the impression that fifty per cent are colour-blind and the other half suffering from astigmatism. Frequently you will see a man wearing a striped suit, a check shirt and a spotted tie. And the odd part about it is that if you encouraged any one of them to dress in a plain colour suit—say clerical grey—a white shirt, a grey tie and a maroon waistcoat, he would consider himself overdressed. Only because he would look so much smarter.

Of course some men are not good shoppers and some shop assistants are particularly good salesmen—especially if there is some line they want to get rid of. Or it may be that with the best intentions in the world they will force a sale of something because they have been *told* it is in the fashion.

So here, ladies, is the Terry-Thomas maxim number two. The secret of dressing well is to have a simple plan and stick to it; to avoid like the plague all those things that can lead quickly to a confusion of colour and design—coloured shirts, patterned suits and ties inspired by Picasso. So get the old man into this way of thinking with, if necessary, a little artful persuasion. " Really, John, I do think dark grey suits you. It makes you look so much younger. . . ." He will assume younger to mean slimmer by the way you say it.

You will notice that I haven't mentioned anything about fancy waistcoats. You did? Good show! Well, why should I, anyway? They are a family matter entirely. Some families go in for flowered wall-papers, some don't. Some like fancy waistcoats around the place, others don't. I'm keeping out of *that* kind of argument.

Once you have got your husband moving in the right direction it is equally important to see that he keeps it up. Suits always pressed, shoes polished, and shirts of snowy whiteness (somebody's wife uses you know what). There must be no shabby old suits " good enough for the office, my dear."

Actually I imagine that a lot of men excuse their clothes because of the work that they do. But when you come to think of the smartness of a soldier (or a policeman for that matter) and then consider what they do, there doesn't seem to be very much point to that argument.

Of course accessories are important—hat, gloves, cane or neatly rolled umbrella, handkerchief just emerging from the breast-pocket. Well-trained husbands will soon get the habit. But button-holes are a much more tricky question. Have you ever noticed a man at a wedding, whether his own or somebody else's, wearing a flower? He looks slightly self-conscious, don't you think?

The answer, of course, is that the florists usually paint the lily, or carnation. Instead of leaving the flower as it was picked, they strap it to a piece of parsley, purple-sprouting broccoli, or a large lump of fern, and the result is more like a window-box than a button-hole. All quite unnecessary, and it again brings us back to my point of simplicity.

But I'm sure that this article would be incomplete without a tale with a moral for the " ever-loving " who may have it in mind to buy her spouse a tie for his birthday. It concerns the wife who spent an enormous amount of time selecting two ties which she proudly presented to her husband on his birthday morning, and then went downstairs to cook the breakfast. This left him with two choices where one might have been difficult. After much deliberation, he chose one and proudly joined his wife. She took one look and said, " Oh—so you don't like the other one, eh?"

The moral is this: in moments when family peace is at stake, be wise, say nothing and let the old man please himself. You can soon get him back into line again. Cheers.

Furness

The author informally dressed for motoring

Peter North

Not a word about fancy waistcoats

What better authority could you want than the man who has twice been voted one of England's eleven best-dressed men and awarded a Golden Oscar this year as Radio's best-dressed star?

About the new Salk immunization plan.

Is it effective? Is it safe?

Will it be used here?

BY LINDSAY WILLIAMS

Anti-polio vaccine

THE FACTS

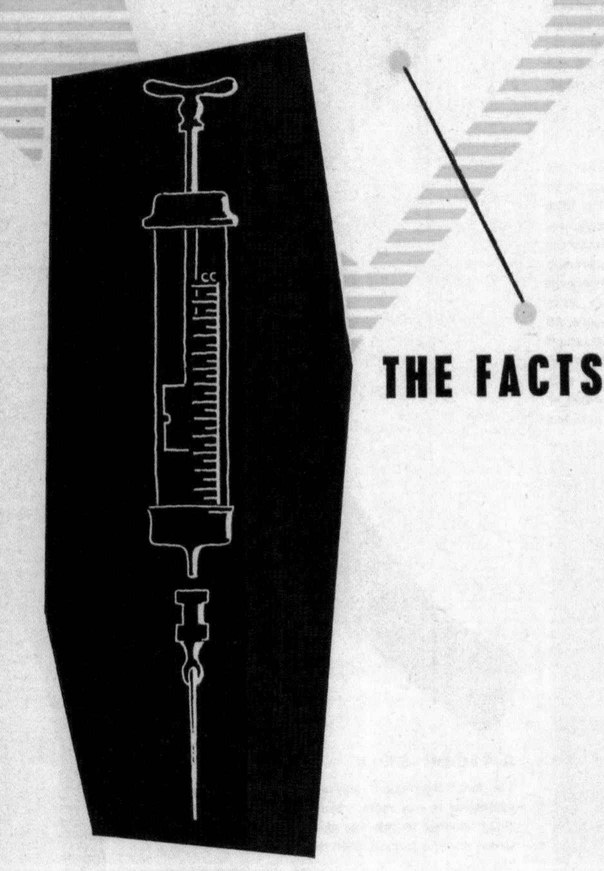

FROM the quiet college town of Ann Arbor in the State of Michigan, U.S.A., news came on April 12th of one of the most sensational medical discoveries of all time. Before a battery of powerful lights and TV and newsreel cameras, two men announced to 150 reporters and 500 scientists the results of the largest medical test in American history—perhaps the world.

Paralytic polio could be prevented. That, in essence, was the news that fifty-four-year-old Dr. Thomas Francis, noted American epidemiologist, announced in an hour-and-a-half-long speech. As he sat down, his audience rose to give a tremendous ovation to the man who had made it possible—Dr. Jonas Edward Salk, of the University of Pittsburg.

From Michigan the news flashed round the world. In the U.S., where the vaccine had been stock-piled in enormous quantities, the six producing firms rapidly made plans for nation-wide distribution, so that mass vaccination could be carried out before the onset of the coming polio season. What amazing news it was. Paralytic polio, which had crippled so many, was at last beaten.

The discovery of the Salk vaccine—though subsequent events were to raise doubts as to whether the victory was quite as complete and decisive as was at first thought—was the solution to one of the most intriguing medical puzzles that has ever baffled doctors. They had conquered yellow fever, typhoid, typhus and a host of other fevers by means of vaccines But they could not fathom polio. They could not apply the usual techniques of immunization because these would not work.

As long ago as 1796, famed Edward Jenner, seeking an answer to the dreaded smallpox, had demonstrated the basic principle of immunology. Namely, that if a patient is inoculated with a form of the disease-causing germ so mild that the disease will not flare up, the body can be tricked into building up a reserve of powerful antibodies in the blood. Consequently any subsequent infection will be blasted away on the spot. Jenner's vaccine came ready-made in the form of cow-pox and not till more than a hundred years later were immunologists able to tackle other infectious ills.

But the acquisition of knowledge about antibodies in due course enabled the immunologists to perfect other vaccines. They discovered that, by growing bacteria in culture media, they could extract their deadly poisons (so-called toxins), turn them chemically into harmless toxoids, and inject them, thus building up a stock of antibodies in the blood that would confer the vital immunity. If they could not extract the poisons, injections of dead bacteria were just as effective.

This basic principle of immunology worked well against various diseases caused by bacteria—typhoid, diphtheria, lockjaw and the rest—but when doctors came to tackle diseases caused by those midget microbes, the viruses, they ran up against a medical brick wall. Viruses could not be induced to grow in culture media like their big brothers, the bacteria. Until some means of coaxing them to grow could be found, immunologists were helpless against them.

It was suspected, as long ago as the turn of the century, that polio was a virus disease. Not that anyone had seen the virus (it was, in fact, not until just under two years ago that it was first photographed under the wonderful electron microscope), but the cause of any infectious disease not produced by bacteria visible under an ordinary microscope was assumed to be a virus.

But polio, if indeed it were a virus disease, was a problem all on its own. For, not only was the virus never seen, but no one could find the slightest trace of it in the blood of a polio patient. Its presence could easily be tested, even if it were too small to be seen. A blood specimen could be injected into a susceptible animal, such as a monkey. If the virus were in the blood, the animal would develop (*Continued on page* **93**)

A TRAIL TO FORTUNE

by the sea

Has private enterprise a chance today? Here is a family which has proved beyond doubt that it has—when backed by determination, courage and hard work

ONE sunny windy Easter in the early thirties, Mr. and Mrs. Robert Scott took a week-end off from their little general shop and sub-post-office in a Kentish village, and went to a sub-postmasters' conference at Great Yarmouth on the East Coast. Walking along the wide flat streets when her husband was at meetings—sniffing the salt fresh wind, watching sun-splashed waves lapping on the wide flat sands, Alice Scott took a fancy to Yarmouth.

"Wouldn't it be nice," she sighed to her husband that evening, "if we could just *stay* here?" And then went on, "But why shouldn't we? Why not sell the business and run a boarding-house here?" With that remark she not only changed the lives of her husband and herself, but started a ripple which spread out and out and is still spreading.

To start with, Robert Scott was not enthusiastic. He had done some pretty fundamental house-moving already. The family had originally had a baking and catering business in Wales, but Mr. Scott's health broke down and the move to Kent had been a help. To give up a profitable, peaceful business in a pleasant village, for something as unknown and strenuous as a boarding-house in a strange town . . . to uproot four children, two still at school . . .

But his objections were as nothing compared with those of his daughter Hilda. It wasn't *fair*; she *couldn't* leave; she had been engaged to Norman Bassett more or less ever since they'd met over a snowball fight when they were both fourteen, but they couldn't afford to get married yet, and how *could* Mum and Dad be so unreasonable as to expect her to ruin her whole *life* . . .?

Mum was not being firm for firmness' sake. She had a sound business sense and she was certain that this move would change the life of the whole family for the better. She knew already what house she wanted to buy—a twelve-bedroomed place near the sea, lighted, like a lot of Yarmouth lodgings in those days, by oil-lamps and candles. By that June she had talked her husband round; soothed Hilda into finding herself a job; arranged for her to live with Norman's parents after the move. She had managed to buy the Yarmouth house on a mortgage; persuaded the Yarmouth bank manager into giving her an overdraft for re-decoration and extra furniture. Leaving (*Continued on page* **136**)

BY DIANA AND MEIR GILLON

Straight-from-stove-to-table

is the sensible idea behind these

good-looking dishes and pans

Left: The pan our model holds in her hand is a sample of the hand-made pottery available in various good designs. It can be used for cooking over an asbestos mat. From Ian Fraser of King's Road, S.W.10

Below: the handsome Danish casserole on the left, with its swimming fish decoration and looped handle, and the two heavy green long-handled enamel pans come from Heal & Son

Below: Pretty square dish to contain a good square meal. In white with green leaf design, also from Heal's. This is a many-purpose piece, useful for hot or cold meat or vegetables, or even fruit

And here is the newest version of the old swan dish. They will never be swans, but are far from ugly ducklings. They aren't strictly for cooking, but can be used to good effect, to hold sweets, small fruits, hors d'œuvres or a flower decoration. They come from Liberty, Regent St., London, W.1

Below: For cheese enthusiasts, a really roomy container, deep rose pottery with wooden stand. Like the soup tureen below, it comes from Heal's

The striking Domino Hot Pot, above left, is by Denby Ware in black and white, and is designed with its own stand and night-light holder to keep it as warm as you want. Above right is a matching casserole, and there are many other matching pieces—such as a teapot and cup—all obtainable from the John Lewis Partnership shops. Denby, long known for their sturdy, simple ware, have now, by choosing black and white, put themselves into the smart set as well

For prices and stockists of merchandise in this feature, see page 228

Below: Known as a soup tureen, this generous rose-red dish could also be used for serving one of those useful all-in-one meals, such as pot au feu, or a casserole recipe for lots of guests. These cooking-pots are so inspiring that they send you to your recipe book looking up meals to use them for. Right: Ian Fraser's irresistible glossy black earthenware cider jar with plain wood tap

Serving vessels of rare distinction;

handsome to look at,

handsome in the measure of trouble they save you

My Ideal....

"I would not have believed that a domestic boiler could do so much and yet be so little trouble. Stoke it twice a day and set the thermostat on the front to the water temperature you require; that is all you need to do! It is very economical on fuel, and the rocking grate makes it amazingly simple to clear—you can also, when necessary, dump the incombustible material into the ashpan without raising any dust."

The Ideal No. 1 'Autocrat' supplies *really* hot water—800 gallons from only 1 cwt. of coke a week, or up to 3 times this quantity according to the amount of fuel used. Where hot water requirements are moderate, this boiler has sufficient power to heat a radiator or towel rail. It is finished in Cream and Black enamel and the overall dimensions are :—Height to top plate 25¾", Width 17", Depth 18".

You can see this remarkable new boiler in our London showrooms, Ideal House, Great Marlborough Street, W.1, or at your local Builders' and Plumbers' Merchants.

IDEAL No. 1 'Autocrat' DOMESTIC BOILER

PRICE complete with Stoking Tools **£23**
(Extra for Ireland & Channel Isles)

Extra if boiler Bower-barffed (Rust resistant treatment for soft water districts)—£3.4.6.

IDEAL-Standard

IDEAL BOILERS & RADIATORS LTD • IDEAL WORKS • HULL

THE STUDIO

Conducted by Harriet Reeder

Rex Smith

HOW TO MAKE A TELEPHONE SHELF

Some people love telephoning, but no one loves the telephone itself. Even less endearing are its multitude of books which must be accommodated. Here is a chance to make your own solution to the problem, which is also the answer to the too-narrow hall, or the bed that leaves no room for a side-table. This telephone shelf, designed by Raymond Elston, costs about 16*s*., less if you can pick up odd pieces of Warerite. The dark panel is red, and meant to take the telephone, the white one can be scribbled on and afterwards wiped clean. This is how to make it.

TOOLS REQUIRED

Tenon saw; mitre block; square; rule; screwdriver; hammer; plane; bradawl; brace and bit.

Above: the underside of the shelf.
Below: a diagram showing how the parts are assembled

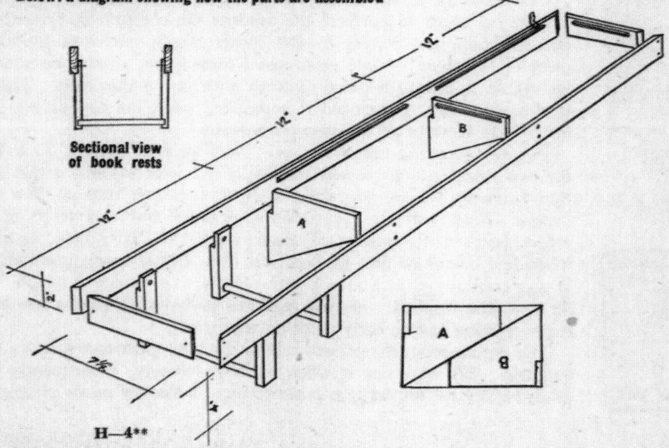

H—4**

MATERIALS REQUIRED

Frame

2 pieces of wood 36 ins. by 2 ins. by $\frac{1}{2}$ in.
2 pieces of wood $7\frac{1}{2}$ ins. by 2 ins. by $\frac{1}{2}$ in.
1 piece of wood $10\frac{1}{2}$ ins. by 6 ins. by $\frac{1}{2}$ in.
1 piece of wood 20 ins. by 1 in. by $\frac{1}{2}$ in.
6 ft. (approx.) of $\frac{1}{2}$-in. quadrant beading
15 ins. of $\frac{3}{8}$-in. dowling

No particular type of wood is essential. This example was made in mahogany.

Panels

2 pieces of Warerite approx. 12 ins. by $6\frac{1}{2}$ ins.
Glue, panel pins and screws

The pieces of wood should be bought slightly oversize and accurately cut to these measurements. Firstly, the four pieces that make the basic frame should be mitred. This could be done by cutting to a pencilled line of 45 degrees, though an accurately fitting mitre is more easily achieved with the help of a mitre block. These pieces are then glued and panel-pinned to form a rectangle. Next make the two triangular pieces, AB, which at the same time serve as supporting brackets and the divisions between the Warerite panels and directory-holder. These pieces come conveniently from one piece of wood, as can be seen from the diagram. After sawing diagonally into two, cut off 3 ins. of the points and then make the slot of 2 ins. by $\frac{1}{2}$ in. at the broad end. With careful, accurate workmanship these two pieces should fit snugly within the frame. Mark their positions on the frame and, with a bradawl, bore two holes at each position as indicated in the drawing, glue the surfaces to be joined and screw together. (Brass countersunk raised-head screws look well and won't rust.)

Now cut the Warerite to fit the two right-hand panels. It may be wise to make cardboard patterns and cut the Warerite from these. To support these panels, pin and glue the quadrant beading round the inside of the frame, allowing just enough room for the thickness of the sheet. When the glue is set, fit into place the tailor-made panels, gluing them to the beading, using books to weight them down till dry.

The directory rack now remains. It is made from the dowling and the piece of 20 ins. by 1 in. by $\frac{1}{2}$ in., the latter being cut into four pieces of 5 ins. each. At one end of each on the 1-in. face, drill a $\frac{3}{8}$-in. hole, but stop just before it goes right through. At the other end, on the opposite face, cut a shoulder 1 in. down and to half the thickness. Cut two pieces of dowel to fit between the 5-in. uprights as they are shown in position in the drawing. Glue an upright on to each end of the dowel bars so that you have, as it were, a pair of U's. Mark their positions within the frame, then glue and screw into place.

Lastly, bore three holes in the back rail to take the screws that will support the whole shelf from the wall. Finish with button polish or beeswax.

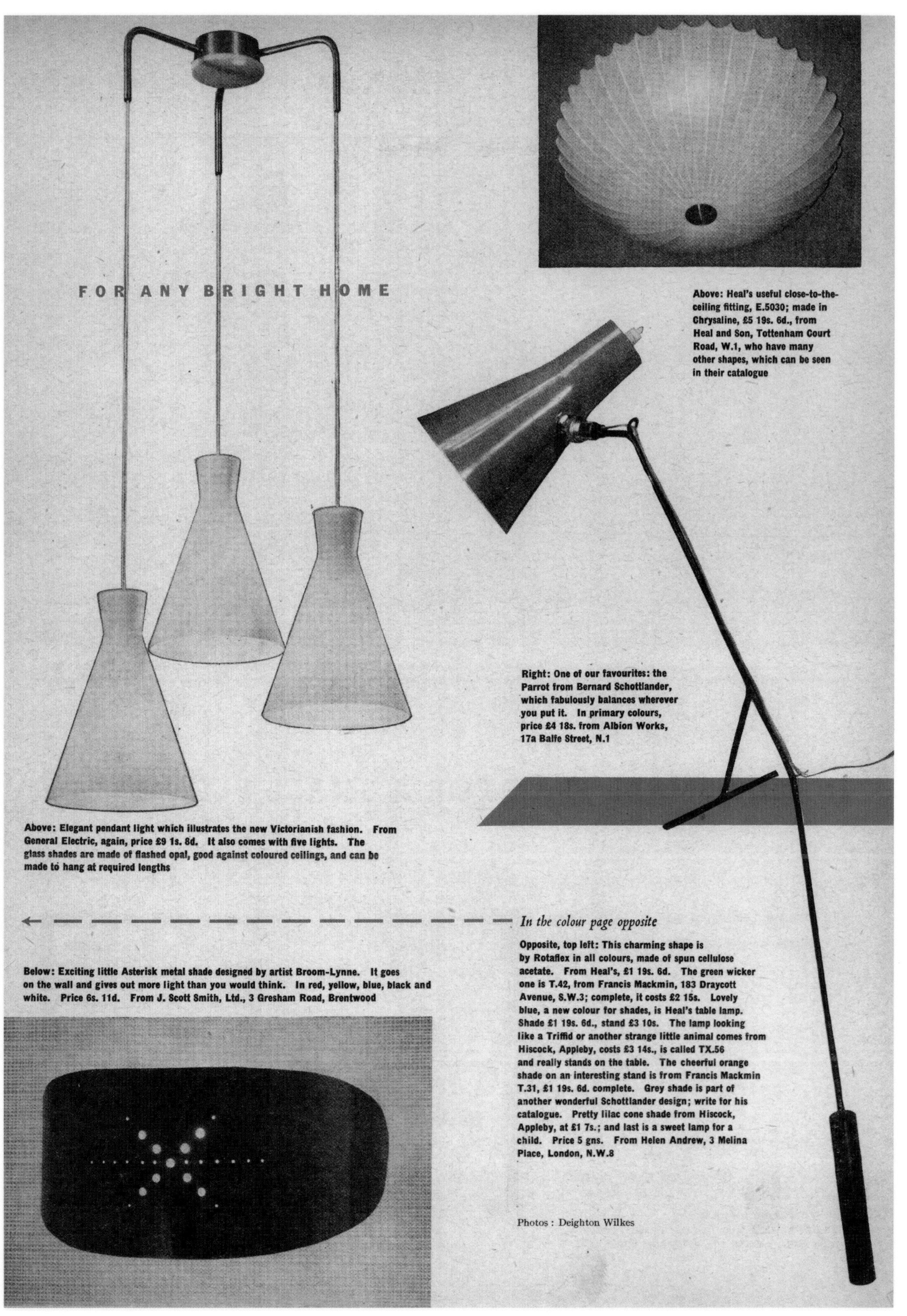

FOR ANY BRIGHT HOME

Above: Heal's useful close-to-the-ceiling fitting, E.5030; made in Chrysaline, £5 19s. 6d., from Heal and Son, Tottenham Court Road, W.1, who have many other shapes, which can be seen in their catalogue

Right: One of our favourites: the Parrot from Bernard Schottlander, which fabulously balances wherever you put it. In primary colours, price £4 18s. from Albion Works, 17a Balfe Street, N.1

Above: Elegant pendant light which illustrates the new Victorianish fashion. From General Electric, again, price £9 1s. 8d. It also comes with five lights. The glass shades are made of flashed opal, good against coloured ceilings, and can be made to hang at required lengths

Below: Exciting little Asterisk metal shade designed by artist Broom-Lynne. It goes on the wall and gives out more light than you would think. In red, yellow, blue, black and white. Price 6s. 11d. From J. Scott Smith, Ltd., 3 Gresham Road, Brentwood

In the colour page opposite

Opposite, top left: This charming shape is by Rotaflex in all colours, made of spun cellulose acetate. From Heal's, £1 19s. 6d. The green wicker one is T.42, from Francis Mackmin, 183 Draycott Avenue, S.W.3; complete, it costs £2 15s. Lovely blue, a new colour for shades, is Heal's table lamp. Shade £1 19s. 6d., stand £3 10s. The lamp looking like a Triffid or another strange little animal comes from Hiscock, Appleby, costs £3 14s., is called TX.56 and really stands on the table. The cheerful orange shade on an interesting stand is from Francis Mackmin T.31, £1 19s. 6d. complete. Grey shade is part of another wonderful Schottlander design; write for his catalogue. Pretty lilac cone shade from Hiscock, Appleby, at £1 7s.; and last is a sweet lamp for a child. Price 5 gns. From Helen Andrew, 3 Melina Place, London, N.W.8

Photos : Deighton Wilkes

Edited by Ethne Davies

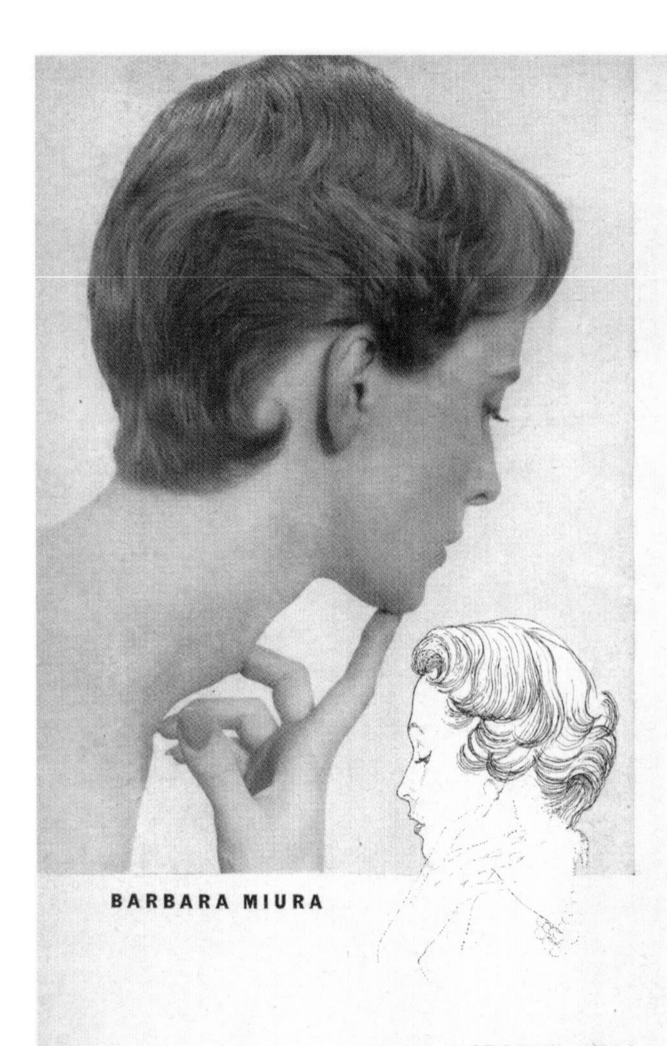

BARBARA MIURA

WHAT COMES NATURALLY

to the hair itself has determined these highly individual styles

● The trend for hairdressing to become determined by the hair's own characteristics may well herald a new era in hair-styling. We have come a complete circle from the bushes of hair piled on the head, at the turn of the century, through the sheared crops that were a result of a reaction to war of the 1920s and the contrived arrangements of the '30s and '40s. Now we have what seems to us, at least, the logical development that nature knows best—trimmed and encouraged by all the art of the hairdresser. The beauty of it all is that it can apply alike to straight, curly, thin, thick, strong or fine hair, but, like all forms of perfected skill, it must be done by an expert.

Our five personalities, who all run homes in addition to careers, particularly needed this new approach to styling. All had found previous styles needed once-weekly setting. Those with straight short styles needed alarmingly frequent permanent waves and all had to "pin up" at night.

Their hairdresser brushed and combed patiently in all directions to determine first the way of the natural growth. This, incidentally, can vary from one side to another and can add much interest. The length adopted was determined by how the hair curled at different lengths. Many heads, for instance, curl or wave when cut to boy's length; some only wave when grown to eight or more inches. They all stress the absence of artificiality, ease of setting and strong affinity with each individual personality.

JEANNE HEAL

ENID MUNNIK

ELIZABETH SEAL

ELIZABETH HAMILTON

John Cole: at Studio Five

Barbara Miura,
whose career as one of London's dozen top models has been interrupted twice: once for the birth of Anita and once for James. Her husband boasts of her cooking. Hair by René

Jeanne Heal,
one of TV's best-known interviewers, runs a charming house in London and a seaside cottage in addition to her job, and is the mother of two live-wire children. Hair by Daphne Vernon

Enid Munnik,
mother of three, is the wife of Roy Boulting of film esteem. In addition to entertaining and painting—her great interest—she has found time to become a top model. Hair by French of London

Elizabeth Seal,
who made the headlines with her part in *The Pajama Game*. She's domestically minded when not rehearsing hard, and initially she took the scissors to herself. Now goes to José and Franke

Elizabeth Hamilton,
whose perfect face and measurements have made her familiar to magazines and papers here and abroad. She maintains a modern flat and her great hobby is anything out of doors. Hair by French of London

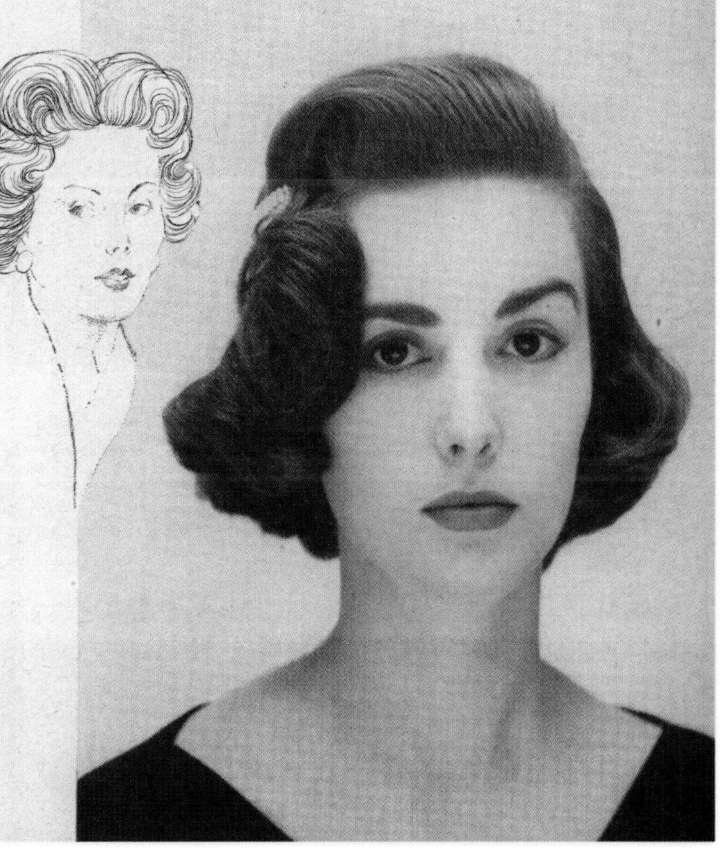

Recipes tested by Muriel Grimshaw • Described by Margaret Sherman

THERE ARE SO MANY WAYS WITH CHEESE

Hans Schwarz

Your cheeses can be tangy or mellow, hot or cold, sweet or savoury. Do you explore them as you might?

"There's always bread and cheese" is a comfortable English assurance now that our famous regional cheeses are with us again. Noble Stilton, homely Cheddar, crisp-flavoured Wensleydale can be meals in themselves. But there are dozens of others to investigate, either cooked or "raw."

When you buy cheeses, let your principle be "buy little, and often." In cooking cheese, the less you cook it the better. Take special care with sauces, adding the cheese to the hot, cooked sauce, and just allowing time for it to melt.

First, here are three piping-hot dishes for cold March evenings. It's the cheese that makes all the difference.

MINESTRONE SOUP

1 quart good stock
Seasoning
1 lb. mixed vegetables
1 dessertspoonful tomato purée
3 oz. spaghetti
1 oz. bacon trimmings
Bouquet garni
2 oz. grated Parmesan

Place the stock in a saucepan and season carefully. Use as wide a selection of vegetables as is available; carrots, turnips, onions, peas, swedes and celery. Cut into thin slices of rough shape. Bring the stock to the boil, add the vegetables, tomato purée, spaghetti broken into ½-in lengths, bacon trimmings and bouquet garni. Simmer for 15–20 mins. (longer if vegetables are old). Remove bouquet garni; serve minestrone hot, offering grated cheese separately.

Cheese—grated Parmesan or Cheddar—is the finishing touch to spaghetti in the party-style (see page 86); it is good as a rarebit garnish to brown onion soup (see this page); and many cheeses are best just as they come from the dairy or shop in all their shapes and sizes

BROWN ONION SOUP
(illustrated opposite)

3 oz. dripping
1 lb. onions
2 oz. flour
1 dessertspoonful tomato purée
1 quart brown stock or water with a bouillon cube
Seasoning
1 slice Welsh rarebit

Melt the dripping; peel and slice the onions. Fry the onions in the hot fat till a good brown colour. Stir in the flour and cook gently till chocolate-brown colour. Add the tomato purée, stir well and gradually add the liquid, stirring all the time. Bring to the boil, skim and season. Cook for 1 hour in a covered pan. Serve with diamonds of the rarebit.

CREAM OF ONION SOUP

3 oz. margarine
½ lb. onions
3 oz. flour
1 pint milk
1 pint stock or water
Salt and pepper
Bouquet garni
Slices red Cheshire

Melt the margarine, toss the sliced onions in the pan, stir in the flour and cook over a low heat till sand colour. Stir in the liquid gradually. When the soup boils, season well. Add the bouquet garni, but remove after ½ hour. Cook the soup for 1 hour and strain or not according to preference. Top each plateful with a square of cheese.

DAMSON COCKTAIL
(serve as hors d'œuvre)

¾ lb. damsons
2 oz. walnuts
2 oz. grated cheese
Paprika pepper

Stewed fresh fruit or the bottled type may be used. Stone the fruit and arrange in cocktail glasses, chop the walnuts and mix with the grated cheese (try Stilton or Wensleydale). Sprinkle over the fruit and shake a little paprika pepper on each.

Another fruit-and-cheese combination to try is halved plums piped with cream cheese or halves of plums sandwiched with slices of cheese, arranged on shredded chicory or lettuce.

SCALLOPS MORNAY

4 scallops
A bay leaf
A parsley spray
A thyme sprig
Water
Salt and pepper
2 oz. margarine
2 oz. flour
½ pint milk
Liquor from fish
3–4 oz. grated cheese
Tomato and parsley

Ask the fishmonger to give you the top shells of the scallops, but the fish from the lower shell. Strip off the black beards if this is not done already. Wash the scallops well, taking care not to break the orange parts. Place in a shallow pan, add the herbs and water to cover, season, and simmer with the lid on

Bread
Rice
Coffee

Deighton Wilkes

KITCHEN KALEIDOSCOPE

Excuses are no longer enough.

Your kitchen should—and can—be the gayest room in the house

for key, see overleaf

77

Travels in Tasting

Two travelling journalists cook up a ragout of gastronomic souvenirs

BY BARBARA WACE AND ANNE DEVESON

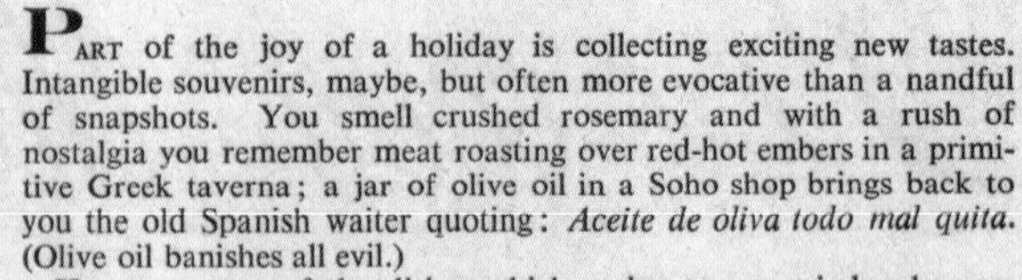

PART of the joy of a holiday is collecting exciting new tastes. Intangible souvenirs, maybe, but often more evocative than a nandful of snapshots. You smell crushed rosemary and with a rush of nostalgia you remember meat roasting over red-hot embers in a primitive Greek taverna; a jar of olive oil in a Soho shop brings back to you the old Spanish waiter quoting: *Aceite de oliva todo mal quita.* (Olive oil banishes all evil.)

Here are some of the dishes which spring to our minds when we talk over our various journeys. They are strictly *our* souvenirs in tasting, and in no sense a gastronomic guide. Each traveller has his own special meals to remember, and their background events.

Perhaps the most striking thing one discovers is that every country (except our own) prides itself on being a nation of gourmets. Food is an opening gambit of conversation.

We discovered this first in Holland. Confession that we liked their custom of eating cheese for breakfast never failed to gratify our hosts. An old gentleman wearing spats whom we met in a 'bus was so pleased that he insisted we should be his guests for Indonesian *rys tafel.* We managed only a third of the dozens of side dishes, but even so it took us every minute of three hours to finish—as he had warned us. There was a wonderful recklessness about that meal: the possibility of missing our boat because we took so long, and, if we didn't miss it, the reasonable certainty of sea-sickness.

" Nonsense," said our friend. " You'll sleep better than ever."

He was right.

In Switzerland our culinary quest met with a different reaction. We had ordered *fondue* in a tiny mountain village, not far from Geneva. The waitress disappeared into the kitchen, voices were raised and then Madame herself bore down upon us, large and terrifying in black. She poured out a flood of incomprehensible French.

" *Les Anglaises n'aiment pas le fondue,*" was all we could gather. The English reputation for conservatism in food had travelled far. We had to do a lot of soothing before we got our bubbling dishes.

After *fondue,* tackling spaghetti was child's play. All the different kinds of *pasta* would fill a dictionary. A *pastificio* near Naples, working in his whitewashed basement, gave us thirty for a start. It was he who described the Neapolitan fisherman's dish, *spaghetti al olio, aglio e*

(*Continued on page* **50**)

Switzerland

FONDUE: Bubbling hot cream of Gruyere cheese, white wine, seasoning, kirsch. Hot-plate keeps it simmering, while each person dips bread spiked on fork into mixture. Kirsch, drunk separately, helps counteract richness.

Holland

Rys Tafel (Indonesian speciality): Huge bowl rice, chicken, spices, supplemented by dozens little dishes at regular intervals—cucumber in coconut milk; nuts; mushrooms; all kinds fish, sweet and sour sauces, etc.

Bruine Bonen met Spek: Brown beans and bacon, like American Boston Baked Beans, served with potatoes and lettuce.

Blinde Vinken ("Blind Finches"): Beefsteak rolled round slice lean pork or veal, gherkin in centre. Browned in butter, simmered till tender.

Spain

PAËLLA: Classic rice dish, hundreds local variations. Basic ingredients besides rice: chicken, white fish, mussels, lobster, red pepper, peas, tomatoes, garlic, saffron. Meat and octopus may be added, rabbit instead of chicken. Whole moistened with stock.

COCIDO: Made with chick-peas (*garbanzos*), vegetables, potatoes, black pudding, beef, perhaps chicken, bacon, ham, marrow, pigs' trotters, dumplings of bread, eggs, meat. Served as three-course meal: broth, sometimes with noodles added; chick-peas, vegetables, potatoes; meat, etc., with hot tomato sauce.

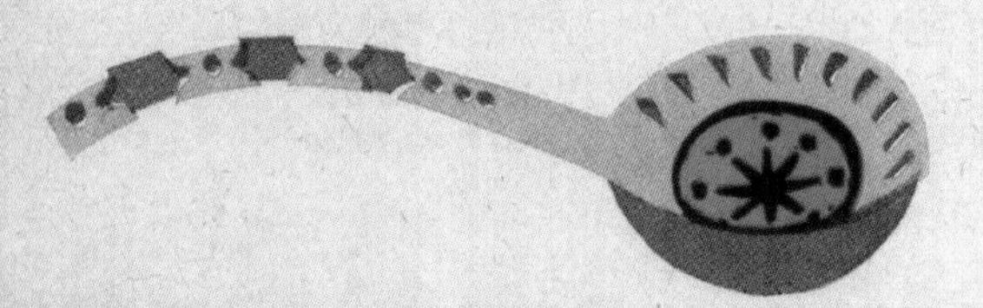

Mediterranean Countries

BOUILLABAISSE: Potent stew every sort of fish, garlic, onions, oil, tomatoes, saffron, black pepper, herbs. Liquid strained off, poured over fried garlic bread, served as soup. Fish, with parsley, dished separately. *Bouillabaisse* never mushy, as each fish added separately, thus soft and firm-fleshed alike come to perfection at same time.

OCTOPUS: from 6 inches span to 3 feet or more. Fresh or dried, cut in pieces, stewed for hours with onions, tomatoes, garlic, herbs, wine. If cooked in own ink, stew black, richly flavoured. Young octopus can be slightly dried, cut in pieces, grilled over hot embers, eaten as hors d'œuvre. Very small **INK FISH** delicious dipped in batter, fried crisp brown.

Greece

Souvlákia: Lamb skewered on sticks, seasoned with wild herbs, grilled (preferably outdoors).

Dolmádés: Tiny parcels savoury rice, wrapped in vine leaves, cooked in stock. Usually served with lemon and olive oil sauce.

Moussaka: Minced meat and aubergines, topped with Béchamel sauce, sprinkled with cheese, baked in oven. Rich but delicious.

Portugal

BACALHAU: *Dried, salt codfish in many disguises. For instance:*
PASTEIS DE BACALHAU, *fish-cakes, lightened with stiff-beaten egg-whites, served with black olives, green salad;*
BACALHAU GUISADO, *codfish casserole with roast potatoes, boiled vegetables, hard-boiled eggs, olive oil.*

Italy

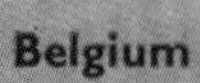

PIZZA: Piping hot rounds doughy paste, smothered in cheese, anchovy, black olives, tomatoes, etc., fried crisp brown.

SPAGHETTI AL OLIO, AGLIO E ALICE: Great mound of spaghetti, cooked in garlic water, glistening with oil and more chopped garlic. Round outside, standing on heads, is ring of anchovies.

CROSTINI DE FEGATINI: Chicken livers, chopped ham, browned in butter, cooked in stock, lemon-juice, black pepper for 10 minutes. Served on croûtons fried bread.

RISI E BISI: Venetian risotto of rice, green peas, butter, cheese.

Belgium

Écrevisses à la Liégoises: Liége crayfish, cooked with butter, cream, in white wine sauce.

Carbonade Flamande: Flemish standby, bacon, beef, onions, touch of garlic, slowly simmered in beer.

Witloof: Chicory, cooked numerous ways: casseroled with milk, butter, nutmeg; roasted in butter; baked in Béchamel sauce; ham wrapped round each head, and cheese sprinkled on top. Whole browned under grill.

Yugoslavia

ČEVAPČIČI: Two different sorts meat, made into rissoles, skewered, grilled.

DJUVEČ: Irish stew—Serbian edition. Highly seasoned with paprikas.

GH—6

DRAWINGS BY HAROLD BARTRAM

Summer charade

SCENE: AT THE BEACH

Mother's pride and joy in a Bairnswear T-shirt, 6*s.* 11*d.* from Selfridges, set off with a snorkel tube and diving mask and has come up with a crab. All that other clutter they made poor father pack into the boot—the fish-print Tri-ang-Raft to paddle round on and the Li-lo whale; the giant Palicraft beach ball and the one with the printed world to throw around; to rest their weary bones the convertible Li-lo bed-chair, and Sea-Esta sun-seat and Spanish-style beach towels for the film star touch. To wear, one has chosen a spotted towelling jacket over yellow pants. Rima, about 11 gns. at Wakeford's, Chelsea, and Florence Wood of Leeds, and, keeping it sunny all the way, yellow sail-cloth espadrilles to match, 6*s.* 11*d.* at most Lotus and Delta coastal shops, e.g. Llandudno, Margate, Guernsey. The other lass is in brother's Toplin shirt (quick-dry, no-iron), 39*s.* 6*d.* at Selfridges, Oxford St., W.1, and Lewis's, Manchester, with it Tyrolean shorts in Super-Tremendo cotton. She made them to Simplicity printed pattern No. 1660 (3*s.*, bust sizes 30, 32, 34 and 36 ins.) and found the baby coolie, 12*s.* 6*d.*, the bottle-carrier, 12*s.* 6*d.* and raffia mules, 32*s.*, all at Eaton, along with the gorgeous sea-shells—she thought no beach would be complete without them

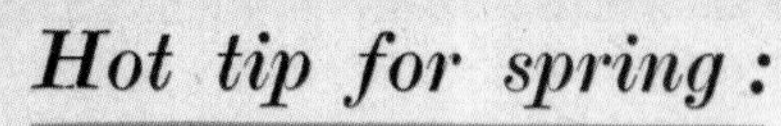

Hot tip for spring:

TAKE A BOATER.....

Make a band of amber velvet ribbon and stitch a yellow rose under the brim where it suits you best

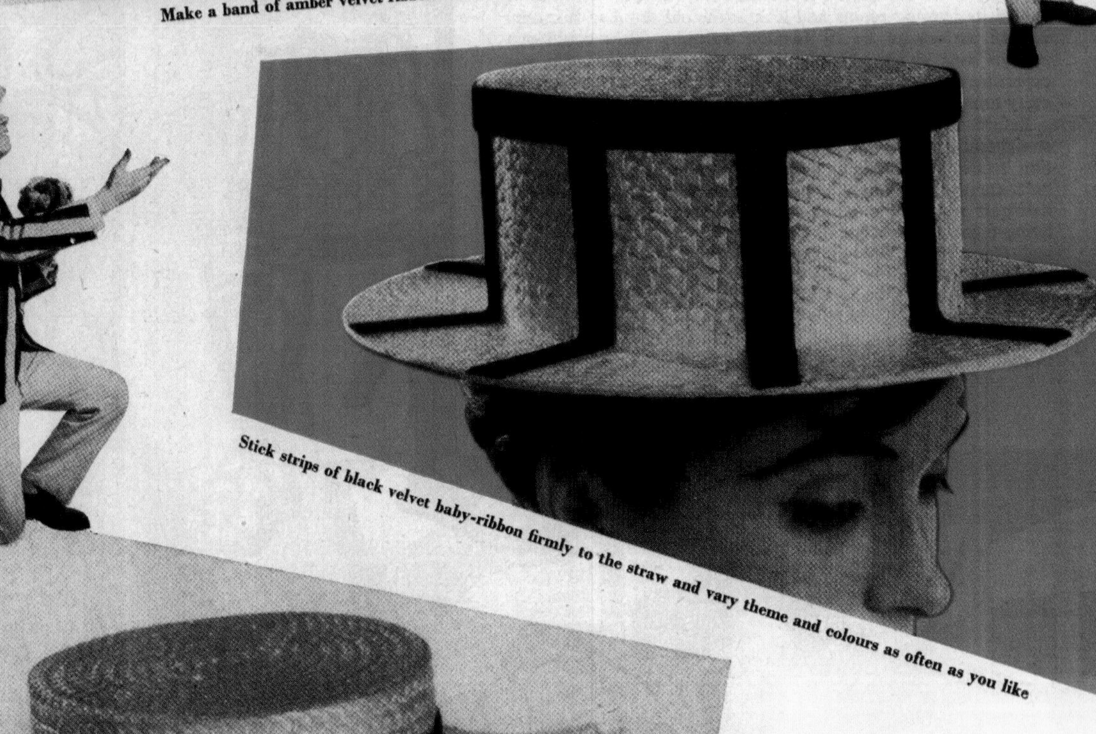

Stick strips of black velvet baby-ribbon firmly to the straw and vary theme and colours as often as you like

Take deep rose ribbon for this band, and tuck and stitch on permanently pleated edging in a pastel shade of rose. Many lovely colour schemes for this

For a guinea or so buy the smartest hat shape of all; then trim it from one of our ideas

Tack on a double coil of swan's-down for a hat so feminine, so *dernier cri* in shape and trimming, you will wear it all through summer

FASHION

Edited by Ethne Davies

Roll a chiffon scarf, thread it on a diamanté buckle and let the ends trail romantically. This one is powder blue

Keep your boater absolutely plain and wear it over a chiffon scarf caught tightly to the head. Most exotic over white

Boaters by G. A. Dunn and Co. Ltd. Accessories by Dickins and Jones

Photographed by Hughes-Gilbey

We believe that readers of Good Housekeeping have the courage and the desire to face facts that matter even when they are not pleasant. This article discusses honestly and without compromise a situation that is causing alarm to decent, law-abiding citizens. The article is addressed particularly to those whose activities take them into less reputable neighbourhoods, and to those who fear that young people may unwittingly find themselves exposed to things that are evil. Much that is sensational has been written about this subject. This summing-up is not of that kind. But it is plain-spoken; and if there are readers who have no wish to give these matters thought we advise them, in all deference to their feelings, to pass over these pages

BY CHARLOTTE AND DENIS PLIMMER

But one pale woman all alone,
The daylight kissing her wan hair,
Loitered beneath the gas lamps' flare,
With lips of flame and heart of stone.

Oscar Wilde (*Impressions du Matin*)

A RAZOR flashes in Soho. A street-walker swivel-hips through Curzon Street past shocked American tourists. In Chelsea, Teddy Boys lob milk bottles through the windows of a youth club. Members of Parliament pinion the Home Secretary with imperative questions, while circulation-greedy newspapers scream in banner headlines for a clean-up.

And in a million British homes from Cornwall to Caithness, Enraged Citizen, Indignant Ratepayer and Pro Bono Publico shake worried heads and tell each other that London is going the slippery way of Sodom and Gomorrah.

How justified are the viewers-with-alarm? How imminent is the hour when race-gangs and white-slave rings take over the nation's heart? How wicked—in actuality—is London?

As American writers who have worked in many of the world's great cities, we have tried to put London's sins into perspective. We have dredged our own memories of New York, Paris, Madrid, Rome, Marseilles, Tangier. We have combed Soho's cellar clubs, the back alleys off Stepney's notorious and sorrowful Cable Street, drab Paddington and dingy Notting Hill. We have talked with priests, prostitutes and politicians, with night-club owners and welfare workers. Their aggregate advice: don't believe all you read.

A large-circulation Sunday paper recently printed the following:

"It is reckoned that there are no fewer than twenty thousand prostitutes on the streets. The figure is not unbelievable when it is considered that in the past 12 months London police prosecuted 11,145 girls for soliciting."

Our investigations suggest that the figure of twenty thousand is wildly inaccurate! According to Miss Mary Hamilton, probation officer of Bow Street Magistrates' Court, about 1,300 girls are arrested annually—not for prostitution, which, as the law books stand now, is no crime—but for "soliciting to the annoyance" of passers-by. Specialists in this sordid subject, leaving the widest possible margin for error, assume that only half the streetwalkers in operation are actually arrested. This gives a theoretical total of 2,600. They add to these the brothel girls, the "call girls" who work by telephonic appointment only, and the night-club "hostesses" (not all are full-time prostitutes and many not even prostitutes at all). They thus arrive at a grand total of about 5,000 or roughly *one quarter* of the terrifying figure given in that Sunday paper. (For contrast, Paris, with about one-third London's population, has 30,000 prostitutes, according to a recent article in *The Reader's Digest.* This would make the Paris–London ratio about 18:1!)

We contest even more strenuously the newspaper's statement that 11,145 girls were arrested in one year. The figure, we suggest, refers not to the number of *girls*, but to the number of *prosecutions.* According to Miss Hamilton, a single prostitute may be hauled before the magistrate as many as twenty or

More wicked than any other capital city in the world? This article gives you the straight, unvarnished truth

Photographs: Guy Gravett

thirty times in a twelvemonth, swelling the statistics with every appearance.

It is an old newspaper truism that bad news sells more papers than good. That is why crime news so often takes on larger-than-life proportions in the irresponsible sections of the press. But cold statistics tell a truer story than hot typewriters. Here is how the statistician compares London with New York, both great port cities of similar standards and comparable populations.

According to London's Metropolitan Police Commissioner, a total of 74,461 people were arrested in 1955 for all offences. In New York, says the United States Embassy, quoting 1954 figures (latest available), 1,593,429 people were arrested for all offences. The ratio, 20:1. In 1954, New York had 275 homicides, compared to London's 59 for 1955. It is apparent that in terms of wickedness, London is lagging hopelessly behind her transatlantic sister.

London's bad reputation comes chiefly from the fact that its vice is so shamefully visible. In New York, you never see open solicitation on the streets. You rarely see it nowadays in Paris, nor to any important extent in Rome, Madrid, Athens, Venice, Naples or Tel Aviv, to garner a random harvest. These cities are not, however, any more free from prostitution than London.

Step into any small side-street bar in New York's West Forties, or off Paris's Champs Elysées. Perched like vultures on their high stools, await the B-girls (B for Bar). In New York, visitors too listless to search out the bars can have their hotel bell-boys arrange room service. "Call girls" are available throughout central Manhattan, where the wonderful invention of Dr. Alexander Graham Bell has replaced the old-fashioned red light.

In Rome, brothels dot the centre of the city, and there is occasional street soliciting. And again, hotel staffs know how to supply transient appetites. Even in well-behaved Switzerland, many barmaids or *serviertochters* (serving daughters is the ironic translation) supplement their income with casual prostitution after hours.

Though the Londoner can hardly escape the sight of the streetwalker plying her trade, his chances of ever becoming involved with the professional criminal are, conservatively, a million to one. The London gangster rarely whips out his razor to slash the cheek of an innocent passer-by, but reserves his good Sheffield steel for settling differences with competitive colleagues. The classic instance is the slashing feud which first lacerated the public conscience that day in August, 1955, when Jack Spot and Italian Albert Dimes were accused of slicing each other up on the corner of Soho's Frith and Old Compton Streets over the control of betting pitches.

As for gangsterdom's latest fad, the so-called "protection racket," any Chicago professional would dismiss the whole effort as feeble and amateurish. "Protection" is, theoretically, money extorted by a crook from, say, a shopkeeper as "insurance" against his shop's being smashed up. But Soho's "protectionists" are a thin-blooded lot, easily scared. Instance: a tailor of our acquaintance (a highly respectable citizen brought up in the East End, and nobody's fool) was approached by a couple of well-known gangster's teara- (*Continued on page* **162**)

A street corner in Soho, the district which has been the object of shocked public opinion in recent months

FACE LIFT FOR A BATH-TUB

1. Here is the problem: a very old bath stands on an old lead base which is slightly larger than the bath. New panelled sides must cover this

2. Measure width of top and check it against base. Measure length and depth. Use 2-inch by 2-inch timber for the framework

3. You will need two timbers equal to length, two equal to width, four equal to depth, and, depending on your bath, short pieces for the fixed end

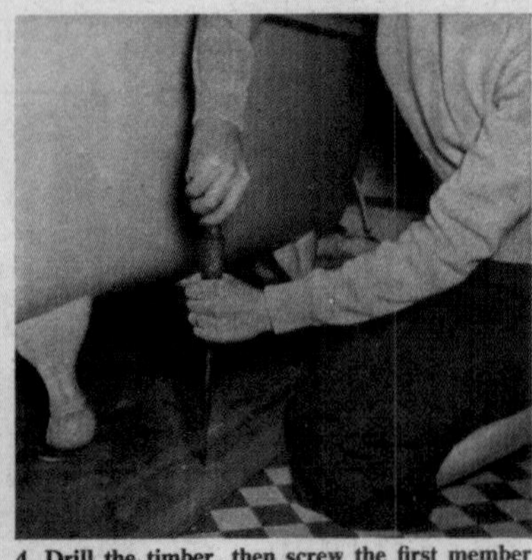

4. Drill the timber, then screw the first member to the floor, just outside the lead base. Then add the floor member at the end of the bath

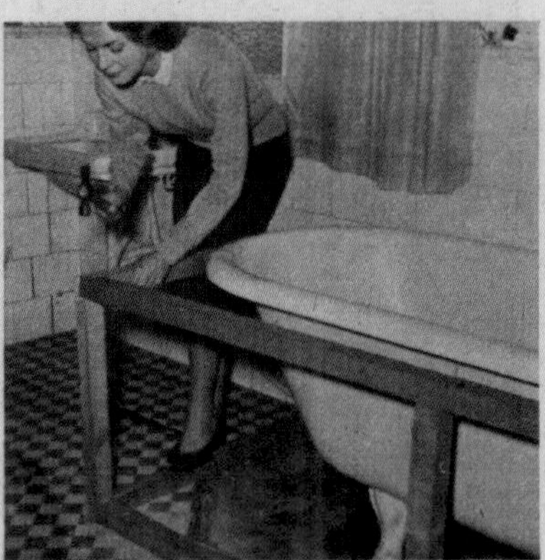

5. Next add the uprights, and remember that—as we show here—you may have to shorten some pieces by 2 inches at the intersections

6. It is a good idea to add struts for extra strength at the corners. Next, cut and fit the hardboard facing for the sides. Secure with panel pins

7. Cover end with hardboard. Reach under it and follow the line of the bath with a pencil. This curve equals the inside shape

8. Cut this curve 1 inch deeper than the line indicates (your line was the *inside* of the bath), fit into position and trim away the remainder, as shown

9. Cut the covering material to fit the hardboard panels (we used Congowall). Apply adhesive, fix the Congowall and firmly rub out the air bubbles

10. For a really neat finish, edge corners with aluminium angle rail. Drill it first, then screw it into position to the timber framing

11. The job is done. There have been smarter bathrooms, but the Congowall is pretty and gay—and never again will the soap get under the bath!

PLASTIC TILES ARE PRACTICAL AND TRIM ROUND THE SINK

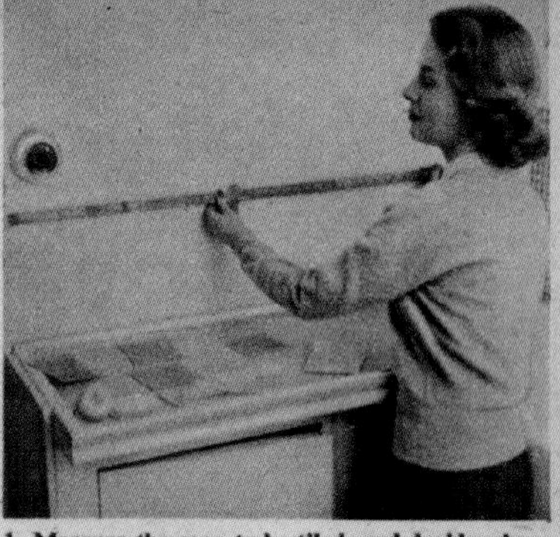

1. Measure the area to be tiled, and decide where you will have your cut tiles (there will almost certainly be some, but you *can* buy half tiles)

2. To tile round a light switch hold the first tile to the wall and mark with a pencil. Repeat with other tiles that will meet the switch

3. Cut round pencil marks, apply adhesive and fit tiles. Cutting plastic tiles is not difficult, but you do need a fine sharp saw

4. Work from this panel. Apply the adhesive to several tiles. Fit them closely and avoid using so much adhesive that it squelches out.

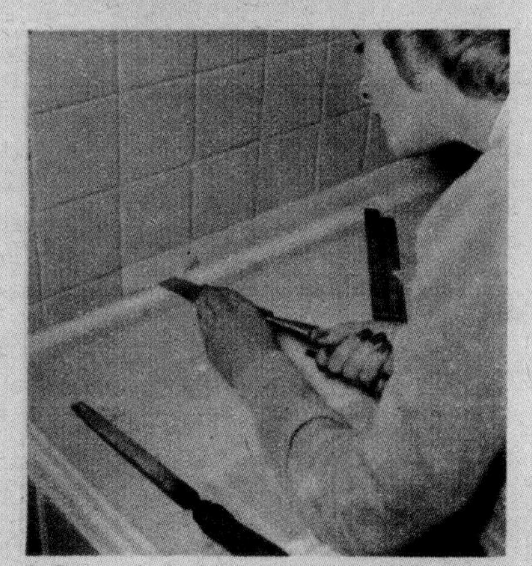

5. Do not deal with the cut tiles until you have fixed all the whole ones. Chisel the plaster so that the tile edges can be set in slightly

6. Measure and cut carefully for these edges. As the draining-board sloped slightly each tile was measured separately—but it was not a long job

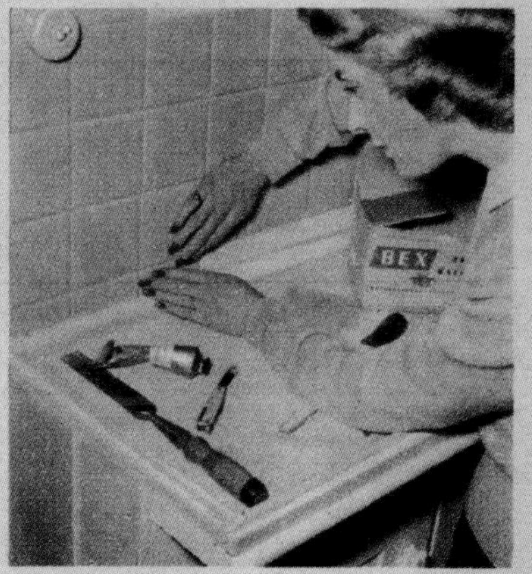

7. Push the cut tiles firmly into place, easing them down into the chiselled groove on the draining-board. Treat the inside wall corner similarly

---

HAS THE BATH ENAMEL CHIPPED?

Once a bath has lost its original porcelain enamel this cannot be replaced with quite such a hard-wearing finish, but it is possible to apply a good bath enamel which will improve its appearance considerably.

Rub down all bare patches with emery-cloth to remove rust spots, then thoroughly wash down with a fairly strong solution of soda and water to remove all traces of grease, then rinse it away. Next, turn taps off tightly to prevent dripping—renew washers if necessary—and wipe down with a chamois-leather.

Buy a special bath enamel and the undercoating to go with it, then use the undercoat on all the bare patches. When it is dry, coat again to build patches level with the main surface—and each time rub away any paint which has overlapped the patches.

When this is finished, give the bath interior a complete undercoating and allow to dry hard, then rub down with medium sandpaper and give another undercoating. Rub down with a finer paper and repeat once more. When you have a good solid effect apply the finishing coat fairly liberally—but not enough to produce "runs."

Allow to dry and harden for at least a week, then fill with cold water and leave for two more days. For a few months always run in cold water before the hot to avoid softening the paint film.

PRETTY PLACES

Good food is better, good wine is finer, good talk is wittier when you properly set the stage

I

2

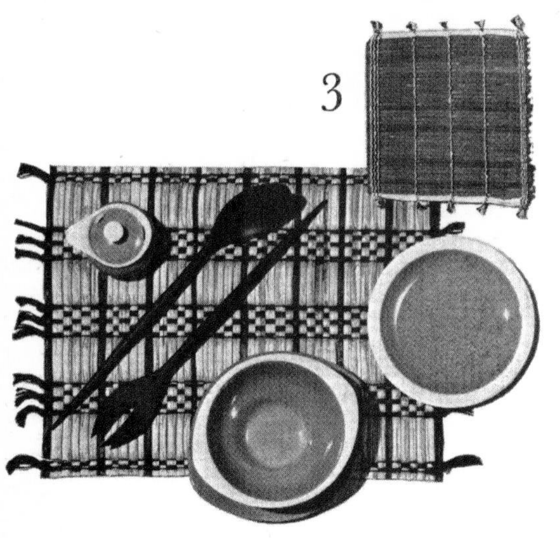

3

I A traditional and timelessly beautiful example of hand-embroidered mats and napkins from Robinson & Cleaver. Cost is 15 gns. for a set for eight people. With it is Wedgwood chinaware; the jug is 27*s*., coffee cup and saucer 17*s*. 6*d*. and ash-tray 24*s*. All from Robinson & Cleaver, W.1.

2 Something for those who like simplicity—a mat in shades of deep rusty-red, pink and white; mat and napkin set for six costs 36*s*. 6*d*., raffia ring is 1*s*. 3*d*., blue soup bowl with lid and saucer is 13*s*. 9*d*., brown and white mug is 6*s*. 6*d*.; and cutlery costs (per doz.) £6 18*s*. 6*d*. (forks), £5 10*s*. 6*d*. (knives), £5 1*s*. (dessert knives), £8 9*s*. (tablespoons), £6 6*s*. (soup-spoons). All from Heal's, W.1.

3 Raffia is for those who like deep texture: here is a place mat, undyed but stitched in black, shown with a small glass mat from a range in paint-box-bright colours. The large mat is 7*s*. 6*d*., the glass mats 18*s*. 6*d*. for a set of six. Wedgwood's Havana Sky side plate costs 3*s*. 9*d*., soup bowl and saucer 10*s*. 6*d*., and mustard pot 8*s*. 9*d*. All from Heal's. Black salad servers, 28*s*. from Liberty, W.1.

4 Lamont's Wrought Iron, a gay printed mat and napkin set for four, costs 25*s*. 6*d*. from Robinson & Cleaver. Four-piece cruet costs 40*s*. 6*d*., and cutlery costs 11*s*. (fork), 9*s*. (knife), and 10*s*. (spoon), from Liberty. The John E. Buck prettily decorated Adam candle is one of a pair costing 7*s*. 6*d*.; the star-shaped holders are 3*s*. 6*d*. per pair from all leading stores.

5 A gay barbecue air comes with this bold printed mat from Liberty. It costs 7*s*. Plain fringed napkins are 4*s*. each. Whangee handled cutlery costs 9*s*. (table knife), 11*s*. (table fork), and 11*s*. 9*d*. (spoon). Copper butter warmer is 37*s*. 6*d*. and a red enamelled steel bowl with cane handle is 32*s*. 6*d*. All from Liberty.

6 Especially elegant is this lime mat with a fine, curving border. A set of six with napkins costs 39*s*. 6*d*. Wedgwood's lovely Dolphin plate costs 31*s*.; the smoked-glass liqueur decanter costs 55*s*. and matching liqueur glasses are 8*s*. each. All from Heal's.

7 This gay peasant design is available in a multitude of colours; we chose vivid, shocking pink. The mat costs 5*s*. and the fringed black napkin costs 4*s*. Black and pink metal bowl costs 6*s*., blue and white mug costs 9*s*. 6*d*., black-handled cutlery costs 7*s*. (large knife), 6*s*. 6*d*. (small knife), and 10*s*. 6*d*. (fork). All from Liberty.

8 Frankly nostalgic and very, very romantic—and here is a way to buy mats to suit each mood and occasion, for these are of printed card and cost only 5*s*. 9*d*. for a set of six. They will not last for ever, but you can use them several times. Beautiful ash-tray by Fornasetti costs an extravagant but well-spent 38*s*. The cutlery costs 10*s*. 9*d*. (fork) and 9*s*. 9*d*. (spoon). All from Liberty.

9 Bountiful vines to foster prosperity—a design that is cheerful to a degree, but simple and elegant, in white on red, and reversed on the napkin. Price 25*s*. 6*d*. for a set for four. The tiny vase for one or two flower-heads costs 34*s*. 9d., the hock glass costs 17*s*. 6*d*., the coffee cup and saucer is part of a set costing 4 gns., and the cutlery is £8 5*s*. per doz. (dessert knives), and £4 12*s*. 6*d*. per doz. (teaspoons). All from Heal's.

4

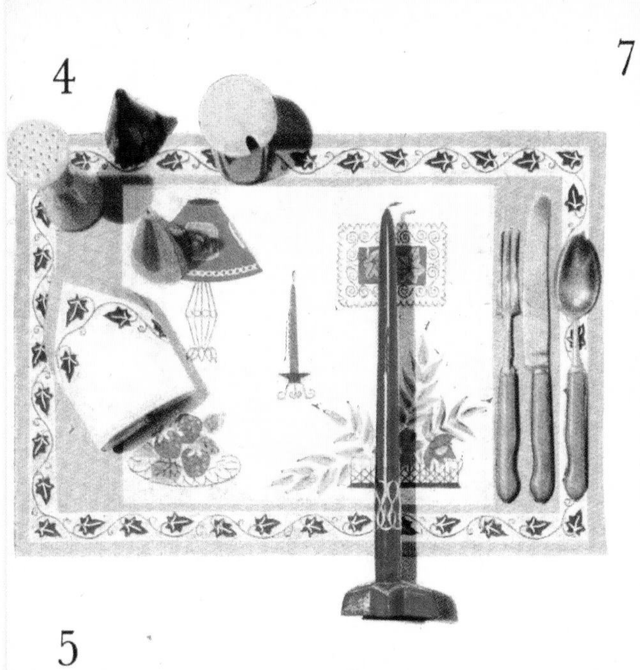

5

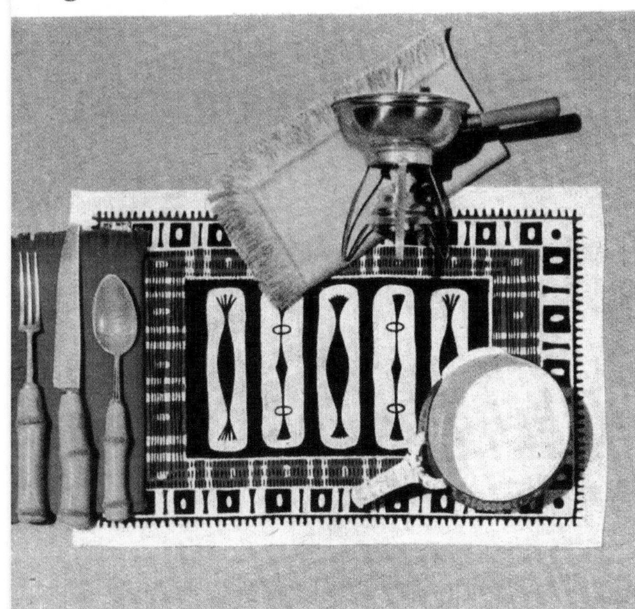

6

7

8

9

Photographs by Deighton Wilkes

MARGARET CHEYNE tots it up and proves it can cost a lot. But convention no longer decrees, she says, that the bride's father must foot the whole bill

"Bless the bride," says everyone. "And bless the bridal arrangements," says the bride's father sometimes, as he ruefully surveys the financial scene. It is true that this is the day the dear girl will remember all her life—or is it true any longer? In any case, can any wedding justify all that?

Verdict seems to be, it can. Perhaps you saw that enchanting film called *Father of the Bride*. Spencer Tracy, as the unlucky fellow in the name part, was pushed around by wife and daughter and prospective son-in-law, by florists, caterers, dressmakers, stationers, waiters and scores of wedding guests—and all for the long-term privilege of paying the bills. But harassed and rueful as Tracy made the bride's father appear, as he shouldered his dogged way through the proceedings, there yet comes a touching and heartening moment at the very end.

What exactly are the costs of a normal church wedding? Of course no wedding can possibly be dubbed as normal, but let's assume we are dealing with a young couple brought up in the kind of homes that used to be called upper middle class. Both have been educated, we'll say, at their parent's expense, and so the parents have less reserve cash than you might suppose. They live in a good residential district, which still keeps some of its character in spite of a new suburban glitter about the High Street. True to the diehard traditions of their upbringing, the young couple will want—or will easily be persuaded by their mothers that they want—a church wedding, with relatives and close friends invited to a reception afterwards. Perhaps fifty guests is a good round number for the reception, but there will be some other meal-and-accommodation problems to be solved, too. Some relatives will come from far afield and, not being great travellers, will be quite helpless about arranging their own meals and overnight stay. It actually happened that one bride we knew, parentless and just dressing in her little flat for a 2 p.m. wedding, was confronted at 12.50 p.m. with four hungry relatives who had motored up from Cheltenham and obviously expected to lunch with her before the wedding *and* spend the night in her flat afterwards.

At its very lowest a wedding of the type we visualize, with any reception afterwards, is going to cost some £175. We have worked out a list of expenses, based on actual research in the kind of district described. And note, please, that the prices are approximate, since *all* caterers, florists, wine merchants and even vicars begin their preamble with the magic words: "Of course it's impossible to give a definite figure: it depends so much on exactly what you want." They might add, "and upon *when* you want it, too," for they can be quite intimidating about their advance bookings, and the days on which they are still open for additional orders. So, if you are wanting a nicely arranged but not exorbitantly costly wedding, you must start to plan several months ahead.

(*Continued on page* **173**)

just how much can a

Photo: Brien Kirley. Dress made from Simplicity printed pattern No. 4698 in Witchcraft lace; "Radiant" head-dress and veil

Wedding cost?

A good first game, as the children chatter to each other and late-comers can join in.
PROVIDE IN ADVANCE—numbered slips of paper with the jumbled up letters of the names of well-known characters, e.g. Liberace, Pooh, Cinderella, Stirling Moss; pins; paper and pencil for each player.
HOW TO PLAY. Pin a slip to the back of each guest and set them to work sorting out the names.

A not-so-strenuous variation of musical chairs.
PROVIDE IN ADVANCE—Hats (any kind) for each player but one.
HOW TO PLAY. Hats must be put on, then quickly passed round, each one in turn being worn, while the music plays. When it stops, the child who has no hat is out.

There'll be much more fun for everyone if you

PARTIES are meant to be enjoyed by *everybody*; grown-ups and children, hosts and guests alike. Some people need no telling, but if you are one of those in whom the thought of a dozen rowdy children on your hands strikes terror, don't despair. A few simple rules, careful, but not over-elaborate planning, a voice that carries—and you can feel safe and serene.

Three years of age is early enough to begin party-going. Before that age a child only tends to get trampled on. For the very little ones, boys and girls from three to six, we have a Family Centre leaflet all their own: *Party Games for Small Children* (with instructions for singing games and suggestions for arranging the party), which we should be pleased to supply.*

On these pages we have in mind the next age group, roughly six to ten, the age when children must be on the go all the time when they are playing. They will listen and watch if there is a short entertainment, a film show, puppets, or conjuring, but they all like a few games, and are happier if they are organized.

Before the party, write out a list of games from which to choose, allowing about seven to ten minutes for each one. Don't let any item drag on too long. Be sure you are clear about the instructions yourself. Begin with an ice-breaker, a game in which the children move around and talk and late-comers can join in. No. 1 fills that role.

Alternate noisy games with quiet ones, though be prepared to scrap any which do not catch on well. Concentrate on games in which everyone has something to do, either all together or in teams. Avoid those in

5 ABSURD STORY

A sitting-down game for a change.
PROVIDE IN ADVANCE—The outline of a simple story.
HOW TO PLAY. An adult tells a yarn, introducing an obvious absurdity from time to time, e.g. "Two children went for a walk one summer's day, and as they walked, they kicked the snow." The children must shout "No" at each absurdity and the adult then asks for the correct version, and proceeds.

6 DUMB CRAMBO

An easy version of ever-popular charades.
NO PREPARATION NEEDED.
HOW TO PLAY. The children divide into two teams, and one goes outside. The others choose a word which rhymes easily, e.g. "read." They recall the others, tell them that the word rhymes with "need" and ask them to act in dumb show or with appropriate noises what they think the word is. The actors may guess "feed" and pretend to share a meal. This will be greeted with boos, and they try again until they hit on the right word.

9 SPOT THE MISTAKES

A test for the observant.
PROVIDE SHORTLY IN ADVANCE—A number of fairly obvious changes in the room, e.g. a stool placed upside down, a clock which tells the wrong time, a fork placed in a flower vase; pencils; paper.
HOW TO PLAY. Ask the children to jot down the things they notice are wrong in a given number of minutes.

Plenty of bustle and noise.
PROVIDE IN ADVANCE—wrapped sweets or peanuts, hidden all over a room.
HOW TO PLAY. Divide the children into groups of about four, each with a leader and the name of an animal. Set the children searching for the hidden objects. As soon as one is found the child begins to baa like a lamb or hee-haw like a donkey, and continues till his leader hurries to the spot to collect the spoil. No one else may claim it. Leaders will have plenty of demands on their attention.

3 TWIRLING THE BOARD

Easy to organize.
PROVIDE IN ADVANCE—a bread board.
HOW TO PLAY. The players sit in a circle. Each is given the name of an animal, e.g. donkey, pig, cat. One player spins the board in the centre and calls out the name of an animal. This character must catch the board before it falls and spin it again. If he fails, he must pay a forfeit.
Suggested forfeits: Sing a verse of a song, touch his toes without bending his knees, kiss a girl.

4 BONNET RACE

A simple team game.
PROVIDE IN ADVANCE—2 bonnets tying under the chin.
HOW TO PLAY. Form the players into two lines. The leaders each tie on a bonnet, untie it and pass it on to the next player. The first team to complete the operation wins a prize.

without Panic

follow these rules suggested **BY NORA ARIS**

which individual children take long turns, while the others just look on. Get your "props" ready beforehand—pencils, slips of paper, beans, or whatever you need—but don't embark on many games which need elaborate preparation or involved explanations. There is no need to wear yourself or the children out.

Provide a generous supply of token prizes, chocolate animals, coloured pencils, or miniature cars, for instance, and make sure that everyone gets a look-in. There can always be a prize for the last as well as the first. Children care much more about the look of the thing than its value.

The party tea is the highlight of the occasion. Make the table look really festive with a bright paper serviette in each glass, a gay cap by each named place, plenty of colour on the plates, and a really pretty (but not too rich) cake as the centre-piece. Remember that children like a lot of quickly eaten dainties (chocolate biscuits, cheese straws, tiny sandwiches, iced animal biscuits), and that they appreciate savoury as well as sweet food. Jellies and soft drinks are *de rigueur*. To help with your party catering, there is *Good Housekeeping's Party Fare* booklet (price 1s. 6d., at most bookshops and news-stands). And now relax and enjoy the afternoon.

---

*To order a copy of *Party Games for Small Children*, send a self-addressed label and a postal order for 1s. to the Belgrave Library, 22 Armoury Way, London, S.W.18. The Belgrave Library can also supply a copy of *Good Housekeeping's Party Fare* (1s. 8d., post paid).

7 TOM TIDDLER'S GROUND

An active game for out of doors.
PROVIDE IN ADVANCE—wrapped sweets or tiny toys.
HOW TO PLAY. Mark off part of the garden in which the "treasure" is scattered around. The "treasure" is guarded by "Tom." The others try to cross the border to grab the treasure. If anyone is caught on Tom Tiddler's Ground, he must join in catching the others.

8 UNTYING THE PARCEL

Fast and furious.
PROVIDE IN ADVANCE—a small present wrapped in numerous layers of paper, each tied with string; a dice; a spoon and fork.
HOW TO PLAY. The players throw the dice. When one throws six, he runs to the parcel and begins to unfasten it, using only the spoon and fork. His place is taken by the next player to throw six. The prize is won by the player who eventually comes to it.

11 BLACK MAGIC

Everyone loves a bit of mystification. Only two people should know the trick.
NO PREPARATION NEEDED.
HOW TO PLAY. Send one child "in the know" out of the room. The rest decide on any object in the room which the child outside must find out, e.g. a vase, a chair leg. The child is called in. The other conspirator touches various objects round the room with a pointer, asking "Is it this?" for each one. He touches the correct object immediately *after* touching something black (the poker, for instance) and the child then of course answers "Yes" to the query. All the other children who don't know the trick will try to work out their own systems, and will offer to have a go, becoming more and more mystified as they fail.

12 THE PARSON'S CAT

To finish up—something quiet, which can be broken off easily.
NO PREPARATION NEEDED.
HOW TO PLAY. All the children sit down round the room. Choose a letter (say A) and go round the circle giving adjectives beginning with A to describe the cat. He can be active, amiable, angry and so on. Change the letter before the supply of adjectives runs right out.

Will the

A both-sides-of-the-Atlantic survey of the modern breed of youth, by a man-and-wife team who've lived over there and here

Gaye and Barton rock it around the clock

Left: In the groove and out of it

Photos: I.N.P., Keystone

Real gone hep cats demonstrate: dig that crazy down beat

teenager replace the human being?

BY CHARLOTTE AND DENIS PLIMMER

If you're not a " square " (that means a creep who doesn't know his way around), you're hep to the fact that today's teenager is real cool, a gone cat—and he's here to stay. He's a new kind of biped, jive-talking, rock-and-rolling, fad-crazy, more flamboyant than young people between thirteen and twenty have ever been before—Cleopatra, Romeo, Juliet, Thomas Chatterton, *et al.* notwithstanding.

The spotlight is on teenagers everywhere. As a couple of peripatetic American writers who've stalked this cocky breed on both sides of the Atlantic, we're constantly being asked one overriding question by British adults: " Are yours or ours worse or better? "

Implicit in the question are a number of preconceived ideas, some true, some false:

1. *Most American teenagers go in for gangsterism and marijuana-smoking*

UTTER NONSENSE. Of course we have juvenile delinquents in the States, just as you have here, and a slightly higher percentage. Apparently, our worst is worse than your worst. But in both countries, the bulk of serious delinquency is found only in the slum areas of large cities. An average parent in the United States is as unlikely to raise a juvenile delinquent as you are.

2. *American teenagers are more spoiled than British*

TRUE. The United States has had a kind of youth cult for at least three decades. Remember " Flaming Youth "? Though American tourists in Europe admire antiquities, at home they are equally fascinated by new gadgets, new ways of doing things. This creates a climate where youth, as an end in itself, is admired. Thus you get the teenager in a sometimes top-heavy role in his own household, monopolizing the 'phone or the TV set; dominating the dinner-table conversation; requisitioning the family parlour for youthful parties, and the family car for youthful expeditions.

We heard one interesting, if peripheral, analysis from Dr. Josephine Macalister Brew, prominent British educator. She believes that in new nations, such as America, with a high proportion of immigrant families, the youngest tend to be the most *American*, the most thoroughly in tune with the new country, and consequently able to interpret not only language but cultural ideas to their impressed parents.

3. *American teenagers have greater buying power than British*

DOUBTFUL. A recent survey showed that 16,500,000 U.S. teenagers command a total cash pool of $7,000,000,000. This

(*Continued on page* **206**)

The drink is strictly non-alcoholic; the music isn't

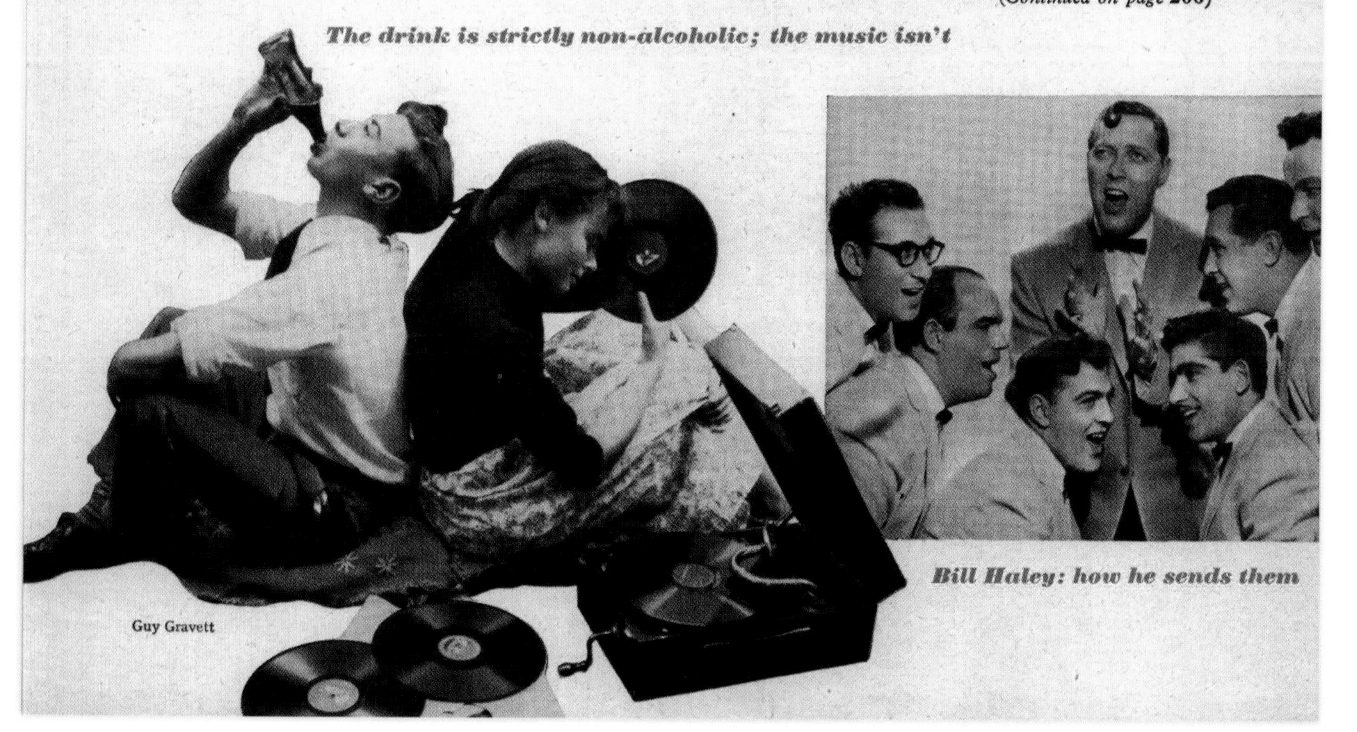

Bill Haley: how he sends them

Guy Gravett

Taking the ache away

Prevention is better than cure—and here we have chosen some domestic equipment specially designed to help you avoid bending, stretching and lifting. Minimize physical strain in other ways too—by arranging the things you use most often where they can be reached most easily

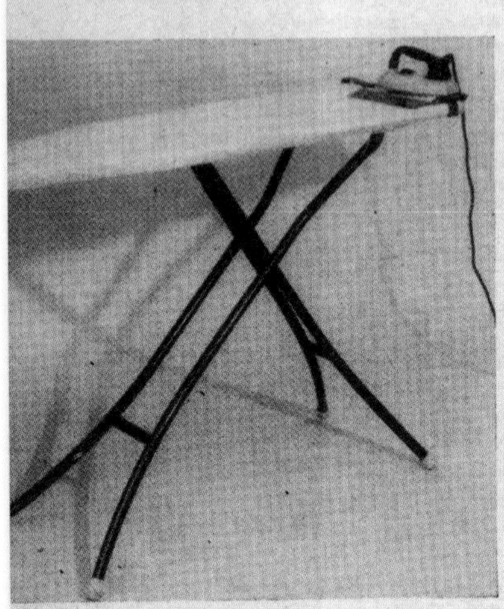

Top corner: the Shopfold folding shopper cuts out unwieldy basket loads. The canvas bag is detachable and the frame folds up for travelling. In green, blue and brown, cubic capacity 1 ft., it costs £2 5s., from the Army & Navy Stores

Above: the Beldray Mark VIII ironing board is easily adjustable to any height up to 35 ins., so you can use it at the level you find most comfortable. Available from Harrods and most good ironmongers, it costs from £5 18s. 2*d*.

Right: sit in comfort to do as many kitchen jobs as you can. The Champion Step-Stool has non-slip steps, which swing away under the seat, and rubber feet to keep it steady. Available from most leading stores, price £7 15*s*.

Above: the Ba-Ba Flick is made of multi-coloured sheep's-wool and is 4 ft. long. Use it for dusting the out-of-reach corners of the room. Available from Harrods and other leading stores, price 10*s*. 6*d*.

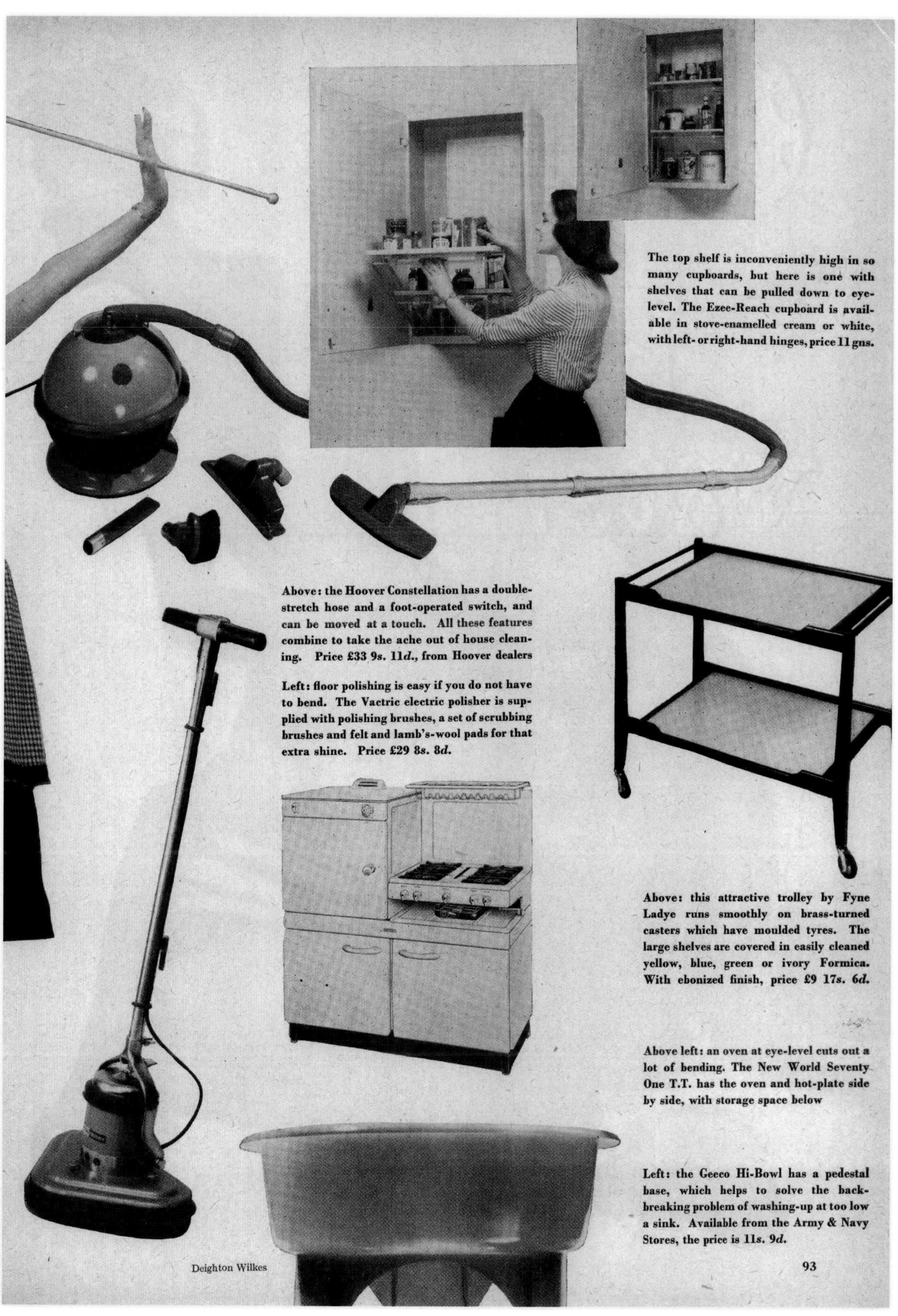

The top shelf is inconveniently high in so many cupboards, but here is one with shelves that can be pulled down to eye-level. The Ezee-Reach cupboard is available in stove-enamelled cream or white, with left- or right-hand hinges, price 11 gns.

Above: the Hoover Constellation has a double-stretch hose and a foot-operated switch, and can be moved at a touch. All these features combine to take the ache out of house cleaning. Price £33 9*s.* 11*d.*, from Hoover dealers

Left: floor polishing is easy if you do not have to bend. The Vactric electric polisher is supplied with polishing brushes, a set of scrubbing brushes and felt and lamb's-wool pads for that extra shine. Price £29 8*s.* 8*d.*

Above: this attractive trolley by Fyne Ladye runs smoothly on brass-turned casters which have moulded tyres. The large shelves are covered in easily cleaned yellow, blue, green or ivory Formica. With ebonized finish, price £9 17*s.* 6*d.*

Above left: an oven at eye-level cuts out a lot of bending. The New World Seventy One T.T. has the oven and hot-plate side by side, with storage space below

Left: the Geeco Hi-Bowl has a pedestal base, which helps to solve the back-breaking problem of washing-up at too low a sink. Available from the Army & Navy Stores, the price is 11*s.* 9*d.*

Deighton Wilkes

LUNCH WITHOUT DON'TS

Diet meals need never be dull, and the pictures on these two pages and on pages 90 and 91 have been planned to show how attractive and appetizing the food in our menu-plan on pages 88 and 89 should be. Above are three of our main lunch dishes. The grilled sole, left, is garnished with olives and lemon. For the dieter, broccoli should be the only accompaniment. The grilled lamb cutlets (top) are shown served up for every one with mint jelly and new carrots. You must restrict yourself to one chop—they may have more and potatoes too, if they like. Leeks au gratin, topped with lean bacon slices, is our third suggestion. Once more you yourself must take only a couple of leeks and one slice of bacon: they can have as much as their appetite calls for

after the fortnight, but if you need to lose a much greater amount, we advise you not to prolong the diet indefinitely but to seek the advice of your doctor.

We include recipes for dishes you may not have cooked before. Take a look at the pictures on this page and page 91 and you will see what we mean by "delicious." You may change and alternate the meals suggested to balance each day's needs, but some, you will see, follow logically, making use of what remains from the day before in an economical everyday manner.

Such obvious points as omitting sugar, chocolates and restricting the amount of bread are so well-known that we have not listed them, but you will not feel the lack of them since there is such a wide variety of other foods. Alcohol, too, must be avoided, of course.

In addition, we give you on these pages and on pages 90 and 91 a fund of fascinating facts all relating to the burning subject of getting slim.

WHAT ABOUT EXERCISE?

Here are some important points about this much discussed aspect of reducing

Does exercise control weight? Regular exercise helps. The habit of walking a few blocks to and from work can easily dispose of three or four thousand calories a month. Exercise makes body fires burn more energetically and use up more fuel (calories). Strenuous exercise may make you hungrier than usual, but moderate exercise does not increase the appetite in proportion to the calories burned.

Is housework exercise? Most housewives need more or different exercise. Doctors rate housework at 70 calories per hour, on the average. The average housewife does 560 calories worth of work in an eight-hour day. An 8 st. 13 lb. woman of moderate vigour spends about the following number of calories per hour in performing her ordinary household tasks:

Table furnishings throughout these pictures from Heal's. Photographs: Chaloner Woods.

DINNER WITHOUT DON'TS

And now we come to some of the main dinner dishes, all with the quality of real family meals with no suggestion of diet austerity. The cod cutlets (top) have been poached in cider and served with tomatoes stuffed with peas—but remember only one cutlet for you, and, as the menu plan shows, with pommes annas are for non-dieters only. Top right we show a lean grilled ham dish topped with pineapple which our menu plan suggests should be served with cauliflower. Below is pigeon roasted in aluminium foil to preserve flavour and food value, but which makes the addition of fat unnecessary. Let the figure-conscious keep to half a bird, sprouts, braised onions and orange slices, but the rest can add game chips. For recipes see pages 88 and 92

Sitting, sewing, writing, peeling potatoes, reading, standing 30
Driving a car 50
Ironing 55
Knitting 40
Washing floors 70
Sweeping with broom 80
Making beds 125
Dish-washing 60

Is play valuable exercise ? Saturday golfers "work" about three times as hard as housewives, but think they're having fun. Playing bridge is as hard work as peeling potatoes. Horseback riding, when the horse merely walks, burns up about 125 of your calories per hour, but if the horse trots, you are exercising at the strenuous rate of 600 calories per hour. Here are other recreations that are surprisingly potent exercises for weight control and physical conditioning:

Dancing, brisk (fox-trot) 215
Waltzing 170
Playing table tennis 250
Gardening 100
Piano playing (fairly fast) 100
Singing 75
Skating 400
Swimming 450

The number of calories spent depends upon your weight and upon the vigour with which you throw your weight about.

Does weather affect exercise? Winter exercise uses more energy than summer exercise. Cold stimulates the body to maintain high muscle tone and to make unnecessarily energetic movements, wasteful of calories. Other things being equal, you need fewer food calories in summer and you will gain weight if you eat as heartily as you do in winter. Profuse perspiring in warm weather is just the body's way of keeping internal temperature from becoming dangerously high.

Can exercise be hazardous ? Heavy lifting by the untrained and exercise continued to extreme fatigue may be injurious. Lifting done with the upper half of the body bent forward—as when leaning over a sink to raise a window, or lifting up a child—can cause severe low back pain. Learn to lift letting your long leg muscles take the strain. Save your back by lifting in line with your centre of gravity, an imaginary vertical line that runs more or less through the centre of your body when you stand erect.

No exercise is too strenuous for a normal person if she stops before she is fatigued or badly out of breath, but competitive sports and games may overtax a person who is not in prime condition.

(Continued on page 90)

The Inside Story of a June Morning

which celebrates with scarlet splendour the Queen's official birthday

BY RENÉ LECLER

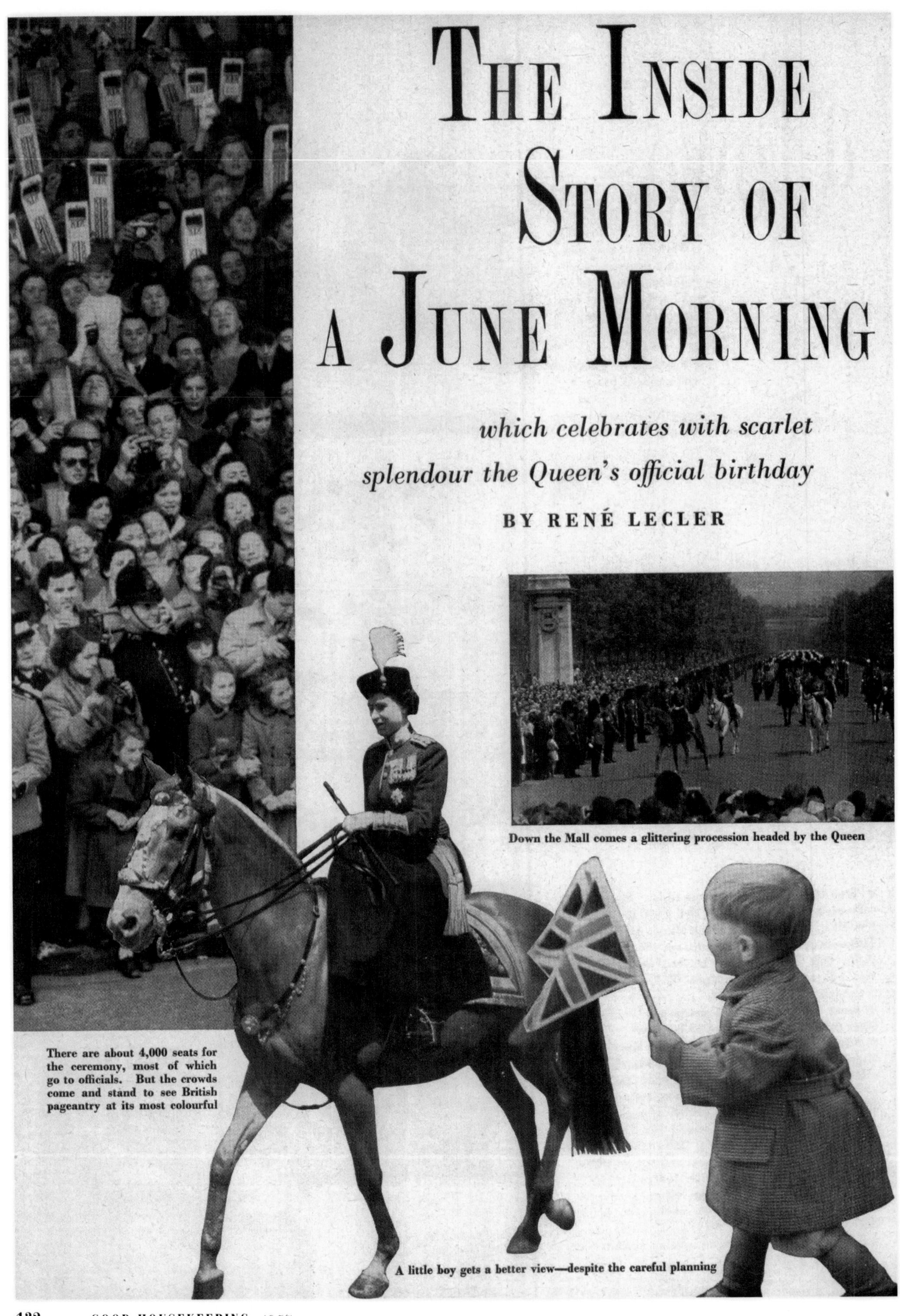

There are about 4,000 seats for the ceremony, most of which go to officials. But the crowds come and stand to see British pageantry at its most colourful

Down the Mall comes a glittering procession headed by the Queen

A little boy gets a better view—despite the careful planning

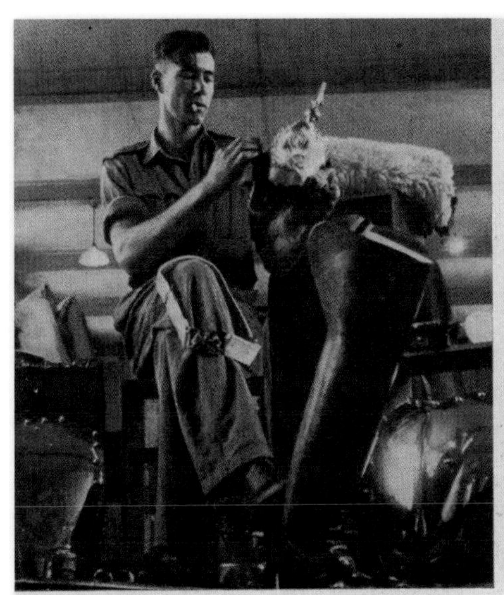

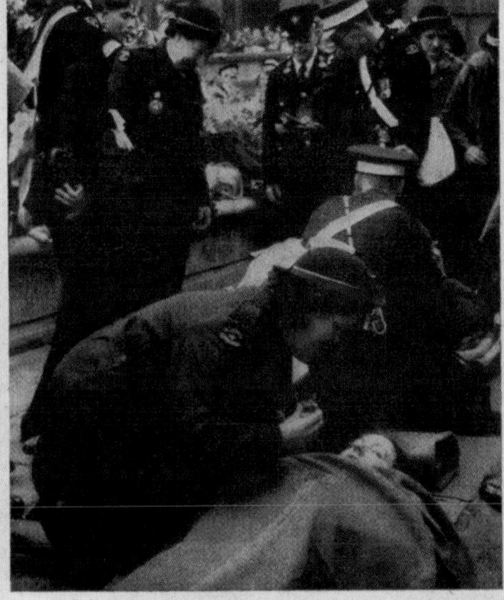

Left: Over forty pieces of equipment are given that extra spit-and-polish that the occasion demands. Right: There's always someone who faints, but the St. John Ambulance Brigade are ready with smelling salts

This year's great parade on the Queen's Birthday, splashing its scarlet and gold across the Horse Guards quadrangle and sending echoes of its martial music floating across the London parks, started, incongruously, one day last November, with a Guardsman on a bicycle. In the darkening gloom of a winter afternoon, he mounted his bicycle just by the War Office arch, pedalled quietly across the vast parade ground, down Birdcage Walk and into the Guards barracks. In his dispatch case he carried an order, signed by the General Officer Commanding, London District, and issued by the Brigade Major, Household Brigade. This order named the First Battalion, Irish Guards, as the unit whose Colour would be trooped on that fine June day, and it detailed eight Guards—each of three officers and seventy-six men—from the Grenadiers, Scots, Welsh and Irish Guards, to take part in the parade. It further ordered that 400 Coldstream Guards should line the Mall.

That piece of paper—its contents terse and to the point—set in motion a vast machine which, in six months, would place in the field 1,651 men for the most gorgeous military show that Britain can put on.

Very soon, regimental sergeant-majors in the various Guards barracks in London and the Home Counties, began looking at their men a little more closely even than usual. In his mind's eye, each picked the tallest, smartest, best-turned-out Guardsmen, those with the best sense of individual responsibility, those who would best do honour to the Queen. In each battalion, the gold sergeants, as the master tailors are called, looked over hundreds of full-dress uniforms and detailed one man, a tradition-loving old soldier, to look after the tall bearskins.

Then, one day in January, a dry day, the Ministry of Works took a hand. A tanker lorry appeared on the vast expanse of the Horse Guards Parade—which is 540 feet long by 370 feet wide—and began spraying the ground with a watered-down solution of calcium chloride. Repeated experiments had shown that this was the best way of settling the dust on London's largest open space. Behind the lorry, a little man with a pointed stick marched back and forth looking for the permanent holes which would hold the tubular scaffolding of the stands.

Four miles away in Clerkenwell, at the No. 1 London District of the St. John Ambulance Brigade, officials began drawing up a list of 300 trained first-aid men and women to look after the crowds because, as one of them put it: "Contrary to tradition, Guardsmen are by no means the only ones to faint on that day. . . ." In Westminster, London Transport officials took out their routing schedules and tentatively arranged to divert ten bus routes on the Queen's Birthday; and in Scotland Yard's Traffic Division plans were laid to make sure that

(Continued on page **163***)*

Photos: I.N.P., Keystone, A.P., Mirrorpic

An Irish Guardsman, representative of the unit whose First Battalion's Colour has been selected for this year's Trooping ceremony

Two pretty subjects for embroidery. The yoke of a gay shortie nightdress and the hem of a waist-slip, both done for us, together with the monogram on the satin nightdress case, by Singer. The nightie in red Viyella (36-in. width, 11*s.* 9*d.* per yard at Gorringes, Victoria, S.W.1, and Kendal Milne, Manchester) is Simplicity printed pattern No. 1431, price 2*s.* 6*d.*, sizes 10, 12, 14 and 16. The tiered waist-slip, made up in fresh, white lawn is Simplicity printed pattern No. S 117, price 2*s.* 6*d.*, in sizes 11, 12, 13, 14, 15, 16 and 18. Gossard bra

Heavenly Stitchery—all machine sewn

with automatic swing-needles at high speed, yet giving all the delicacy of hand work

The Necchi Supernova Zig-Zag machine

At the touch of a button the new machines sew straight or zig-zag, forward or reverse, hem, darn, sew on lace, make buttonholes and stitch on buttons. Pillow-slip embroidery here by Singer, handkerchiefs by Necchi

Few man-made wonders give as much scope for making pretty things as the swing-needle machines. If you're already a proud possessor, you'll know the possibilities, and now, at Christmas, will set it to work on lovely gifts like those we show. If not—a hint in the right place, and who knows? Santa may hang one on your tree. It's well worth a try!

DECORATIONS BY JANET WATT

10 GREEN BOTTLES

You can make your own wine using almost any of the cultivated fruits, edible wild berries, or flowers. These should be in perfect condition. The basic wine ingredients are sweetened juice and yeast.

Have the right equipment and use it with care. This is essential if wine is to be kept from souring.

Start with a mixing-bowl of glass, wood, aluminium or polythene, or an earthenware crock glazed on the outside.

All containers must be scrupulously clean and closely covered with several layers of muslin while the fruit is soaking before the addition of the yeast. This is to prevent bacteria from entering the wine and turning it into vinegar.

FERMENTING JARS AND LOCKS: You can get special glass, stoneware or polythene fermenting jars in 1- or 2-gallon sizes. You will also need a fermentation lock for the neck of the jar when the wine is fermenting. Jars must be kept full during fermentation. Allow surplus wine to ferment in small loosely corked bottles, ready for topping up the jars.

Use a 4-ft. length of rubber tubing, ⅜-in. in diameter, to siphon the wine from one container to another.

CORKS: Use new corks and sterilize them. Don't allow them to dry out after sterilizing as it will be difficult to insert them into the bottles. A special bottle corker will do the job efficiently.

BOTTLES: All bottles must be thoroughly washed and dried before use. Avoid those in which strongly flavoured liquids have been stored, as these may taint the wine. Wine bottles can be used for storing still wines. Cider or strong beer bottles are best for storing sparkling wines. Tighten corks only when all fermentation has ceased.

Label the bottles with the type of wine and date. Store full bottles on their sides, either in special wine bins or on shelves in a cool, dark place.

THE USE OF YEAST: Many traditional recipes use brewer's and baker's yeasts, in the proportions of 1 oz. yeast to each gallon of liquid. The yeast is spread on a piece of bread.

Special wine yeast is very satisfactory.

Baker's yeast has the disadvantage that wine made with it is frequently cloudy and covered with a film. Older recipes often give too great a proportion of yeast and a vigorous fermentation results. The quality of your wine will be better with slower fermentation.

There are many different-flavoured wine yeasts, but the "all-purpose sedimentary wine yeast" gives excellent results. We advise the use of a yeast nutrient, too, with some of our recipes. Always use wine yeast in accordance with the maker's instructions.

GENERAL METHOD: The preparation and yeasting of the liquid is given with the individual recipes. The next step is to pour the liquid into a clean fermentation jar until it is filled. Stand the jar on a tray in a warm room. The first fermentation

and they could all be yours—full of sweet wines, dry wines, made at home with pride

will froth vigorously. When it ceases, clean up the jar and insert the fermentation lock.

This process of fermentation, during which the sugar is converted into alcohol by the yeast, varies considerably in duration. External temperature can retard or speed up the process. The ideal temperature is that of a comfortable living-room, about a steady 60° F.–65° F. The process should take about three weeks. Never keep a glass jar of fermenting wine in direct sunshine.

When fermentation stops—that is, when gas bubbles are no longer formed—treat the wine according to type, as follows:

DRY STILL WINES: Keep in a cool room for 14 days, when a deposit will have formed and the wine will be ready for racking. This important process clears the wine by removing the yeast deposits, and prevents over-fermentation. Racking may be necessary several times during the storage period. Siphon the liquid through a rubber tube into a clean jar, taking care not to disturb the yeast deposit; make sure the second jar is quite full.

Insert a cork into the jar and wax the top. Store in a cold cellar for six months, then rack off the clear liquid, bottle and cork firmly. Store bottles on their sides for at least another six months.

It is a great mistake to sample wine before it has had time to mature.

SWEET STILL WINES: Use 6 lb. of sugar instead of the amount stated in the recipes. Allow the wine to continue fermenting until all signs of fermentation cease. Then continue as for dry still wine. If a more controlled sweetness is desired, add ¾ lb. sugar to each gallon of fermented wine, stir until dissolved, re-insert air lock and allow to ferment in a warm room. When fermentation ceases, taste the wine and if necessary add another ¾ lb. of sugar; repeat the process. When the required sweetness is obtained, or fermentation ceases, rack it and store for six months prior to bottling, as for the dry still wines.

SPARKLING WINES: Our recipes are for still wines. Sparkling wines can be made at home, but the method is more complicated.

GRAPE WINE

6 lb. grapes • 1 gallon cold water • 3½ lb. sugar • yeast

Crush the grapes with your hands, then cover with cold water. Leave covered with a thick cloth for 4 days, stirring frequently. Strain through muslin and add the sugar and yeast. Stir until the sugar is dissolved, then pour into a clean jar or cask. Proceed as in general method.

ELDERBERRY WINE

4 lb. elderberries • 1 gallon water • 3½ lb. sugar • yeast

Remove the stalks from the fruit. Weigh and bruise in a bowl. Pour on the boiling water, cover with muslin and allow to stand for 3 days. Strain through muslin. Dissolve the sugar in the juice. Add the yeast. Place in a fermenting jar and allow to ferment. Continue as in general method.

(Continued on page **64***)*

Except where otherwise stated, recipes are for 4-6 servings

GARDEN-FRESH VEGETABLES–

every day of the year

Some of these hot dishes are a meal in themselves. Others will happily partner fish or meat

Peas à la Toscana *Illustrated on cover*

4 oz. bacon • fat for frying • 1 medium onion
10-oz. packet Findus garden peas • a little water
salt • ½ teaspoonful sugar • pinch of allspice

Cut the bacon into small strips, and fry lightly with the onion, cut into thin rings. Add the peas and a little water if necessary. Season with salt, sugar and allspice, and allow the peas to simmer slowly until soft, with a lid on the pan.

Dressed French beans

1 packet Findus green beans • salted water
1 oz. butter • 2 tablespoonfuls mayonnaise or *cream*
lemon-juice • seasoning • fried bread • parsley

Cook the beans in boiling salted water for 15 mins. until tender, and drain thoroughly. Melt butter, add green beans, mayonnaise, few drops of lemon-juice, seasoning; heat thoroughly.

Pile in a vegetable dish and garnish with neat pieces of fried bread and a little chopped parsley.

Beans au gratin *Illustrated*

1 packet Findus green beans or *runner beans*
salted water • seasoning • 2 oz. grated cheese

Cook the beans in boiling, salted water for 15 mins. Drain and season. Pile into a fireproof dish, sprinkle with grated cheese, brown under a hot grill. Try broccoli the same way.

TRY FROZEN FOOD FOR A ZESTFUL CURRY

1 packet Findus corn on the cob • 2 oz. dripping
2 onions • 10-oz. packet Findus garden peas
1 packet Findus green beans
1 dessertspoonful curry-powder
1 teaspoonful curry-paste • 2 cloves of garlic
a few mushrooms • 1 tablespoonful sultanas
stock • lemon-juice • seasoning
cayenne pepper • 4 oz. rice

Cook the corn on the cob, and, when cooked, drain, and remove the corn from the cob. Melt the dripping. Prepare and slice the onions. Fry the frozen vegetables and the onions with the curry-powder and paste for about 10 mins. Prepare and chop the garlic and mushrooms. Add the garlic, mushrooms and sultanas to the other vegetables. Add sufficient stock to cover. Simmer until tender. Add the lemon-juice, seasoning and a little cayenne pepper. Serve with boiled rice.

French-style peas

10-oz. packet Findus garden peas • 3 or 4 lettuce leaves
1 small onion, sliced, or a few spring onions
a knob of butter • salt • a little sugar • water

Defrost the peas, and place in a saucepan with some finely-cut lettuce leaves, slices of onion and a large knob of butter. Season with salt and a little sugar. Pour boiling water over the peas until they are almost covered. Boil, without a lid, until the peas are soft and the water has almost boiled away.

Spinach soufflé *Illustrated*

2 oz. butter • 2 oz. flour • ½ pint milk
half a 6-oz. packet Findus spinach • 3 eggs • seasoning

Melt the butter in a saucepan, blend in the flour and add the milk carefully; cook gently to a thick, creamy sauce. Add the spinach, and let it defrost while the sauce is simmering. Remove the pan from heat, add the egg yolks and season well. Fold in the stiffly-beaten egg whites. Cook in a moderate oven for 30 mins. (375° F.) Serve immediately.

Spinach Mornay

12-oz. packet Findus chopped spinach • 2-3 hard-boiled eggs
½ pint cheese sauce • a little grated cheese

Cook the spinach and drain well, place on a fireproof dish together with quartered hard-boiled eggs, and cover with cheese sauce. Sprinkle a little grated cheese on top and brown in oven or under grill.

Sweet corn pancakes

FILLING:
1 packet Findus corn on the cob • salted water
¼ pint white coating sauce • seasoning

BATTER:
4 oz. flour • pinch salt • 1 egg • ½ pint milk and water mixed
lard for frying • parsley

Cook the corn in boiling, salted water for 10-15 mins.; drain and cool. Remove the corn from the cob and add corn to the white sauce. Season the mixture, reheat.

Sieve the flour and salt. Beat the egg and add to the flour. Add two-thirds of the milk and water, and mix to a smooth batter. Add the remaining liquid, and mix well. Heat some lard in a frying-pan and fry the pancakes. Place some filling in the centre of each pancake. Serve garnished with parsley.

Broccoli and butter sauce *Illustrated*

2 oz. butter • ¾ oz. flour • ½ pint stock or *water • seasoning*
1 packet Findus broccoli spears • salted water • melted butter

Melt the butter for the sauce, and add the flour. Gradually add the liquid and season. Bring to the boil, stirring all the time. Cook the broccoli in boiling, salted water for 6-7 mins. Drain and pile into a vegetable dish. Sprinkle with melted butter and serve with the hot butter sauce.

Our picture shows buttered broccoli, corn on the cob, individual spinach soufflés and beans au gratin ⟶

Cookery photographs by Chaloner Woods, ovenware and tableware from Heal's and Wuidart

the way to success

A STORE cupboard filled with jars (and possibly cans) of home-preserved fruit and vegetables has been the pride of generations of housewives. In olden days, the " know how " was handed down from mother to daughter but just occasionally seemingly inexplicable troubles did occur. Perhaps some jam did not set, perhaps it became mouldy, or there may have been a bout of sickness after partaking of home-bottled vegetables or meats.

Today, rule-of-thumb methods have been replaced by scientific knowledge. With this more definite information there is no reason why everyone who is prepared to work accurately and carefully should not be rewarded by one hundred per cent success.

With bottling and canning it is, of course, what you *don't* see that is the most important part of the operation—the destroying of hordes of bacteria, yeasts and enzymes present in the food and those in the surrounding atmosphere also can cause not only trouble but possible danger unless they are rendered innocuous by the preservative process. The problem is how to destroy these, how to ensure the right amount of heat—for too much may spoil the food; too little may result in incomplete sterilization.

Steps to avoid re-infection of the food afterwards are equally important. An immense amount of work has been done on this subject in recent years, and correct and safe procedures have been worked out by various bodies, including Long Ashton Research Station and the Ministry of Agriculture and Fisheries.

Fruit is the easiest and safest of foods for home preservation, largely because it contains a certain amount of acid, which inhibits the development of putrefactive bacteria. And usually (but not necessarily, of course, in bottling) sugar or sugar syrup is added, which has preservative qualities. Vegetables, on the other hand, contain little or no acid. Some, particularly peas, contain an appreciable amount of protein, which makes them more difficult to sterilize safely under domestic conditions. We do not, therefore, advise bottling or canning these at home, unless a pressure cooker is used with an adequate pressure gauge to maintain a pressure of 10 lb., thus ensuring that a temperature considerably higher than normal boiling point is reached. With root vegetables it is essential to follow reliable instructions implicitly, after very thoroughly washing and scrubbing the vegetables.

The most difficult foods to preserve safely under home conditions are the protein foods, including meat, fish and poultry, and there is a very real element of risk in attempting to do so. Such risk may be small—but it may be fatal. This is why we do not advise the home preservation of these foods.

Jam making is a simple enough process, but here, too, the scientists have been at work. Their findings can help you turn out bright-coloured, well-set jams of which you can be truly proud. Of course, the same germ killing is essential, but the sugar solution in itself ensures that jams and marmalades are taken to a sufficiently high temperature (about 220° F.).

Pectin, which causes jam to set, is present in varying amounts in the cell walls of fruit. Slightly under-ripe fruit contains proportionately more pectin than over-ripe fruit. But, since its flavour is not fully developed, use one part fruit slightly under-ripe and three parts ripe when possible. The use of over-ripe fruit, in which the pectin has deteriorated, often results in a poor set. Other reasons for a poor set may be under-boiling before adding the sugar, or over-cooking after adding it; so it is important to follow instructions on these points. Pectin is dissolved out when the fruit is boiled, but if it is boiled for too long its setting properties are lost. A certain amount of acid is also necessary for the pectin to set the jam, and it changes some of the cane or beet sugar to " invert " sugar, thus reducing the danger of the jam crystallizing during storage.

Most fruits picked at the right stage have enough pectin and acid of their own for jam making, but there are some, such as strawberries, blackberries, sweet cherries, rhubarb and marrow, which need added acid and pectin to make a good preserve. In some cases this is done by adding one fruit to another, for example, red currants with strawberries, in other cases by adding a little lemon juice.

BY PHYLLIS L. GARBUTT, A.R.I.C.

JAM MAKING

We have already stressed the importance of choosing the freshest and best fruit. Before you start, it should all be washed carefully. The first stage in the actual jam making is to cook the fruit, so as to soften it and release the pectin and the acid. This is best done slowly; the fruit and water should only simmer. Extra acid, if needed, is added during this stage.

Never be in a hurry over the cooking. The quantity of water and the cooking time need to be varied for different types of fruit, and the fruit skins must be really soft, as tough skins in jam are most unpalatable and hard to digest. Fruits such as black currants, damsons and plums need at least ½–¾ hr. cooking. This preliminary cooking may be done very satisfactorily in a pressure cooker —in this case the quantity of water can usually be halved, as little is lost by evaporation. It should be remembered also that in most domestic-sized pressure cookers the amount of fruit dealt with at one time would be smaller, as the pressure cooker should never be filled above the safety level recommended by the manufacturers.

The addition of sugar It is clear from our readers' queries that many people imagine there is some advantage in using, say, cane rather than beet sugar, or lump sugar rather than granulated. In fact, there is no difference in the keeping qualities of jam made from any of these sugars. Preserving sugar, as such, has one advantage, however: it does dissolve more easily—a factor which is, of course, of importance. It used to be cheaper, too, but unfortunately this is no longer true.

No matter which sugar is used, it must be completely dissolved *before* the mixture comes to the boil again. This is why some recipes state that sugar should be warmed while the fruit is cooking, as it helps it to dissolve more quickly. This is not essential, but it is important to stir the jam while the sugar is dissolving.

Boiling the jam As soon as all the sugar is dissolved, bring the jam rapidly to the boil and allow to boil quickly. At this stage a large, shallow preserving pan has great advantages, as it enables the jam to boil quickly without boiling over. Always remember: slow cooking before the sugar is dissolved, and hard, rapid boiling after.

Testing for setting point There are several reliable ways of deciding whether the jam is ready to set, but it is at this stage that many housewives experience difficulty. Providing the fruit has been properly cooked beforehand, it is usually necessary to boil for approx. 5–20 mins., while some jams need as little as 3 mins. When testing jam, particularly in the later stages, always lower the heat, so that it does not go on cooking after it has reached setting point.

Of the many different methods of testing jam, the most common is the "plate test." A little jam is put on a cold saucer and allowed to cool. If the surface is set and crinkles when it is gently pushed with a finger, the setting point is reached. You only need use a tiny spot of jam on the saucer.

One very reliable method is to use a sugar thermometer. When the jam reaches 220° F.—providing the pectin and acid content are correct—setting point has generally been reached. With some jams, temperatures of 221° F. or 222° F. may give better results, but this is a matter of experience. One note of warning here: make sure the thermometer is accurate. Check it from time to time by taking a reading in boiling water (this is, of course, 212° F.).

During testing, fill a jug with boiling water and keep the thermometer in this when it is not actually in the jam. Stir the jam thoroughly before using the thermometer. Sugar thermometers are not expensive and can be obtained from most large chemists. In households where jam is often made, they are a good investment.

Readers often send us queries about the yield of jam, and this is easy to ascertain. As the sugar content of the finished jam should not be less than 60 per cent, a recipe that needs 3 lb. sugar should yield 5 lb. jam.

Potting and storing The jars must be clean and sterilized, and should be warmed in an oven just before use. When you buy packets of covers, be sure that they are the correct size for your jars. Wax covers in particular must fit exactly, otherwise the resulting air spaces will increase the risk of mould contamination.

(*Continued overleaf*)

Preserving sugar is here being added to the partially cooked jam. Cane, beet, or lump sugar can be used equally satisfactorily

A little jam is being tested on a saucer to determine if it has reached the setting point. This is one of the simplest tests

The prepared jam being poured into the sterilized pots, which have been kept in a warm oven until they are ready to be used

THE MODERN WAY • No. 3

Washing-up

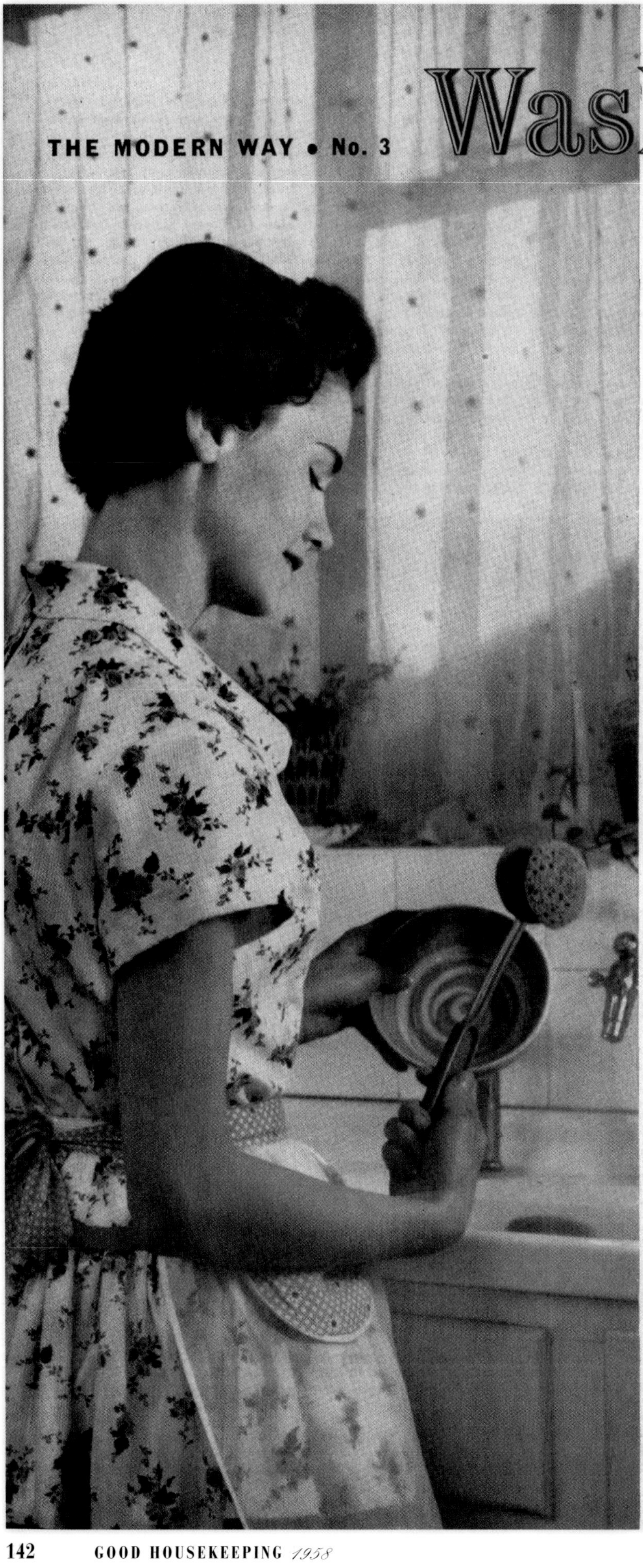

THE GOOD HOUSEKEEPING INSTITUTE,

28-30 GROSVENOR GARDENS, S.W.1.

PRINCIPAL,

PHYLLIS L. GARBUTT, A.R.I.C.

MANY experts are disturbed by the spread of bacterial infections through improper "washing-up." One scientist said to me recently, "If you could get more people to realize that under adverse conditions washing-up can easily contaminate rather than reduce microbial infection of food utensils, you would be doing a valuable piece of work."

Forks, spoons and drinking vessels can all be potential means of spreading infection. Sinks, draining-boards, washing-up water and tea towels have all been incriminated at times.

Perhaps it's time we all gave second thoughts to this chore which, because of its familiarity, is often undertaken with nonchalance. It might be wise to think anew about ways in which washing-up could be made safer and less irksome.

Good organization is as important in washing-up as in any other job. It makes it much easier and more pleasant, too, if dishes are sorted, scraps of food removed, glasses and cups emptied and everything stacked neatly beforehand. Naturally the washing-up should start with the cleanest articles—the silver and glass. Follow on with the crockery, and finish up with the dirtiest—the saucepans and baking tins.

The kitchen sink

The sink, with its surroundings, is the king pin of washing-up. Whether it is of stainless steel or good vitreous enamel is largely a matter of personal choice. Both are easily cleaned and can be kept in a much more hygienic condition than the old type of glazed earthenware sink. Wherever space allows, a double sink is preferable so that one side can be used for washing-up and the other for rinsing.

The height of the sink. Nowadays the top rim of the sink is usually 35 or 36 ins. from the floor, a convenient height for most people.

The floor you stand on. The floor has a good deal to do with your comfort—even for a chore like washing-up. Try to have one that is slightly resilient. If the kitchen floor is a hard one, say of quarry tiles, a suitable mat in front of the sink can make a world of difference. An easily cleaned comfortable mat, which we are at present testing in the Institute, has a plastic-covered upper surface and a foam plastic base which grips even a highly-polished floor.

Good lighting. This is another "must," and an additional lighting point over the sink can be not only cheering but also a real aid to efficiency and cleanliness.

Rex Moreton

The draining-board. Fortunately it is becoming more and more usual for the draining-board to be made in one piece with the sink so that there are no chinks and gaps where dirt and microbes can penetrate. There is also the great advantage that the surface itself will be non-porous and easily cleaned. The old absorbent wood draining boards can be a real menace and a potential source of contamination unless strict attention is paid to scrupulous cleanliness.

Stacking and drainage space

Even in some modern kitchens, space for stacking and draining crockery and cooking utensils is inadequate and, on occasions, the floor has to be used for the overflow of saucepans. Practical tests carried out at the Institute proved that a 32 in. by 18 in. area is needed for the tidy stacking of china and cooking utensils used in the preparation and serving of a typical main meal for a family of four or five people. A minimum space of 18 ins. by 18 ins. is required for draining, since everything is seldom drained at once. Where this amount of space cannot be managed, a mobile trolley or small table can be drawn up for stacking.

Mechanical dish washers

From the point of view of hygiene, a mechanical dish washer has much to commend it. Not only can very hot water be used, but articles are very thoroughly rinsed with sprays of hot water and dried without the use of tea towels which, as we mentioned, can in themselves be a source of infection.

In the United States there are many small dish-washing machines which can be conveniently fitted in line with other unit furniture. In this country, however, they are mostly larger machines and the necessary space cannot always be afforded. Apart from considerations of hygiene, many people think in terms of the labour saved with a dish-washing machine. This may be a real advantage if there is a large household of ten or twelve people, or if a good deal of entertaining is done. However, some of the more difficult articles, such as saucepans and baking tins, still have to be done by hand. Even assuming it's a large household, one person using a machine can often accomplish the work of two people without a machine.

For a small household of three or four people, the usefulness of a dish-washing machine of the usual size available here is, perhaps, a little more questionable. This is because the stacking, unloading and cleaning of the machine may take as much time as a small wash-up done by hand.

One of the larger machines recently tested by the Institute takes a load of twenty plates, fourteen cups or glasses, fourteen saucers or small plates and thirty pieces of cutlery. It washes by direct impeller action and then gives two rinses. Washing and a double rinsing take three gallons of hot water for each load.

For hand washing-up, a good supply of really hot water at not less than 120° F. is important, not only for hygienic cleanliness, but also for removal of grease and easy washing-up generally. If your supply is limited, the installation of a small gas or electric sink heater might help.

Soap or soapless detergent?

Soapless detergents are widely used by most people, since they make no scum in hard water and, of course, are excellent for removing grease. Tests have indicated, however, that soap possibly has greater germicidal properties. If detergents are used, they should be carefully chosen, since some can cause staining of silverware and cutlery. Quite a number of readers have written to us recently about unaccountable dark or straw-coloured spots which have appeared on their silver, and also occasionally about discoloured patches on stainless-steel cutlery. The Master Silversmiths' Association published a report a year or two ago stating that such stains were apt to occur when there was undissolved salt on articles washed in synthetic detergents containing oxygenated compounds found in many washing powders now on the market. To avoid such discolouration, washing with a mild liquid detergent or soapy water is recommended in preference to a powder. If powder is used, it should be a mild one containing no oxygenated compounds and care should be taken to dissolve it completely before starting the washing-up. Oddly enough, to remove, or at least reduce, any stains which may have already formed, treatment with a salt solution is advised, followed by rinsing and a rub with rouge or a silver powder containing rouge.

A very little detergent goes a long way; too much is not only wasteful but serves no useful purpose. A few drops of liquid detergent are all that is necessary for the average sink or bowl. A convenient plastic pack from which the small amount necessary can be gently squeezed is now on the market. For cleaning the sink, there is a useful powder preparation containing a chlorine bleach which has both germicidal and bleaching properties.

The effect of synthetic detergents on the skin was one of the points investigated by the Committee on Synthetic Detergents, appointed by the Ministry of Housing and Local Government, which reported in 1956. The committee found no evidence of any greater degree of skin trouble caused by the use of detergents than by the use of soap products. This corroborates the result of some research work we ourselves undertook a few years ago on this subject. Nor did it find that detergents had any greater effect on sink or wash-basin outlets, waste pipes, etc., than other commonly used household products such as soda or bleaches.

Dry them or drain them?

From the point of hygienically clean china and of saving labour, much can be said for draining rather than drying, provided the articles are thoroughly rinsed after washing in plenty of clean, really hot water. For draining, there are many easily cleaned plastic coated drainers on the market. Whichever method you choose, some things—such as glass and silver—must still be rubbed up for a good shine.

Finally, just to give a rough idea of what can happen to dish-water at its worst, it is worth referring to an investigation that was carried out in certain establishments where hygienic conditions were, in some cases, rather questionable. Tests were made to find the number of bacteria present in dish-water, sinks and dish-cloths at various stages of washing-up. In some cases, the count amounted to tens and hundreds of thousands, and in one or two of the worst, between one and two millions per millilitre, in unheated rinse sinks. Such results as these, of course, are very abnormal and indicate really gross carelessness of a kind which, fortunately, is seldom found. No doubt, also, most of the bacteria were relatively harmless, although others probably represented at least latent dangers.

As a matter of interest, in this investigation, the lowest counts occurred where a liquid detergent hypochlorite mixture was used. One feels the trouble need not have occurred at all if the ordinary rules of hygiene had been more strictly observed—if attention had been paid to such things as clean hands, plenty of clean hot water, frequently boiled dish-cloths, disinfected mops, clean sinks and draining boards.

Take a fresh view of your household's most regular chore.

Foresight and the right equipment make it easier,

more hygienic—almost, in fact, a pleasure

THE FIRST TEN YEARS OF A KING-TO-BE

1948

Charles Philip Arthur George, one month old and a king-to-be, but also a beautiful baby, truly his mother's pride and joy

A family affair. Londoners stop by the gates of the Palace to read the news. November 14th, 1948. It's a boy and mother's doing well

The christening with, besides the Princess and her son, the Dowager Marchioness of Milford Haven and Queen Mary. Standing are Lady Brabourne, the proud father and grandfather, David Bowes-Lyon, the Earl of Athlone and the baby's aunt, Princess Margaret

Charles was nineteen weeks old and weighed 16 lb. 3 oz. There is something of his grandfather in him

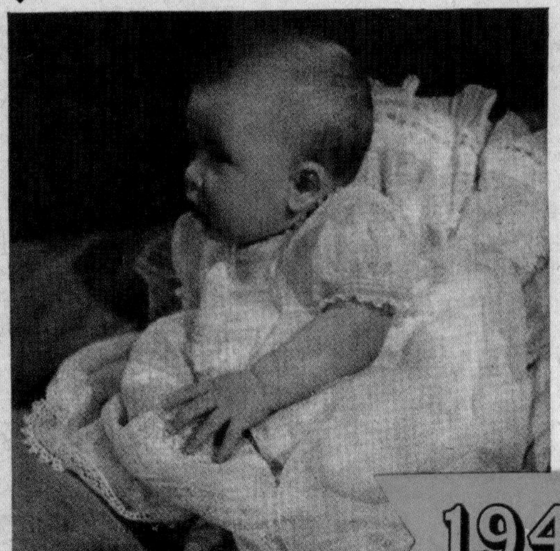

1949

One candle on 40 lb. of cake. If you want to know, it took 6 lb. of currants, 3 lb. of sultanas and a pint of rum

The first cuckoo clock made entirely in Britain was a gift for the first baby in the land

1950

ONLY a while ago he was a little boy looking out of a car window at the world about him. Now he is ten, a schoolboy proud of his school cap, pleased to be among his fellows. Then, all of a sudden, he becomes His Royal Highness the Prince of Wales. These ten years of Prince Charles' childhood have been happy years, secure years in the midst of a family that makes its own happiness and creates it for others. This family album proves that.

Now, Charles is growing up, sturdy, independent, already showing that self-assured personality that is the stuff of Royalty. Soon now—how very soon—that fanfare will sound on the old walls of Caernarvon to herald his young manhood and make him truly the Prince of Wales.

▲ The most endearing picture of the year. A princess joins the family and her gallant brother gree her. The medallions adorn his new bed

▲ Cats can look at kings, so there is no reason why little princes can't go for a ride in the park

◀ There ought to be a sweet in there. Grannies always carry sweets in their handbags. This one's no exception

1951

◀ It's Charles' third birthday. He has a lot to tell his grandfather. About that birthday cake, for instance

1952

▲ Now he has learnt to wave properly. But with flowers for the Queen Mother in the other hand, it is not so easy

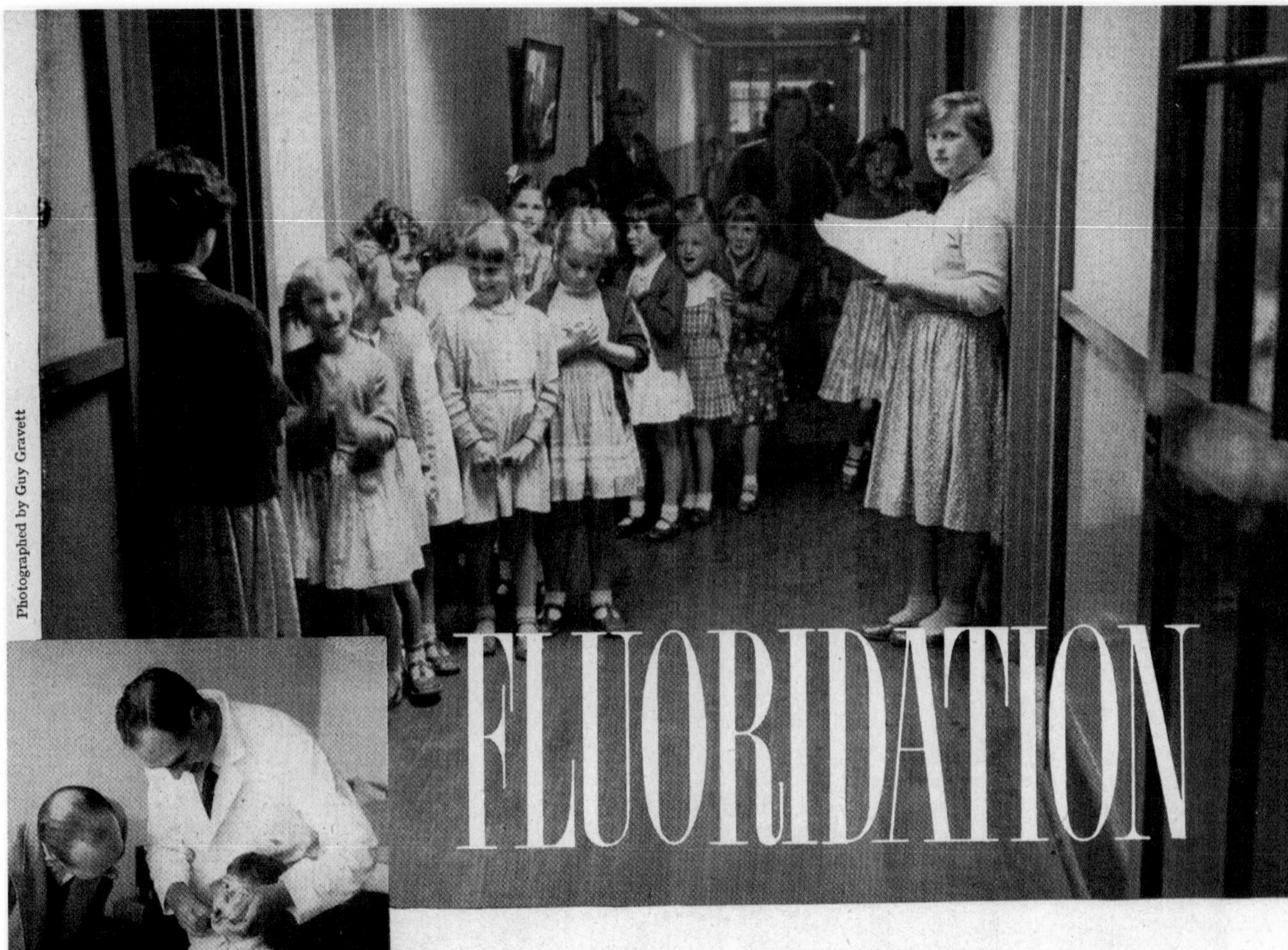

Photographed by Guy Gravett

FLUORIDATION

Let's have a look at those teeth! In Slough, whose water has natural fluoride, school inspections prove that the unseen element strengthens children's teeth

YES OR NO?

Should they treat our drinking water to do us good? A searching inquiry into the facts behind a stormy controversy

BY RENÉ LECLER

FILL a glass with water from the tap in your home. Add to it the tiniest imaginable quantity of a harmless-looking white powder, too small for the clumsy spoon to hold, too tiny even to pinch between your fingers, actually one part white powder to a million parts of water. Doctors, dentists and public health authorities all over the world believe that by so doing you will give your children better, sounder teeth, that you will save them from the ordeal of the dentist's chair, for some time at any rate. A simple enough matter, you say?

Yes, it is simple. An easy, safe-as-houses way to prevent, or at least retard, dental caries, the world's most universal ailment. It is far simpler than vaccination or immunization; easier than swallowing vitamins by the bottleful, perhaps safer than all the things we do to our cakes and pastries to make them last longer or to our bread to make it look whiter.

Yet this simple matter of adding a substance called sodium fluoride to our drinking water is dynamite. In recent years it has aroused more controversy, more bitterness, more misunderstandings than almost any other subject on the domestic scene. It has set neighbour against neighbour and city council against voters: there have been court cases, cries of mass poisoning, dictatorship and compulsory medication. Communism has been blamed and so has Fascism. As a last resort the rights of the individual have been invoked—and all the time the dentist's drill drones on and on.

"Do we really need that pinch of white powder?" you might well ask. Unfortunately we do. The facts speak for themselves. We have far too few dentists and our teeth are getting steadily worse—among the worst in the world. Table indulgence is

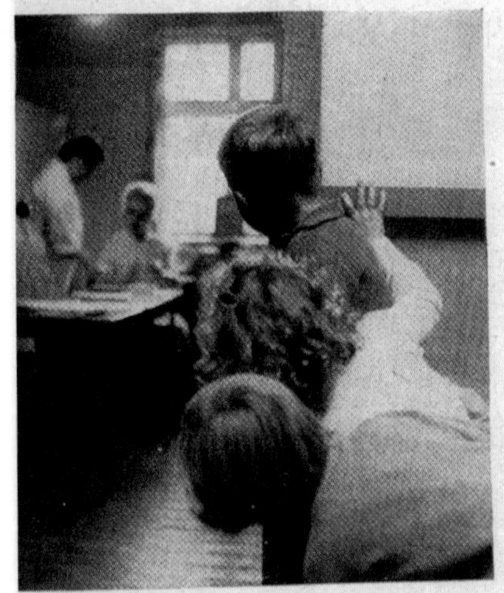

In Britain today there are children of three with complete sets of dentures. Dentists cannot keep up with the work and they say that fluoridation is the answer

to blame for this. We don't eat enough of the right foods and far too much of the wrong ones, with sugar at the top of the list, in those delicious sticky toffees, those rich treacle puddings, those chocolates with deceptively lovely centres. With an annual consumption of 105 lb. of sugar per head of the population, we have the world's biggest sweet tooth, and it's a bad tooth.

In Britain today there are children of three with full sets of dentures. It is a rare child who has not been to the dentist's many times before he reaches the age of ten or twelve. One recent survey showed that among a hundred typical youngsters of fourteen, only two had reasonably sound teeth.

That is where fluoride comes in, as an element which will help to make our teeth stronger, more resistant to decay, longer lasting. Its story is fascinating. Like so many things in science, it started at the wrong end of the stick. Scientists first discovered its harmful effects, then its beneficial ones. As an element, natural fluoride is widespread in nature. Tea contains a good deal of fluoride, so does fish. Red wine has a fluoride content and so has beer, though brushing your teeth with pale ale won't do much good since fluoride, to do the maximum good, must pass into the system before the birth of the child. Much of the world's water supplies, depending on their geological birthplace, have some fluoride in them. Some have as much as fourteen parts per million. The richest fluoridated water in Britain, in parts of Essex, has six parts per million.

Back around the turn of the century when dentistry graduated from the string-and-door-knob methods to an exact science, American dental experts discovered that in certain areas, the enamel of people's teeth had an odd, mottled look. There were no differences in diet but an analysis showed that water supplies in the mottled teeth areas contained fluoride, sometimes four or five parts per million. Then the experts discovered something else: while their patients' teeth were undoubtedly unsightly, they were also much stronger and far more resistant to decay. Studies in other countries yielded the same answer: where there was mottling of the enamel, there were fewer cavities, fewer toothaches. Tests also showed that water containing one part per million of fluoride caused no mottling at all and preserved the hardness of the enamel.

The experts began spreading the knowledge they had acquired. They made speeches and began writing the first of over 3,000 reports that have accumulated over the years from places as widespread as Texas and India, Belgium, Britain and Venezuela. With slow deliberation, dental authorities in America and Britain embarked upon some research projects that turned out to be among the most brilliant in modern preventive medicine.

The classic example was the now historic case of the "Newburgh–Kingston Study." In 1944, American medical authorities picked two small towns, Newburgh and Kingston, lying thirty miles apart on the west bank of the Hudson River in New York State. The two communities were very similar in most respects. Newburgh added one part per million of fluoride to its water; Kingston retained its normal, non-fluoridated water. In each city about five hundred children were periodically examined, not only in the dentist's chair, but also for possible effects on their general health. In 1954, the teeth of Newburgh showed 58 per cent less caries than those of the Kingston children. The latter also had eight times as many missing first molars as their neighbours in Newburgh. There had been no change in the health of the Newburgh children.

The action of fluoride was known in Britain, too, and the war brought out some interesting sidelights. Doctors in charge of the school population of (*Continued on page* **182**)

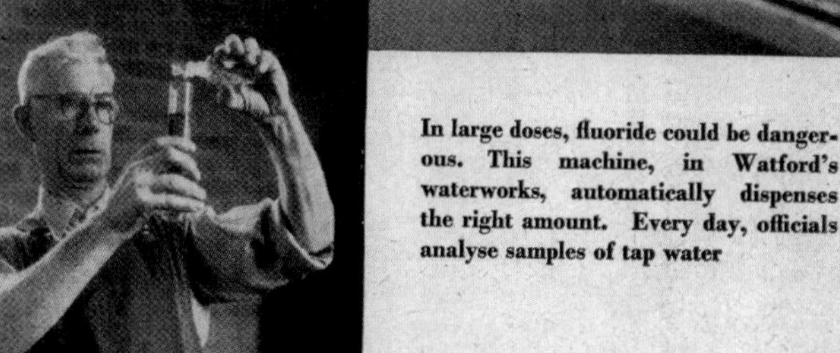

In large doses, fluoride could be dangerous. This machine, in Watford's waterworks, automatically dispenses the right amount. Every day, officials analyse samples of tap water

Dr W. Alcock, Watford's M.O.H., (below) says: "I am certain that fluoridation will reduce dental decay"

Some claim fluoridation is medically unsound and against human rights

Brian Foxwell (left) refuses to drink Watford's water and cycles four miles to fill his bottles from an "untainted" tap. In Andover, Mrs Olive Harvey (centre) dug her own well in her garden and invited people like the man on the right to help themselves. Now her fight has stopped fluoridation in the town

CHARLOTTE AND DENIS PLIMMER *visit the school in Paris where*

TOP DEBS

H.R.H. Princess Alexandra

Bobo Sigrist

H.R.H. Princess Elizabeth of Yugoslavia

H.R.H. Princess Margarethe of Sweden

Daphne Fairbanks

LEARN SAVOIR VIVRE★

Henrietta Tiarks

Tessa and Marina Kennedy

Aerofilms

Dorothy Wilding, Camera Press, Associated Press, Keystone

In historic Cliveden House, high on a wooded hillside above the Thames, a seventeen-year-old girl stood ready to receive the most distinguished guests of the evening. She was Daphne Fairbanks, daughter of American screen and TV star, Douglas Fairbanks. The occasion was Daphne's coming-out party. And the guests she awaited were Her Majesty the Queen and the Duke of Edinburgh.

Few teenagers could meet such a social challenge. Even for Daphne, whose father had trained her to be as at home in London as in Hollywood, in Paris as in Washington, the moment was electric. But when her royal guests arrived, Daphne's composure was enamel-smooth, her dark eyes calm, steady and smiling.

At least part of the credit for Daphne Fairbanks's poise on that star-dusted evening goes to a firm-featured, vital, middle-aged woman named Mademoiselle Anita, one of the most remarkable personalities in the field of international education—and one of the most curiously elusive.

Mlle Anita's school in the heart of Paris, near the Arc de Triomphe, is the stuff of legend. It is never advertised. It distributes no educational brochures. It is listed with no school agency. So great is its directress's passion for anonymity that few even know her last name or the land of her birth. Though she is a handsome woman, she will not, for undisclosed "personal reasons," allow herself ever to be photographed.

All this, not surprisingly, has lead to a great deal of cloak-and-dagger speculation among some of her students. Completely discounting the possibility that she could be a sphinx without a secret, they like to identify her as a member of one of Europe's exiled noble—or even royal—families. Polish or Spanish are first choices.

Whatever the origins of the educator herself may be, her student body certainly comes from the world's most stratospheric social levels. A classmate of Daphne's, Henrietta Tiarks, deb of the season in 1957 both in London and New York, said to us, "A girl simply doesn't go to Paris without going to Mlle Anita's."

Anita's pupils are the daughters of diplomats, authors, politicians, bankers, industrialists. They are also the daughters of royalty.

Over the years, she has enrolled girls from every royal family—reigning and non-reigning—in Europe. Princess Alexandra was one of her students. So was the granddaughter of the King of Sweden, Princess Margarethe, whose romance with Robin Douglas-Home has made headlines for the past year or so. When we visited Mlle Anita's, her student body included three nieces of the Queen of Denmark and one Siamese princess.

The school has two purposes. One is to provide an intensive but essentially normal education for its 250 or so French (*Continued on page* **95**)

★ *Expressing in almost untranslatable form the elusive qualities of the school's principal, as well as her philosophy on femininity today*

WORDS AND MUSIC BY THE FOOT

Lovers, schoolteachers, hostesses, businessmen, are cashing in on the immense versatility of the tape-recorder, the modern " magic box " of sound

BY MATTHEW PARIS

Did you ever receive a spoken love letter from a man you had never seen? Quite by accident the other day I heard of a woman who did. She had been corresponding with an Australian farmer, and was surprised one day to learn that he had sent her a tape recording. She had no tape recorder so, when the tape arrived, she went along to a local dealer and persuaded him to let her play it on one of his machines.

When she came out of the audition room she looked confused, pleased and rather embarrassed. The tape had finished with a proposal of marriage, she told the dealer. Could she have a tape to record her answer? " She didn't buy a tape recorder," he says, " but a few weeks later she came in to tell me she was flying to Australia to get married."

How would one begin such a letter, I wondered? " Dear Miss Smith? " " Dear Joan " seemed too formal in speech, and the telephonic " Hallo, Joan " too casual. The dealer didn't know, but he was sure there was no magic formula. Alan Wilson, a serviceman in Malaya, sent twelve miles of taped endearments to his sweetheart in Devon before she agreed to marry him.

This was a use of tape recorders which I had never heard of before. I wanted to know about other ways in which this latest " magic box " is enriching our leisure.

I went along to the largest suppliers of tape recorders in the country. I spoke to secretaries of tape recording clubs, and inquired among friends and acquaintances.

Playing Cupid, I soon found, is only one of hundreds of uses for tape recorders. The machine, which began as an expensive toy for broadcasting studios, and was then taken up by scientists and radio amateurs, is now used by thousands of ordinary families for recording music, the voices of their children, the fun at their parties, bedtime stories, and for helping to learn a musical instrument or polish a language.

Where the television screen often seems to hypnotize a family into silence and make all visitors seem intruders, the tape recorder, enthusiasts pointed out, restores the balance by taking an evening at home right back to the party spirit of pre-war days. Everybody joins in.

Sandy Saunders, whose West Middlesex club has been in existence five months, and includes a number of lady members, had a lot to say about the fun and excitement a tape recorder can add to a party.

" With a little imagination," says Saunders, " you can use your tape recorder to make any party go. Apart from the fun to be had from recording and playing back everyone's party piece, there are lots of games you can play. Pre-record a number of snatches of different well-known tunes, and get your guests to see how many they can identify. Record sounds from around the house—a washing machine being emptied, an egg whisk, a hair-dryer, taking the joint out of the oven, a child playing with a push-and-go toy—and include them in a quiz. Some are much harder to guess than you'd think."

It's also good fun to leave a tape recorder running for half an hour in some obscure corner, and let it record whatever conversation it hears, and then play it back. " Be careful what sort of party you choose for this," warns (*Continued on page* **98**)

HOLIDAY PLANNING

1959 the Good Housekeeping way

Brittany

Italian lakes

reece

and

adventures

for the fancy free

THE start of a new year is an ideal time for holiday planning, so we have set ourselves to pick out three types of holiday-maker and to seek in one of the not-too-distant European countries the answer to the chief requirements of each. We have prepared two special pages of useful facts to ease the planning of these holidays and to help holiday-makers to feel at home when they get to the country of their choice.

In addition a final page has been devoted to assorted suggestions for those who like to adventure on novel holidays in rather unusual places, particularly in the company of people who share a common enthusiasm for some special form of sport or recreation. These we picture as being a little more experienced and wanting ideas rather than detailed directions.

All prices quoted are correct as we go to press, are usually the lowest available for the particular type of holiday quoted and may be affected by high season or other charges.

Compiled by LORNA BRAITHWAITE
Family Centre Holiday Expert

Mrs Braithwaite will gladly give further information on any type of holiday mentioned in this brochure, though she herself cannot undertake to plan detailed routes for individual readers. She can, however, give the addresses of organizations who are prepared to do this. Write to her at The Family Centre, Good Housekeeping, 30 Grosvenor Gardens, S.W.1, enclosing a stamped self-addressed envelope.

Mirrorpic

THE QUEEN: her first seven years on the throne

A word and picture record of change and achievement

HOW SHE HAS CHANGED

1952

1958

Poise

The Queen was not yet twenty-six when she ascended the Throne on that sombre day in February 1952, and early pictures of her reign suggested that she was not, at first, completely steeled to the almost overwhelming strain of her new rôle. At first she followed her father's example in most things: it was the easiest way. But gradually she matured as a woman and emerged a Queen.

Today she always manages that most difficult thing: to be just right on all occasions. Her poise has created comments all over the world. One prominent American editor once said of her: "Americans are filled with admiration at the virtuosity with which the Queen fulfils her job," and one French statesman, watching her walk down the stately staircase of the Paris Opéra, went on record with: "What presence; even the way she holds her hands is right . . ." Her self-confidence is remarkable. One politician who watched her during a recent State banquet remarked: "The Queen knows all the answers . . ." Serenity of this kind has to be learnt the hard way.

Fashion

Before her accession it was quite clear that the Queen did not attach great importance to questions of fashion. Nor was there any reason why she should, having not yet been called to fill the primary position in the Royal Family. In those days she pleased the rank and file, if not the extremely fashion-conscious, by the simplicity and comfort of loose coats, tweed suits, low heels, and her avoidance of ultra smart clothes obviously designed to rivet public attention.

But the way a Queen dresses is important in a world that watches her as the very embodiment of the Commonwealth she rules, and our pictures show how brilliantly the Queen adjusted herself to the change.

Last year America ranked her among the world's ten best-dressed women and one usually sharp-tongued American columnist described her progress through the State visit as being "one stylish dress after another." French fashion experts went even further. During the Paris visit, one of them described the peacock-blue outfit the Queen wore as "*ravissant et sensationnel* . . ."

The Queen, who always had a sense of colour, now links this with a flair for simplicity and elegance of line. Wherever she goes she is envied—and copied.

1952 1953 1958 1958

1953

1957

Pastimes

The Queen has always enjoyed watching horses, and early in her reign she was often unkindly criticized for being seen too often in the Royal box of Britain's great racecourses. But, like all intelligent people, the Queen moves forward in her interests and, for her, racing has led to horse-breeding. With her famous horse, Aureole, as its mainstay, her stud is one of Britain's finest, and her own horses have twice, in 1954 and 1957, led her to the top of the list of racing owners. Her knowledge of form has become almost legendary. France's Marcel Boussac places her among the world's five or six foremost authorities on the breeding of race-horses.

Photos: Keystone; Associated Press; Central Press

How to help your

Lord Attlee's wife travelled with him as chauffeuse and companion on his strenuous election campaigns

An understanding wife gave George VI confidence to carry the burden of kingship

Lord and Lady Douglas—"the chic ex-model and the genial giant"—off to Moscow together

Former stage star Mrs John Profumo brings inimitable grace to her real-life rôle of politician's wife

If you know the answers, good luck to you. You don't need this advice. But others may like a tip or two. Here are some shining examples of success in the important twentieth-century art of wifemanship

BY GWEN ROBYNS

IN the art of wifemanship, how-to-help-your-husband-get-along is becoming increasingly important.

It's true that it has always been, throughout history. How would Disraeli have managed without his Mary Anne to connive and push him on? The course of English history might have been very different if Sarah Jennings, wife of the Duke of Marlborough, had not caught Queen Anne's ear and pleaded for her man to be given a chance.

Nearer our times, it was a Scots girl, Elizabeth, who turned a shy, stuttering, awkward sailor into the most loved and respected king in British history.

Today it's more important than ever before, because it is the bosses who have suddenly become acutely wife-conscious. In this "attaboy," competitive age, John Smith's wife behind her kitchen sink has become a V.I.P. For she is the one human element who can finally make or break her man. In America she has already assumed enormous importance. For some time it has been recognized procedure in Big Business there to interview the

husband GET AHEAD

Mrs Peter Thorneycroft has many public engagements. Impeccably tailored, she always looks the part to perfection

Candid yet discreet, Lady Churchill has practised wifemanship with superb success for fifty-one years of marriage

Eye-catching as ever, Lady Docker dances with Sir Bernard at a "smart set" fancy-dress ball

Dame Margot Fonteyn helped her husband by silence under reporters' gruelling pressure

wife, as well as the husband, when he applies for a top-line job.

Pick up any American magazine and you'll recognize the familiar pattern. . . . Ambitious young business executive has difficulty in getting along with his ulcerated employer. One day baby-doll wife invites boss home to supper and serves him bilberry pie "just like my mom used to make." End of story. Hank gets his promotion and Betty Ann writes a testimonial for Aunt Sarah's pie mix.

You may say that it can't happen here. Britain is still a male-dominated country. But just as surely as the ten-shilling broiler chicken has staked a claim on the Sunday joint, the idea of wife-vetting is catching on.

As one managing director of a large firm told me, "I don't care what their wives look like. When the time comes and the money is there, a bit of beauty treatment and a good dressmaker can work a miracle. What I am interested in is their attitude to their husband's job. Whether they take it seriously as a joint effort and not just the means of a monthly pay cheque. It's the long-term policy that marks out the future executive and not a flash-in-the-pan coup."

Moral: As long as your husband is on the job, whether he comes home for dinner at 6 p.m. or 8 p.m. shouldn't matter to you. Overtime, business trips and entertaining on-the-hop business V.I.P.s should all be accepted as an integral part of wifemanship. That is, if you want your husband's promotion!

The maëlstrom of public life always spotlights the exceptional cases. But on a lesser scale the same problems apply behind the lace curtains in every suburban street. I doubt if any wife in Britain, apart from the Queen Mother, has accomplished more for her husband than Lady Churchill. Hers is the backroom method practised to perfection.

Through fifty-one years of marriage she has done her job so well that the world is oblivious of the fact that she worked at it at all. (*Continued on page* **162**)

the Four Ages of Woman

The age of sparkle, enthusiasm and experiment

Luzzatto

For a woman there is no best, happiest or most elegant age. If she is clever, she will use all the wiles of her youth, or her experience, to look simply stunning from childhood to grandmotherhood and beyond. She will choose her clothes and her furniture to flatter and enhance her own personality, rejecting expensive whims and approving only those things which are both elegant and timeless

At 20, a girl likes to indulge herself. She plays records over and over again; wears bright, bright red with charming assurance. She wants to bring the voice of her favourite recording-star faultlessly into her room. So, having found a teak cabinet that might have been designed for her alone, she herself selects the high-fidelity recording and tape equipment to put into it. Her wool hopsack winter shirt-waist (left) shows her sure touch—how well she knows herself. It is so well-cut it will always have a crisp shape and a fresh look.

● Cabinet only, £37 10*s*., Heal's, Tottenham Court Rd., W.1. Dress by Polly Peck, 10½ gns., at Woollands, Knightsbridge, S.W.1, and Diana Warren, 78 The Promenade, Blackpool

At 30, a woman conducts herself with an elegance it has taken her most of those years to learn. She dresses in a discreet, but definitely head-turning way; maintains a home that is remarkable for its combined serenity and vivacity. She knows the value of a suit that is timeless, made in jersey to move with ease while it quietly flatters; and furniture, Scandinavian and sculpted in teak, that is timeless and flattering too.

● Susan Small Casual, 16½ gns., at Galeries Lafayette, Regent St., W.1, and Huntbach Ltd., Hanley. Trolley, £15 1*s*. 6*d*., Liberty, Regent St., W.1. Coffee set, £9 15*s*. 9*d*., Heal's. Both imported by Scandia. Picasso *Tête de Femme* from Lefevre Galleries. Flowers from Moyses Stevens.

Serene, perfectly poised and enviably elegant

Her husband's career calls for graceful formality in his home

the Four Ages of Woman

Compiled by Ethne Davies and Pamela Westland

At 40, a woman has an assuredness that younger women are still striving to attain. She knows that her husband, by now reaching the peak of his career, relies on her to be perfect in every detail. When they entertain, as they often must, she chooses (left) a dinner dress that is for ever. A line so feminine you can trace it back to past beauties, almost to the time of the ballad *Greensleeves*. Here, entirely today, it is made from blue and silver matelassé.

● Jean Allen gown, 29 gns., at Harvey Nichols, Knightsbridge, S.W.1, and County Clothes, Cheltenham. Arm-chair, with petit-point embroidery on back, seat and arms, £59 10*s*., chosen from a wide range in the second-hand furniture department of Harrods, Knightsbridge, S.W.1

At 50, a woman's life is at its fullest. Her husband, her family and several social organizations all make heavy demands on her time. Yet she remains enchantingly unruffled. For the countless activities of her day she dresses slimly, serenely, in a tailored grey Prince-of-Wales check dress. Her most cherished piece of furniture is her walnut writing-table, for it is here that she relaxes to write those long, news-filled letters that mean so much to her grown-up sons and daughters.

● Dress by Marcusa, 9½ gns., at Debenham & Freebody, Wigmore St., W.1, and Griffin & Spalding, Nottingham. Writing table, £58 10*s*., chair, £47 5*s*., at Maples, Tottenham Court Rd., W.1

Her busy social life encourages perfect grooming

THE LEGGY LOOK

BEAUTY • *Edited by Ethne Davies*

It's a bare-legged look today: seamless stockings grace legs on view in this high-hem Charleston age

62

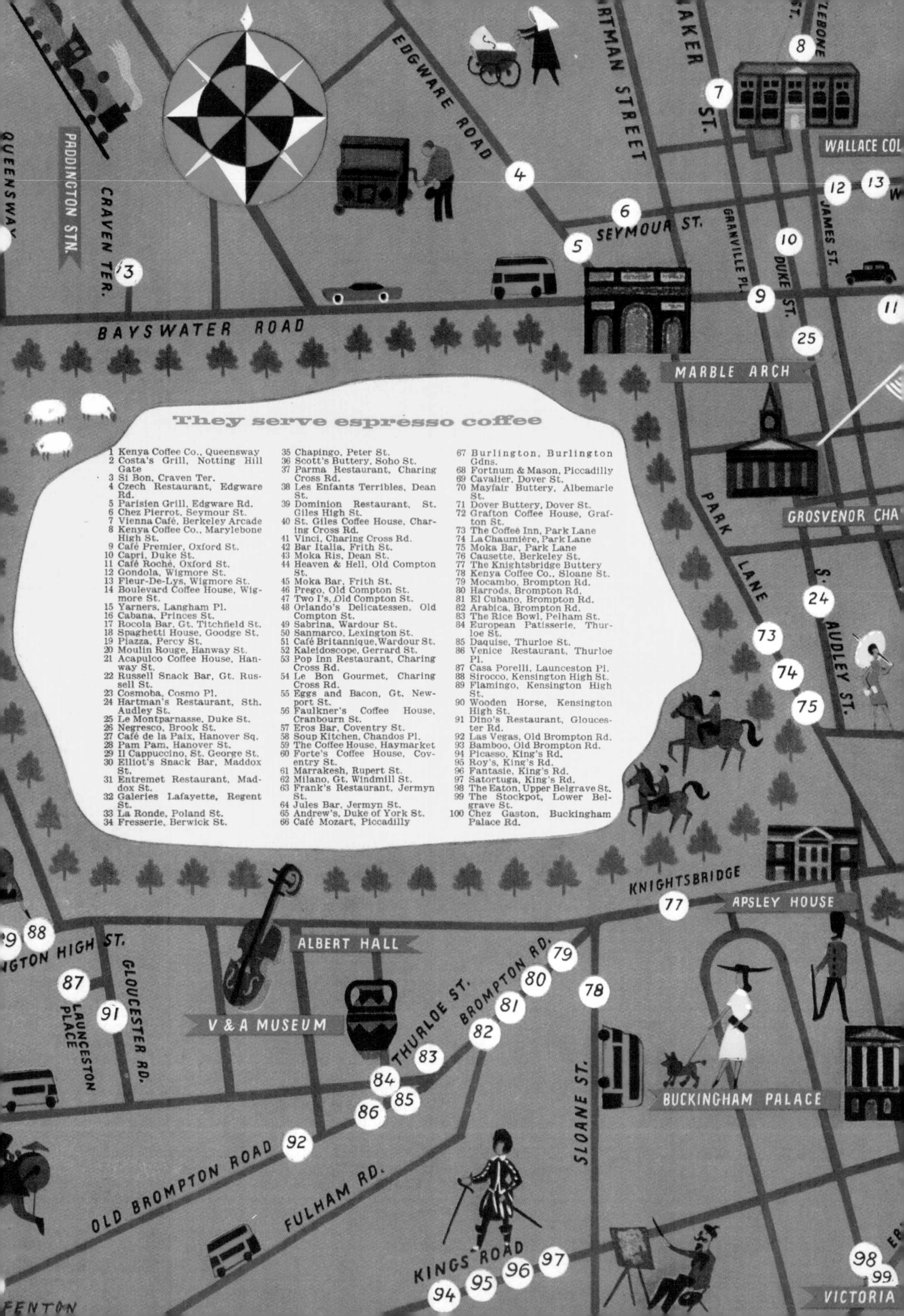

They serve espresso coffee

1 Kenya Coffee Co., Queensway
2 Costa's Grill, Notting Hill Gate
3 Si Bon, Craven Ter.
4 Czech Restaurant, Edgware Rd.
5 Parisien Grill, Edgware Rd.
6 Chez Pierrot, Seymour St.
7 Vienna Café, Berkeley Arcade
8 Kenya Coffee Co., Marylebone High St.
9 Café Premier, Oxford St.
10 Capri, Duke St.
11 Café Roché, Oxford St.
12 Gondola, Wigmore St.
13 Fleur-De-Lys, Wigmore St.
14 Boulevard Coffee House, Wigmore St.
15 Yarners, Langham Pl.
16 Cabana, Princes St.
17 Rocola Bar, Gt. Titchfield St.
18 Spaghetti House, Goodge St.
19 Piazza, Percy St.
20 Moulin Rouge, Hanway St.
21 Acapulco Coffee House, Hanway St.
22 Russell Snack Bar, Gt. Russell St.
23 Cosmoba, Cosmo Pl.
24 Hartman's Restaurant, Sth. Audley St.
25 Le Montparnasse, Duke St.
26 Negresco, Brook St.
27 Café de la Paix, Hanover Sq.
28 Pam Pam, Hanover St.
29 Il Cappuccino, St. George St.
30 Elliot's Snack Bar, Maddox St.
31 Entremet Restaurant, Maddox St.
32 Galeries Lafayette, Regent St.
33 La Ronde, Poland St.
34 Fresserie, Berwick St.
35 Chapingo, Peter St.
36 Scott's Buttery, Soho St.
37 Parma Restaurant, Charing Cross Rd.
38 Les Enfants Terribles, Dean St.
39 Dominion Restaurant, St. Giles High St.
40 St. Giles Coffee House, Charing Cross Rd.
41 Vinci, Charing Cross Rd.
42 Bar Italia, Frith St.
43 Moka Ris, Dean St.
44 Heaven & Hell, Old Compton St.
45 Moka Bar, Frith St.
46 Prego, Old Compton St.
47 Two I's, Old Compton St.
48 Orlando's Delicatessen, Old Compton St.
49 Sabrina, Wardour St.
50 Sanmarco, Lexington St.
51 Café Britannique, Wardour St.
52 Kaleidoscope, Gerrard St.
53 Pop Inn Restaurant, Charing Cross Rd.
54 Le Bon Gourmet, Charing Cross Rd.
55 Eggs and Bacon, Gt. Newport St.
56 Faulkner's Coffee House, Cranbourn St.
57 Eros Bar, Coventry St.
58 Soup Kitchen, Chandos Pl.
59 The Coffee House, Haymarket
60 Forte's Coffee House, Coventry St.
61 Marrakesh, Rupert St.
62 Milano, Gt. Windmill St.
63 Frank's Restaurant, Jermyn St.
64 Jules Bar, Jermyn St.
65 Andrew's, Duke of York St.
66 Café Mozart, Piccadilly
67 Burlington, Burlington Gdns.
68 Fortnum & Mason, Piccadilly
69 Cavalier, Dover St.
70 Mayfair Buttery, Albemarle St.
71 Dover Buttery, Dover St.
72 Grafton Coffee House, Grafton St.
73 The Coffee Inn, Park Lane
74 La Chaumière, Park Lane
75 Moka Bar, Park Lane
76 Causette, Berkeley St.
77 The Knightsbridge Buttery
78 Kenya Coffee Co., Sloane St.
79 Mocambo, Brompton Rd.
80 Harrods, Brompton Rd.
81 El Cubano, Brompton Rd.
82 Arabica, Brompton Rd.
83 The Rice Bowl, Pelham St.
84 European Patisserie, Thurloe St.
85 Daquise, Thurloe St.
86 Venice Restaurant, Thurloe Pl.
87 Casa Porelli, Launceston Pl.
88 Sirocco, Kensington High St.
89 Flamingo, Kensington High St.
90 Wooden Horse, Kensington High St.
91 Dino's Restaurant, Gloucester Rd.
92 Las Vegas, Old Brompton Rd.
93 Bamboo, Old Brompton Rd.
94 Picasso, King's Rd.
95 Roy's, King's Rd.
96 Fantasie, King's Rd.
97 Satortuga, King's Rd.
98 The Eaton, Upper Belgrave St.
99 The Stockpot, Lower Belgrave St.
100 Chez Gaston, Buckingham Palace Rd.